Games against nature

Games against nature: an eco-cultural history of the Nunu of equatorial Africa

ROBERT HARMS

Yale University

CAMBRIDGE
UNIVERSITY PRESS

PUBLISHED BY THE PRESS SYNDICATE OF THE UNIVERSITY OF CAMBRIDGE
The Pitt Building, Trumpington Street, Cambridge, United Kingdom

CAMBRIDGE UNIVERSITY PRESS
The Edinburgh Building, Cambridge CB2 2RU, UK   http://www.cup.cam.ac.uk
40 West 20th Street, New York, NY 10011-4211, USA   http://www.cup.org
10 Stamford Road, Oakleigh, Melbourne 3166, Australia
Ruiz de Alarcón 13, 28014 Madrid, Spain

First published 1987
First paperback edition 1999

Printed in the United States of America

A catalog record for this book is available from the British Library

Library of Congress Cataloging in Publication data
Harms, Robert
Games against nature.
(Studies in environment and history)
Bibliography: p.
1. Nunu (African people) 2. Human ecology – Congo
(Brazzaville) I. Title. II. Series
DT546.245.N86H37   1987   967:24   87–11749

ISBN 0 521 34373 9 hardback
ISBN 0 521 65535 8 paperback

Contents

List of maps

Preface

I FIRST ENCOUNTERED the Nunu in 1975 while I was collecting oral traditions on the history of the slave and ivory trade along the middle Zaire River. Although the main focus of my research was the Bobangi, who dominated the commerce of the middle Zaire in the nineteenth century, I was also interested in understanding the effects of the slave trade on the populations living in the hinterlands of the trading centers. Because the Nunu inhabited three geographical regions—the riverbanks, the inland swamps, and the farmlands behind the swamps—they presented an excellent opportunity for studying the impact of the slave trade on peoples living in different environmental zones.

My visits to the swamps and the farming regions proved frustrating at first. The oral traditions I collected contained little or no information on the slave trade. Direct questions about the slave trade drew mostly blank stares and shrugs. The evidence clearly indicated that the Nunu had been neither suppliers nor purchasers of slaves on a significant scale. It forced me to acknowledge that, contrary to my presuppositions, life in the eighteenth- and nineteenth-century swamplands had *not* been dominated by the spectre of the Atlantic slave trade.

I gradually began to understand that Nunu history was animated by a dynamism of its own. The Nunu were important not because they were spectacular, but precisely because they were ordinary. The processes of change that characterized Nunu history were far more typical of the forest peoples as a whole than were the spectacular transformations of the Bobangi traders. Convinced that the Nunu had a story worth telling, I continued my investigations of the Nunu fishermen in tandem with my research on the Bobangi traders. Language posed little difficulty, for the Nunu dialects were almost identical to that of the Bobangi, which I gradually learned to speak with reasonable fluency.

The fieldwork among the Nunu revealed the need for new thinking about equatorial African social structures. I had gone to Africa equipped with the latest anthropological models showing how lineage structures dominated power and exchange relationships in African life. The first doubts as to the usefulness of such models were expressed to me by the anthropologist Pierre Van Leynseele, whom I visited in Belgium. "If you want to understand the river peoples," he told me, "you will have to ignore the dominant anthropological models." Van Leynseele's advice notwithstanding, I at first concentrated on reconstructing lineage systems, patterns of circulation of wealth, and lineage alliances. Yet all of this information seemed curiously divorced from the central concerns of both modern Nunu life and Nunu remembrances of their past.

I listened again to the tape-recorded stories I had collected. They stressed individual initiative and achievement. They told of conflict among individuals instead of communal harmony. I therefore began to focus on the aspirations of individuals and the competition that resulted. As I did so, I began to realize that the Nunu settlers on the floodplain of the Zaire had a great deal in common with our own pioneer forebearers in the United States.

When my book on the slave trade appeared in 1981,[1] it gave scant attention to the Nunu (whom I called Moye, using the riverine term). I used Nunu data primarily to contrast the older patterns of river life, as exemplified by the riverine Nunu, with the economic and social innovations of the Bobangi. This contrast was valid in the context of the river communities; but it nevertheless left the impression that the Bobangi traders represented an island of dynamism in a sea of tradition-bound societies.

When I took a fresh look at my Nunu data in the spring of 1981, I realized that the dynamics of Nunu history became fully visible only when traced across several environmental zones. The links between the zones were provided by the small-scale

---

[1] Robert Harms, *River of Wealth, River of Sorrow: The Central Zaire Basin in the Era of the Slave and Ivory Trade, 1500–1891.* (New Haven, 1981).

migrations that dominated Nunu oral traditions. When the places mentioned in the oral traditions were located on maps and correlated with aerial photos, they revealed a process of environmental diversification. Ethnographic and linguistic data confirmed that environmental diversification correlated closely with cultural diversification. The dialogue between people and their environment, in short, was a major force in Nunu history.

I returned to equatorial Africa in 1981 to collect new data on Nunu interaction with their environment. Along with my mosquito net, notebooks, and tape recorders, I also carried romantic notions that held that the forest peoples strove above all to live in harmony with their environment and that embedded in their social systems was a variety of ritual, social, and economic sanctions to minimize their impact on nature.

What I found was very different. My first interview on the subject took place in a canoe while I was poling through the swamps with Nsamonie, an old man who turned out to be a valuable informant. After Nsamonie had delivered knowledgeable discourses on the migration and spawning habits of the fish and on the various methods of catching them, I asked him if he ever worried about killing off too many fish. He burst out laughing. "The fish come from the river," he said. "The supply is infinite." Nsamonie's concern was how to *maximize* his impact on nature. Conservation was not an issue as long as resources remained plentiful.

When I began to write the manuscript, I felt a certain ambivalence toward the project as a whole. Was I merely describing a quaint curiosity in a small corner of the rain forest? Or did my data fit into a larger historical pattern? The ambivalence began to dissipate when I received copies of two dissertations on the peoples living between the Zaire and the Ubangi, one by Pierre Van Leynseele and the other by Mumbanza mwa Bawele.[2] I was fascinated by the dissertations. They were about

---

[2] Pierre Van Leynseele, "Les Libinza de la Ngiri: L'Anthropologie d'un Peuple des Marais du Confluent Congo-Ubangi," (Diss., University of Leiden, 1978); Mumbanza mwa Bawele, "Histoire des Peuples Riverains de l'entre Zaire-Ubangi: Evolution Sociale et Economique (ca. 1700–1930)," (Diss., Zaire National University, 1980).

competition as well as community, about strategies as well as structures. Their findings resonated with my Nunu data. It was left to Jan Vansina to draw on his incomparable knowledge of Africa's forest peoples to confirm that the phenomena we had uncovered were indeed part of a larger pattern. In a series of articles beginning in 1980, he described the socioeconomic processes of the forest peoples as being more open, fluid, and competitive than I had previously imagined.[3] I was delighted. Together, these creative scholars provided the context I needed to connect my Nunu findings to larger historical processes.

My analytical focus on the logic of individual actions created a different kind of problem. In a narrative that covered three centuries and five environmental zones, a systematic approach to the reconstruction of decision making was necessary in order to ensure a coherent analysis. Although I had sometimes mused about the usefulness of game theory and had even presented a paper on the subject,[4] I nevertheless failed for a long time to see the relevance of a gaming approach to the history of the Nunu. Eventually I began to understand that I could not talk about competitive strategies without also talking about goals and rules. Game theory provided a useful way of thinking about strategic decision making in competitive situations. Once I began to experiment with the idea, more and more pieces of the Nunu puzzle fell into place.

As should by now be obvious, this work is the result of stimulating dialogues with a variety of people over more than a decade. My first debt is to my Nunu informants such as Nsamonie, Lila, and Etebe, who patiently tore down my

---

[3] Jan Vansina, "Lignage, Idéologie et Histoire en Afrique Equatoriale," *Enquêtes et Documents d'Histoire Africaine*, 4 (1980):133–55; Jan Vansina, "Towards a History of Lost Corners in the World," *Economic History Review*, 35 (1982):165–178; Jan Vansina, "The Peoples of the Forest," in *History of Central Africa*, edited by David Birmingham and Phyllis Martin, 2 vols. (New York, 1983) I:75–117; Jan Vansina, "L'Homme, les Forêts, et le Passé en Afrique," *Annales: Economies, Sociétés, Civilizations*, 1985:1307–34.

[4] Robert Harms, "Social Choice and Political Economy in Precolonial Africa: A Game Theory Approach," Paper presented at the annual meeting of the American Historical Association, December, 1983.

stereotyped views and taught me to ask new questions. My thought was further stimulated by Mumbanza mwa Bawele and Pierre Van Leynseele, creative scholars of equatorial Africa whose works have in some ways anticipated the path that I am following. I owe an equally great debt to my senior Yale colleague Leonard Thompson, whose lively mind encouraged me to push in new directions and whose devotion to rigorous scholarship and clear writing helped me to transform vague ideas into readable prose. Jennifer Widner drew on her skills as a political scientist to help me to apply game theory terms in a consistent way.

Anyone who reads the footnotes in this book will notice the pervasive influence of Jan Vansina. His pathbreaking ideas on the processes and structures that have influenced the history of the equatorial forest helped to create the larger context within which this study is situated. He drew on his awesome knowledge of equatorial African history, ethnography, and linguistics to make a critique of the manuscript so meticulous as to question the tone patterns of certain Nunu words. Any remaining errors are entirely my own.

The original fieldwork on the Nunu was carried out under a grant from the Social Science Research Council and the American Council of Learned Societies. The follow-up trip in 1981 was funded by the Center for International Studies and the Whitney Humanities Center, both at Yale University. The archival research was aided immeasurably by archivists such as Mrs. Van Grieken at the Archives Africaines in Brussels, Mr. Luwel and Ms. Van Geluwe at the Musée Royal de l'Afrique Centrale, Tervuren, Belgium, and Rev. A. B. Amy at the Baptist Missionary Society in London. While in the field I received much needed aid and comfort from the missionaries of the Baptist Missionary Society, the Lazarist fathers, and the Sisters of Charity. The actual writing of the book was partially supported by a Mellon Fellowship at Yale's Whitney Humanities Center and a Morse Fellowship from Yale University. The maps were drawn by Claudine Vansina and paid for by a Griswold grant from the Whitney Humanities Center. I am immensely grateful for all this help, and I hope that those who invested energy and money in this project will feel rewarded by the results.

Preface for the paperback edition of *Games Against Nature*

by Robert Harms

WHEN I WROTE *Games Against Nature,* the term "environmental history" was not yet part of my vocabulary. The environmental theme that would dominate the book emerged from two sources. The first was my experience of motoring, paddling, and poling a dugout canoe through the Equatorial African swamplands that were once inhabited by people who called themselves Nunu and being struck by the astonishing array of micro-environments packed chock-a-block into a region only 40 kilometers long by 20 kilometers wide. Often, on a voyage of ten kilometers or less, I could observe a total change in the landscape, almost as if I had left one world for another. Moving from north to south I passed from tropical rain forest to a forest-savanna mosaic, to grassland. Moving from west to east, I passed from the powerful, if lazy, waters of the Zaire River to the still waters of the swamps, and to dry land crisscrossed with creeks and bogs. To travel, in this region, was to observe a continual transformation of the landscape.

The second source was the historical accounts told by the inhabitants themselves. To my Nunu informants, historical knowledge was, above all, knowledge of the names of long-abandoned settlements now marked only by small clumps of palm trees, abandoned clearings, earthen dams, and man-made ponds. These were the landmarks by which canoes navigated. Traveling through the region with local companions made history come alive. "See those trees? That was the village of X." "See that clearing? That was made by the inhabitants of Y." "See that dam? It was constructed by the ancestors of Z." History was inscribed in the landscape, and a person who knew how to read—really read—that landscape also knew its history. To recount history was to recount movement across the landscape: movement across a succession of micro-environments.

To the inhabitants of the swamplands, "history" was first and foremost environmental history. It was the history of how their ancestors had cleared land, planted trees, built dams, and dug ponds. Although I first came to the swamps with the naïve dichotomy in my mind about how the industrialized West tries to conquer nature, whereas the inhabitants of Africa's equatorial rain forest live in harmony with nature, I was quickly disabused of this by my informants. To them, nature was always a managed nature, a transformed nature. My informants harbored no romantic notions of pristine nature unspoiled by humans. People, trees, animals, fish, and a variety of spirits all shared a single environment. History was the story of the ways people shaped and managed their environment to suit their own purposes. That was the history that people recounted to me.

But there was also a counter-narrative that remained implicit, like a counter-current running beneath the surface of the water. That was the story of the ways the people themselves had changed and adapted when they moved across the landscape from one environment to another. Nunu in the floodplain of the Zaire River fished more than they farmed, whereas those in the wetlands to the east farmed more than they fished. Nunu in the heavily forested northern parts made very few dams, whereas the southern grasslands were studded with dams. The human adaptations to the environment were inscribed into the landscape just as surely as were the human transformations of the environment, but they had not become part of the local historical narrative. Nobody told stories about how people had bent before the power of the trees, the grasses, and the waters. This was a story that I would have to explore in interviews and field observations.

The two themes that emerged from my research on the Nunu can form a useful definition of a people-centered environmental history: It is the story of the ways that people alter their environment, but it is also the story of the ways that people alter their own thinking and behavior to adapt to its opportunities, dangers, and constraints. At the 1997 meeting of the American Society for Environmental History, Philip Curtain made the astute comment that environmental historians of the United States tend to focus on the former theme, whereas environmental historians of Africa tend to focus on the latter. The narrative and counter-narrative of the history of the Nunu show, however, that the two themes cannot be separated. People were adapting to their micro-environments even as they were transforming them.

The term "adaptation" comes to us from evolutionary biology, and it usually refers to adaptations by plants or animals for purposes of survival. It is seen almost as a natural process. Humans, however, have a wide range of choices over where to settle and how to adapt. Therefore, rather than taking adaptation as a natural—almost unconscious—process, we must ask: "Adaptation for whom?" and "Adaptation for what purpose?"

The first of these questions—"Adaptation for whom?"—leads us directly into the issue of social structure. Nunu societies were by no means egalitarian. Each dam, pond, palm tree, or cleared field had a named owner. During the eighteenth and nineteenth centuries a class of "big men" had developed who controlled the dams, ponds, and dugout canoes that were essential for serious fish production, and a class of clients who worked for them. Clearly, the kinds of technical and social adaptations that had been going on since the ancestors of the Nunu first settled in the swamps had, on the whole, worked in favor of the owners. The inequality of ownership also affected the way people viewed the carrying capacity of the land and the way they defined overpopulation. Most people who left the settled areas for the frontier did so not because there was no land, but because they lacked access to a dam, a pond, or a canoe. It was the social order, more than the environment, that was shaping migratory processes.

If this social order is viewed from afar over a long stretch of time, it seems remarkably fixed and stable: New generations of property owners replaced the old, and new generations of clients succeeded their elders. But if we look at the oral histories collected settlement by settlement and family by family, a very different picture emerges. It was commonly said, for example, that ownership of dams and ponds passed along matrilineal lines from a man to his sister's eldest son. But the detailed histories showed that, in many cases, the property went to someone else, sometimes to someone who was not even a member of the lineage. Moreover, the histories told of dams and ponds that passed from one lineage to another lineage as a result of warfare or debt. In short, there was a great deal of fluidity and individual competition in the social order.

In fact, any free male member of Nunu society, whether high born or low, had the possibility of acquiring property and thus becoming a "big man." One way to achieve this was by moving to the frontier and establishing ownership of resources unavailable to him in the settled areas. The other way was by currying the favor of his patron and proving himself to be a more worthy successor than his competitors. This could be accomplished by social networking, success in fishing, or, most importantly, heroism in war.

If the social division between "big men" and clients was one of the enduring structural features of life in the swamp, from the eighteenth century onward, life on a day-to-day and year-to-year basis was shaped by the strategies of competition that included migration, fish production, social networking, and warfare. The stories told by Nunu made this abundantly clear. Stories of migration stressed the independence and possibilities for success offered by the frontier regions. Stories of war stressed the competition among warriors within a war band as much as they described fighting between opposing groups. If the shaping of the environment was the major theme to emerge from Nunu oral traditions, then the theme of social competition to determine who would direct and harness the processes of environmental adaptation and change was a close second.

This brings us to the other question raised earlier: "Adaptation for what purpose?" If we want to find the driving forces behind the processes of migration, adaptation, environmental transformation, and warfare, we have to look to culture, or, more specifically, to socio-political ideology. One component of this ideology was the idea that the social unit composed of the "big man" and his following transcended the lineage. This socially constructed unit included lineage members, but it also included non-lineage clients, slaves, wives, and in-laws. The very pattern of inheritance referred to earlier, which often diverged from the rules of lineage succession, is a testimony to the power of this idea. A related component was the ideology of social and geographical mobility: the notion that the humblest free male could become a "big man" if he went about it in the right way. The very founding myth of the Nunu—the story of Botoke—emphasized how a poor outcast could become a "big man" through his own efforts.

The ideological notion that the frontier offered a mechanism for social mobility encouraged ambitious young men to move beyond the fringes and settle new lands, even if the new environment was significantly different from the one they had left. Thus, migration proceeded from the flooded forests to the flooded grasslands to the drylands and the riverbanks. Migrants had the idea of replicating the success of their mythical ancestor, Botoke, and of gaining the wealth and honor that they lacked in their homelands. But new environments contained different resources and required different labor processes for their exploitation. New forms of labor mobilization had to be developed and new social contracts on cooperation and distribution had to be hammered out.

Some of the biggest changes involved the division of labor and the distribution of resources between men and women. In the swamps, for example, men controlled fish, which they could trade for agricultural products, whereas in the nearby drylands women controlled the farm crops, which they could trade for fish, leaving men out of the equation. It was such shifts in the division of resources that helps to explain why Nunu men in the nineteenth century resisted moving to the drylands for so long, even though the edges of the swamps had become overcrowded and fish were becoming scarce. Stories that Nunu still tell about the village of Minsange, on the edge of the swamps, confirm this process.

The process of migration across a series of distinct micro-environments thus involved not only a series of environmental adaptations but also a series of major social changes. By the early twentieth century, the region inhabited by the Nunu contained at least four distinct socio-economic systems that were clearly based on adaptations to four different micro-environments. What they all had in common was the ideology of the "big man" and the permanent competition for control of natural resources, although the powers and prerogatives of a "big man," and the means to control natural resources, were different in each place.

If the stable structures of Nunu society in the eighteenth, nine-teenth, and twentieth centuries were provided by the division between property holders and their clients and the social solidarity provided by the matrilineages, then the continual migration, the incessant competition, and the development and unraveling of personal followings became the dynamic processes that animated Nunu history. The problem that I faced when I sat down to write this book was how to discuss the historical interaction of structure and process in four distinct, but related, societies, and to do so in a consistent and systematic way. I searched for an overarching metaphor that would provide a common terminology for discussing a variety of changes that took place within the context of certain long-term continuities.

The image of the game that is evoked in the title of this book provided the overarching metaphor that I was looking for. Games are forms of competition; they are highly dynamic; and their outcomes are influenced by individual actions. But games are also highly structured and played according to commonly understood rules. Rules can be broken and they can be changed, and thus the game itself, not just the action within it, must be seen as dynamic. The game metaphor thus allowed me to distinguish, in a systematic way, between different forms and different rates of change. Tactics can change rapidly. Strategies, which involve sequences of tactics, change more slowly. Rules change more slowly still. Slowest of all to change are the objective and goal of the game itself. Distinguishing among tactics, strategies, rules, and goals gave me a way of discussing complex changes in a series of related, yet distinct, societies in a systematic manner.

Although the potential utility of the image of the game first came to me when I was reading books on game theory, the theory of games is not applied in a formal way in this book. Formal game theory begins with certain assumptions about how a universal "rational actor" calculates advantage and risk. These assumptions are then translated into mathematical formulas, which can be applied to a variety of situations to predict what the most "rational" course of action would be in a given situation. Because this book is a work of history, I am not trying to predict what people will do or what the logical normative behavior would be in a given situation.

To the extent that formal game theory may be said to have influenced my analysis at all, it is used in reverse. We know from the oral traditions and the evidence inscribed into the landscape what the ancestors of the Nunu did, but the evidence itself tells us very little about why they were doing it or what they were thinking. We can, however, try to reconstruct the logic of their actions. If large numbers of people were independently following similar courses of action (such as migrating eastward), then it can be assumed that there was a larger culturally sanctioned logic at work to which a variety of individuals were responding. We can then work backward from the actions themselves to ask what social goals were motivating this action and what rules were shaping its course.

The concept of "rules" is used rather vaguely in this book to refer to the constellation of opportunities and constraints that influenced the choices and actions of Nunu settlers. Constraints were imposed by laws, social norms of behavior, enemies or rivals, natural environments, and limitations of technology. The nature of the constraints faced by Nunu settlers could evolve slowly over time, as happened in the swamps in the eighteenth and nineteenth centuries, or it could change rapidly, as happened after the colonial conquest. Despite drastic changes in the nature of opportunities and constraints in the colonial period, competition over resources and the desire to be a "big man" did not disappear; they just took new forms that were more in line with the new "rules." The use of the term "rules" is thus a metaphorical way of discussing some of the issues that anthropologists now refer to in terms of "structure and agency."

Although social competition for control of resources remained a feature of Nunu society during the colonial period, a totally new form of competition for resources also emerged. That was the competition between Nunu producers, who wanted to appropriate the resources of the swamps, rivers, and forests for their own gain, and the Belgian colonial state, which wanted either to appropriate the natural resources of the forest and swamps or at least to control their exploitation and marketing. At this point, the game image becomes more complex because competition for resources was being carried out on two different fronts at the same time. It was in the context of this new, more complex, set of "rules" that Nunu began to abandon the swamplands. Abandoned villages, eroding dams, and silted up ponds became part of the environmental legacy of colonialism in this region.

By the time the colonial period came to an end on June 30, 1960, most of the Nunu had abandoned the swamps for the high banks of the Zaire River, and the series of distinct Nunu societies based on environmental differences that had thrived in the eighteenth and nineteenth centuries had all but disappeared. Yet social distinctions based on environmental differentiation re-emerged in the form of political ideology in the post-independence period. Under the new "rules" of political competition in the Democratic Republic of Congo, mobilization of mass support became a necessary strategy and claims based on ethnic affinities became a key tactic. If the reality of differentiation into environmentally defined groups had disappeared, the historical memory of the past, reinforced by mimeographed historical narratives, became the basis for dividing the Nunu politically between swamp and river factions. The impact of environmental diversity lay not only in its physical manifestations; it had also become a socially constructed reality that went to the very heart of people's identity.

Today, very few Nunu still live in the swamps, although a great many of them pass through it in canoes to fish or to visit the dryland regions on its eastern edge. When poling through the floating grasses or paddling among the tall trees, they keep a sharp watch for clusters of palm trees, clearings, or abandoned dams. They know each of these landmarks by name, and each name recalls people and events of a now-distant past. If history, for them, is the story of movement, adaptation, and transformation across a succession of landscapes, then each new voyage through the swamps is also a journey through history.

NOTE: In 1997, the name "Zaire River" was changed to "Congo River," and the nation called "Zaire" at the time this book was written became the Democratic Republic of the Congo.

1. Introduction

TO AN AIR TRAVELER, the equatorial African rain forest looks like a thick, green carpet that stretches to the horizon and beyond. This illusion is interrupted only by occasional roads, rivers, lakes, swamps, patches of intercalary savanna, and clearings for villages and fields. When viewed from the ground, however, the apparent monotony resolves itself into a spectrum of astonishing diversity. The rain forest is home to over 7000 species of flowering plants, and they intermingle promiscuously. More than a hundred species of trees have been identified in a single sample plot the size of three football fields.[1] With so many species competing for space, the floral composition of the forest varies widely from place to place according to altitude, rainfall, slope, ground water, soils, and other factors.[2] The resulting patches, each subtly different from the next, form a mosaic that covers an area roughly the size of continental western Europe.[3]

---

[1] Paul W. Richards, "Africa, the 'Odd Man Out,' " in *Tropical Forest Ecosystems in Africa and South America*, edited by Betty Meggers, Edward Ayensu, and Donald Duckworth (Washington, D.C., 1973), pp. 22–23.

[2] One botanist has identified 19 categories of micro-environments for the Zairian forests alone. See C. Evrard, *Recherches Ecologiques sur le Peuplement Forestier des Sols Hydromorphes de la Cuvette Centrale Congolaise*, INEAC, Série Scientifique, no. 110 (Kinshasa, 1968), pp. 70–71. See also R. Letouzey, "Végétations," in *Atlas de la République Unie du Cameroun* (Paris, n.d.), pp. 20–24. This map of the different forest types in Cameroon is reprinted in Jan Vansina, "L'Homme, les Forêts, et le Passé en Afrique," *Annales: Economies, Sociétés, Civilizations* (1985):1314.

[3] The tropical rain forest covers about two million square kilometers. See Jan Vansina, "The Peoples of the Forest," in *History of Central Africa*, edited by David Birmingham and Phyllis Martin (New York, 1983) I:77. The combined area of Belgium, Denmark, France, East Germany, Italy, The Netherlands, Portugal, Spain, Switzerland, and West Germany is 2.1 million square kilometers.

Human populations inhabit all regions of the rain forest, but they are spread thinly over the land. The estimated population density is less than four inhabitants per square kilometer, and it was roughly the same a century ago.[4] The forest dwellers have nevertheless left their mark on the environment they inhabit. As Paul W. Richards has observed:

> In my opinion the "virgin tropical forest" of Africa is a myth. All we can find today are areas of old mature forest here and there which may have been undisturbed for some years but are certainly not unmodified relics of the original pre-human forest.[5]

The forest, in turn, has affected the lives of the people who call it their home. The forms of social organization exhibited by the peoples of the forest are, in the words of Vansina, "variations on a common theme."[6] The reasons for this are only now being sorted out, but the forest environment may be a significant factor in accounting for the cultural similarity. Moreover, the diversity of micro-environments within the forest may help to explain the cultural variation. The natural boundaries that divide the micro-environments correspond in many cases to linguistic and cultural boundaries, and this correspondence suggests vigorous historical interaction between people and their environments.

In order to take a closer look at how the peoples of the forest have interacted with their environments, this book will examine the history of the Nunu of Zaire, a people who inhabit the southern fringes of the rain forest, about 300 kilometers below the equator. The land they claim as their own comprises a strip of Zaire River floodplain about 40 kilometers long by 20 kilometers wide, a narrow strip of farmland on the eastern edge of the floodplain, plus a strip of high bluffs running along the Zaire for about 60 kilometers. Although the region is small

---

[4] Vansina, "Peoples of the Forest," p. 79. For a discussion of the environmental and historical factors that have limited population density, see Gilles Sautter, *De l'Atlantique au Fleuve Congo,* 2 vols. (Paris, 1966) 2:965–99. On the modern population density, see Pierre Gourou, *La Densité de la Population Rurale aud Congo Belge,* ARSOM, Sciences Naturelles et Médicales, n.s. vol. 1, no. 2 (Brussels, 1955), p. 67.

[5] Richards, "Africa, the 'Odd Man Out,' " p. 25.

[6] Vansina, "Peoples of the Forest," p. 83.

compared to the vastness of the forest, it contains stark environmental contrasts. There are flooded forests, flooded grasslands, dry lowlands, and riverbank bluffs. Today, the vast majority of the Nunu live in crowded towns along the river, but two centuries ago they lived mostly in small homesteads scattered across the floodplain, and in an earlier time they lived far up the Zaire River.

Writing a history of the Nunu that traces several centuries of eco-cultural change is a problematic venture because the types of evidence that are normally used for historical reconstruction are scarce. No literate visitors recorded information about the Nunu or their neighbors before Henry Morton Stanley's descent of the Zaire River in 1876–77.[7] Dynastic oral traditions of the type that historians of Africa have used to recover the histories of African kingdoms are seldom found in the equatorial forest, in part because the political systems that developed there were extremely decentralized and political authority was exercised mainly within the kin group.

The oral traditions told among the forest peoples usually recount migrations of small numbers of people over relatively short distances. When plotted on a map, these movements form no clear pattern in either space or time; instead, they reveal a maze of comings and goings.[8] Despite the justifiable skepticism voiced by academic historians who suspect that migration traditions may well be making statements about cosmology instead of about actual population movements,[9] the stories of

[7] Henry Morton Stanley, *Through the Dark Continent*, 2 vols. (New York, 1879).

[8] See, for example, Georges Van der Kerken, *L'Ethnie Mongo*, 2 vols. (Brussels, 1944) I: map 3; Jacqueline M.C. Thomas, *Les Ngbaka de la Lobaye* (Paris, 1963), pp. 256–57. Mumbanza mwa Bawele, "Histoire des Peuples Riverains de l'entre Zaire-Ubangi: Evolution Sociale et Economique (ca. 1700–1930)" (Diss. Zaire National University, 1980), map between pp. 36–37.

[9] For discussions of migration traditions in central Africa, see Jan Vansina, "Comment: Traditions of Genesis," *Journal of African History* 15 (1974):317–22. Wyatt MacGaffey, "Oral Tradition in Central Africa," *International Journal of African Historical Studies* 7 (1974):417–26. John Thornton, *The Kingdom of Kongo: Civil War and Transition, 1641–1718* (Madison, Wis., 1983), pp. 118–19.

small-scale and chaotic movements collected in the forest ring true. The apparent randomness of the described movements negates cosmological interpretations, as cosmology, by its very design, is orderly.

The migration stories told by the Nunu are rather typical of those found throughout the forest. Although the Nunu retain only the vaguest notions of how they came to settle the swamplands where they now live, they are more precise in preserving the memories of short-range movements of small groups of people within the swamps themselves. Their migration traditions often identify the routes followed by the founders of various settlements. The details of these population movements can be elaborated by using family genealogies. When the names given in genealogies are identified with specific homesteads or villages and plotted on maps, they reveal a similar process of migratory expansion.

The movements of Nunu families as recounted in migration stories and genealogies can be confirmed by physical evidence. Wherever people settled, they built dams, dug ponds, cleared fields, and planted palm trees. Many of the dams and ponds are still in use, although their productivity is now diminishing. Normally, the name of the ancestor who is reputed to have dug the pond or constructed the dam is known, as is the list of successive owners from the founder to the present. These lists may well be telescoped, and they may even have been altered as a result of inheritance disputes, but they nevertheless testify to the links between the first settlers and the present occupiers. In a similar way, the palm trees planted near the old homesteads remain, even though the sites themselves have been mostly abandoned since the 1930s. The names of the former homesteads are still remembered because they serve as navigation aids to fishermen twisting their way through the swamp in tiny canoes. It is therefore certain that the migration stories and the genealogies refer to actual places that were once inhabited by real people.

Like migration tales found throughout the forest, Nunu traditions indicate movements in a variety of directions. Some families moved east, others moved west, and still others moved south. The logic of these movements becomes apparent only when they are correlated with the micro-environments that the

Nunu inhabit. The stories then reveal a pattern of geographical expansion from the swamplands to the surrounding fringe areas. Some people, for example, moved eastward to dryland areas, whereas others moved westward to the Zaire River. Other stories reveal a secondary pattern of movement from one fringe area to another: people from the dryland areas moved to the banks of the Zaire River, and so forth.

When the ancestors of the Nunu changed locations, they were also initiating cultural change. Upon entering new microenvironments, settlers had to devise new methods of production, adopt new forms of labor organization, and create new settlement patterns. Such adaptations, in turn, led to more subtle forms of cultural change. Once these factors are taken into account, it becomes clear that the migration stories can tell us a lot more than just the locations of abandoned homesteads; they also contain hints as to the kinds of cultural changes experienced by previous generations.

Identifying such changes requires ethnographic data. Because no ethnographers ever visited the precolonial Nunu, I have relied on the data I collected during fieldwork in 1975–76 and 1981. Many of the direct ethnographic observations I made during fieldwork were of little historical value because substantial changes had taken place during the colonial period: scattered homesteads were consolidated into villages, and later the swamps themselves were abandoned in favor of the crowded towns along the river. It was therefore necessary to collect data on life as it was before these changes took place.

Fortunately, life in the swamps did not change drastically until 1926, when the Belgian colonizers consolidated the scattered homesteads in order to set up indirect rule via appointed chiefs. Many of the elders I interviewed had spent their early years living in the old homesteads. They could describe their physical layout, their social structure, and their histories. Many of these men had learned to fish before the consolidation of the villages, and their earliest knowledge of fishing techniques and the distribution of the catch came from that period. Some could describe incidents that they had witnessed during that period, as Etebe, for example, had witnessed the ritual killing of a dog at his grandfather's funeral. Other informants could recount stories told to them by their parents. Ekando, for example, could not only tell of his grandfather's exploits during wars, but also describe the resulting scars on his grandfather's body.

Because the changes that arose from the forced creation of villages were so massive, it was relatively easy for informants to distinguish the older patterns of life from contemporary ones, and thus the danger of anachronism was reduced. An old man's recollections may become muddled with time, but this factor could be compensated for by interviewing a variety of persons in different villages. By concentrating on general patterns and structures of everyday life as pieced together from a number of testimonies, the effect of possible distortion from any individual's testimony was minimized.

Although strictly speaking, these data are valid mainly for the beginning of the twentieth century, they can provide a rough guide to some of the cultural changes that occurred in earlier periods if used comparatively. The Nunu area can be subdivided into flooded forest, flooded grassland, riverbank, and dry land. These zones correspond with linguistic subdivisions, which in turn correspond with cultural subdivisions.[10] By comparing the ethnography of the different micro-environments, one can distinguish the cultural traits shared by all of the Nunu from those that are distinct to a single environment. Traits shared by all are assumed to be old unless it can be demonstrated that they are recent innovations. Therefore, they define the more enduring and general features of the Nunu culture. In contrast, if an institution or practice is distinct to a certain micro-environment, we can assume that its existence or persistence has something to do with conditions unique to that area. It therefore represents innovation. Since we know from oral traditions and genealogies the order in which the successive micro-environments were settled, we can infer the order in which these changes occurred.[11]

---

[10] Mayaka Ma-Libuka, "Phonologie et Morphologie du Bobangi" (Mémoire de Licence: Institut Supérieur Pédagogique, Kikwit, Zaire, 1977), p. 1.

[11] For a more thorough explanation of how comparative ethnography can be used to reconstruct the history of equatorial Africa, see Jan Vansina, "Towards a History of Lost Corners in the World," *The Economic History Review* 35 (1982):165–78.

What is missing from the analysis so far is a sense of the people themselves. Why did they leave their old homes? What did they hope to find in their new ones? Why did they change their institutions and patterns of social interaction? The early Nunu left no equivalent of the letters and diaries left by American pioneers, and local migration traditions usually emphasize the paths of the migrations instead of the causes. There is, however, one oral tradition that sets out a general model of migration. This tradition is a cliché, a stereotyped story that is told among various ethnic groups throughout middle Zaire and the lower Ubangi regions.[12] The fact that the story is known by so many different peoples indicates that its value lies less in reconstructing the details of any specific migration than in making a statement about the causes and meaning of migrations in general.

Shorn of variations in detail, the core story is both short and simple. A common villager had been caught sleeping with the wife of a powerful man. Seeing that the jealous husband was making life miserable for him, the unfortunate lover moved away from the village. He went to settle in a frontier area, where he amassed wealth and became a powerful man. A structural analysis of this story that focuses on the obvious oppositions between men and women, spouses and lovers, and power and weakness could miss the basic point. This story is about competition. It is about winners and losers; and it is about losers becoming winners through migration.

The themes of this story correlate well with the findings of recent ethnographic and historical research on the peoples of the equatorial forest.[13] Because the forest societies usually had decentralized political institutions, each settlement enjoyed a great

---

[12] The oral tradition was collected by T.J. Deweerd in 1957, and reprinted in J.J.L. Lingwambe "Histoire Banunu-Bobangi" (mimeographed pamphlet: Kinshasa, 1966), p. 7. For details on the distribution and interpretation of the tradition, see Robert Harms, "Bobangi Oral Traditions: Indicators of Collective Perceptions," in *The African Past Speaks: Essays on Oral Tradition and History*, edited by Joseph Miller (Hamden, Conn., 1980), pp. 185–86.

[13] See Mumbanza mwa Bawele, "Histoire"; Vansina, "Peoples of the Forest"; Vansina, "L'Homme, La Forêt."

deal of autonomy. There was competition within settlements for positions of leadership, and there was competition among settlements as their leaders competed to attract dependents and increase their power. Winners in the competition consolidated their power, and losers often left in hopes of becoming winners somewhere else.

The social competition that has long characterized life in this region provides a key to understanding why some people moved, why others stayed where they were, and why people sometimes left one micro-environment for another. By using ethnographic data to reconstruct the contexts within which they made those decisions, it becomes possible to make reasonable inferences as to the logic of their actions. A reconstructed context would include four elements: the culturally defined goals that motivated individuals; the available resources for meeting those goals; the strategies by which people sought to reach their goals; and the institutionalized norms that structured the competition.

To facilitate the exposition of the various elements that made up that competition, I will occasionally employ images and vocabulary drawn from game theory.[14] Game theorists view a game not as a trivial pastime, but as a context for strategic decision making under conditions of competition and conflict.

---

[14] For an introduction to the basic concepts of game theory, see Martin Shubik, "Game Theory and the Study of Social Behavior: An Introductory Exposition," in *Game Theory and Related Approaches to Social Behavior,* edited by Martin Shubik (New York, 1964), pp. 3–77. For examples of this approach applied to Africa, see Walter Goldschmidt, "Game Theory, Cultural Values, and the Brideprice in Africa," in *Game Theory in the Behavioral Sciences,* edited by Ira Buchler and Hugo Nutini (Pittsburgh, 1969), pp. 61–74; Robert Bates, *Essays on the Political Economy of Rural Africa* (New York, 1983), pp. 7–20; P.C. Lloyd, "Conflict Theory and Yoruba Kingdoms," in *History and Social Anthropology,* edited by I.M. Lewis (London, 1968), pp. 25–61. For an example of the use of gaming terms and concepts to analyze political competition in a totally analogical and non-quantitative way, see F.G. Bailey, *Stratagems and Spoils: A Social Anthropology of Politics* (Oxford, 1970). For an example of the application of game theory to Marxist analysis, see Jon Elster, "Marxism, Functionalism, and Game Theory," *Theory and Society* 11 (1982):455–82.

The game metaphor integrates the disparate elements of a competitive situation. A game has players who seek certain goals. It is played according to mutually understood rules. The players devise strategies, each of which has potential risks and pay-offs. In choosing a strategy each player must take into account not only his own goals, but also the actions of the other players. Strategies to minimize losses can therefore be as rational as strategies to maximize gains, depending on the circumstances. The game is dynamic in that each move can change the context for future moves, and the success or failure of certain strategies can bring about changes in the rules or even in the definition of the game itself.

The Nunu do not describe their social and economic competition in such terms, but they nevertheless have clear understandings of the goals, strategies, tactics, and rules that impinge upon their actions. Fishermen are constantly debating where to fish and which methods to use. A wide range of life situations in Nunu society—birth, marriage, death, sickness, health, and so on—involve the exchange of money, and thus in the course of social life people are constantly planning strategies and calculating advantages. Even the invoking of supernatural forces via diviners and charms involves well-understood tradeoffs. The strategic thinking exhibited in those decisions closely parallels the rationality of game theory models.

A modern example will illustrate the complex nature of decision-making in Nunu society. As I was preparing to leave Zaire at the end of my first research period, a young man offered to buy my outboard motor. He wanted to use it to transport cassava to Bolobo from Tchumbiri, 80 kilometers down the river. According to his calculations, he could make a hundred percent markup because there was a surplus of cassava in the hinterland of Tchumbiri and a shortage of cassava in Bolobo. Lacking the cash to buy the motor, he had arranged to borrow it from his maternal uncle. When the day came to conclude the sale, however, the young man backed out. He explained that his mother had forbidden him to borrow the money because she feared that the transaction would render him vulnerable to being bewitched by his uncle should he fail to pay the debt. In calculating his strategy, the young man was trying to balance gains and risks in terms of three sets of "rules": those imposed by the regional economy, those embedded in the kinship system, and those expressed by local witchcraft beliefs.

In reconstructing the history of the Nunu, neither the historical data from oral traditions and genealogies nor the reconstructed competitive contexts can be considered completely reliable on their own. However, the reliability of the overall analysis can be increased if the two approaches are used concurrently, allowing each to serve as a check on the other. One can ask if the reconstructed contexts of competition help to explain the dynamics indicated by oral traditions and genealogies. Conversely, one can ask if the movements and migrations across diverse ecological zones help to explain why the contexts of decision making changed. If the ethnographic reconstruction provides a satisfactory framework for understanding the movement and vice versa, then the analysis is as reliable as possible, given the limitations of the data. Even with the most careful analysis, the possibility of error remains. But the greatest error of all would be to throw up one's hands in the face of complexity and ambiguity and miss the richness of the Nunu and their history.

2. The antecedents

THROUGHOUT THE 1400-kilometer stretch between Wagenia Falls and the Bateke Plateau, the Zaire River describes a lazy arc through the tropical rain forest. The river's width varies from three kilometers at narrow points to thirty kilometers along the widest stretches. Beyond its low banks lie floodplains that extend up to twenty kilometers inland.[1] When the river rises, the floodplains turn into one of the largest swamps in Africa,[2] and they remain so for up to nine months before the water recedes. The southern tip of the swampy floodplain, an area that I shall call the southern swamps, is the home of the Nunu.

The Nunu say that their ancestors have not always lived in these swamps, but are immigrants from farther up the river. This view is consistent with the geographical and linguistic configuration of the area. The major concentrations of swampland

---

[1] Egide Devroey, *Le Bassin Hydrographique Congolais*, IRCB, Sciences Techniques, vol. 3, no. 3 (Brussels, 1941), p. 22. See also George Grenfell's "A Map of the Congo River between Leopoldville and Stanley Falls, 1884–1889" (London: The Royal Geographical Society). For a general description of the rivers and floodplains of the central cuvette, see R. Germain, *Les Biotopes Alluvionnaires Herbeux et les Savanes Intercalaires du Congo Equatorial*, ARSOM, Sciences Naturelles et Médicales, n.s., vol. 15 (Brussels, 1965), pp. 49–83. The extent of the floodplains is difficult to determine. Maps do not distinguish between the floodplain itself and the inland marshes, and the floodwaters, which are usually hidden in forest or under floating prairies, do not show up on Landsat satellite photos. The Niger floodplain is over fifty kilometers wide in places, but the Zaire floodplain is generally much narrower. J.P. Gosse, *Le Milieu Aquatique et l'Ecologie des Poissons dans la Région de Yangambi*, MRAC, Sciences Zoologiques, no. 116 (Tervuren, 1963), p. 138.

[2] See Keith Thompson and Alan C. Hamilton, "Peatlands and Swamps of the African Continent," in *Mires: Swamp, Bog, Fen, and Moor*, edited by A.J.P. Gore, 2 vols. (New York, 1983), B: 331–73.

are found up the river in the Zaire-Ubangi peninsula, which is inundated from both the Zaire and the Ubangi. This area was ideally situated to be the crucible of interaction and exchange in which the general features of water culture were shaped. By contrast, the swamplands where the Nunu now live represent the southernmost extension of the Zaire floodplain, the place where swampland gives way to the sandy, waterless bluffs of the Bateke Plateau. The Nunu also live on the linguistic periphery of the world of the water people. Although they speak a water language, their neighbors to the south speak languages that belong to a different linguistic subgroup. Because the Nunu inhabit the periphery of both their environmental zone and their linguistic zone, it seems reasonable to suppose that their ancestors came from somewhere nearer to the core.

The Nunu have lived in the southern swamps for at least three centuries, perhaps much longer. The longest genealogies collected from the present inhabitants go back to about 1750.[3] By that time the core areas of the swamps must have already been well populated because the genealogies show migration toward the inland fringes. None of the genealogies go back to ancestors who had entered the southern swamps from elsewhere; neither do they go back to the founding ancestors named in the oral traditions. There is thus a genealogical gap between the time of the first ancestors and the period covered by the genealogies. Although it is impossible to say how many years that gap covers,[4] Portuguese documents reveal that in 1612 there were speakers of a language similar to that of the Nunu already living in the general area of the southern swamps.[5]

---

[3] See genealogies of Ekando, Mongemba, Likinda, field notes.

[4] There are some lists of rulers that may be of some help in calculating the chronology of the settlement of the swamps. Ekando listed eight "elders" who ruled the Moliba area. The last of them saw the coming of the whites. See field notes. Lila listed nine *Ngeli* rulers at Mitima before the coming of whites. Interview: Lila, 7-12-81, Tape 3/1.

[5] The documents mention a place called "Ibar" or "Ybare," located near the Tio Kingdom. They are clearly referring to *ebale,* the word that the Nunu and the peoples farther upriver use for the Zaire River. Antonia Brasio, *Monumenta Missionaria Africana,* 11 vols. (Lisbon, 1953–71) 6:104, 438.

A comparison of traditions from diverse localities in the southern swamps makes it clear that the ancestors of the Nunu did not all arrive at the same time nor did they necessarily come from the same place. In the Nsangasi River valley, for example, one tradition holds that the founding ancestor was Ewando, who entered the valley via a small channel with his wife, Mama Masumbi.[6] Another version holds that the man who first entered that channel was Pembele.[7] Other traditions hold that the main body of settlers came via the mouth of the Nsangasi, led by Bongongolo and Mobangi, names that refer respectively to the inhabitants of the west bank of the Zaire and those of the lower Ubangi.[8] Such diversity of traditions can easily frustrate the historian looking for a neat migration pattern. The Belgian colonial officer Gustin, who tried to sort out the history of the Nunu in 1924, concluded that "The Nunu seem to have come from everywhere."[9]

Several sources indicate the Ngiri River valley and surrounding regions as the homelands of some of the immigrants. One such source is an archaic song that was sung by women as they kneaded cassava flour. It went:

Where do we come from?

We come from Moongo.

Which Moongo?

Moongo of the Libinza[10]

---

[6] Document written by elders of Nkolo-Lingamba, March 3, 1964, in possession of the author.

[7] Interview: Etebe and Ngamakala, 5-22-75, Tape 4.

[8] Interview: Etebe and Ngamakala, 5-22-75, Tape 4.

[9] Gustin, "Les Populations du Territoire de la Mpama-Kasai," 1924, MRAC-E, Prov. Equateur, Distr. Equateur, Terr. Bikoro, 1. By the time I did fieldwork in the 1970s, the Nunu possessed several written histories that were composites of a variety of local traditions, as well as numerous oral accounts of a common origin up the river and a single heroic migration. These accounts were heavily influenced by the cultural unity movements of the early 1960s, when it became important for political purposes to speak of a common origin. Given these circumstances, the composite traditions are more useful for the light they shed on the crisis of the 1960s than for light they shed on the ancestors of the Nunu.

[10] Interview: Lila, 7-14-81, Tape 4/2.

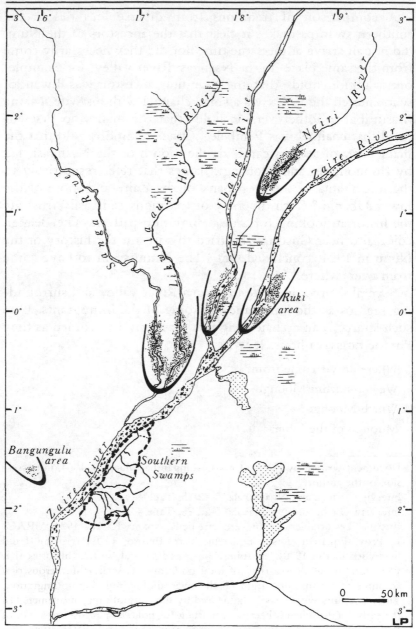

Probable Sources of Immigration into the Southern Swamps

Modern informants interpret the phrase "Moongo of the Libinza" as a reference to the Libinza people who live along the Ngiri.[11] Another hint of a historical link between the Nunu and the Ngiri region can be found in a line of an old war chant which goes "We come from Mutu mo Ese (the head of land)," a term by which the water people often refer to the peninsula bounded by the Zaire and Ubangi Rivers. The Ngiri is located on this peninsula.[12]

To understand why the ancestors of the Nunu left their homes in the Zaire–Ubangi region and what kind of cultural baggage they brought with them to the southern swamps, it is necessary to examine the ideology and practice of social competition among the water peoples living in the area of the Zaire–Ubangi peninsula. Although it is not possible to reconstruct the details of the period between 1500 and 1700, comparative ethnographic data from this and surrounding areas show that the approaches to social organization and competition are surprisingly uniform, and therefore they are probably very old.

---

[11] Lila, "Ekumela e Banunu-Bobangi," manuscript in possession of the author, p. 1. See also references to the Ngiri in Vincent Bokono, "Monkama mo Mibembo mi Bankoko o Ebale e Congo. Bibo be Makonzi na Bitumba bi Bango" (Typescript: Bolobo, 1960), pp. 1–2; J.J.L. Lingwambe, "Histoire Banunu-Bobangi" (mimeographed pamphlet: Kinshasa, 1966), p. 1, tells of the ancestors of the Nunu descending the Ubangi together with the Libinza.

[12] Interview: Mongomo, 12-13-75. There is a discrepancy between this reconstruction, which posits people moving down from the Ngiri area, and the reconstruction of Mumbanza mwa Bawele, which posits people moving up into the Ngiri River valley around 1700. See Mumbanza mwa Bawele, "Histoire des Peuples Riverains de l'entre Zaire-Ubangi: Evolution Sociale et Economique (ca. 1700–1930)" (Diss., Zaire National University, 1980), pp. 37–60. Because the two reconstructions are based on very different sources, there is no way to resolve the discrepancy without additional data. Two observations are in order, however. First, a pattern of contradictory movements is typical of the forest in general. Second, more reliable data as to the chronology of these movements might resolve the discrepancies. All of the movements may have been much earlier than either reconstruction suggests.

THE IDEOLOGY OF COMPETITION

Competition for wealth and power was based on commonly understood definitions of the competitors, the goals, and the stakes. Although the water people did not necessarily think about their activities in such terms, they nevertheless possessed clear models that defined each of these issues.

The model that defined the strategic decision-makers in the competition was that of the segmentary lineage. In the abstract, a lineage was a corporate unit composed of descendants of a certain ancestor. The group regulated marriage alliances, provided a system of insurance and social security for its members, and defended their common interests. The actual structure of the lineages varied widely according to the method of reckoning and the genealogical depth of the calculations, but the abstract model was relatively uniform throughout the area.[13]

The lineage model represented an idealized structure for relationships among lineage members. It ranked members by gender, generation, and order of birth. It outlined who should have authority, who should control material wealth, and who should control ritual power. It also determined who should succeed to office and inherit property. Because ranking was done according to genealogical reckoning, the model made inequality and social stratification seem natural. By emphasizing the succession of generations, it subsumed many of the inequalities of everyday life into a long-term egalitarian vision.

The lineage model emphasized gender differences by defining

---

[13] Jan Vansina, "Lignage, Idéologie, et Histoire en Afrique Equatoriale," *Enquêtes et Documents d'Histoire Africaine*, 4 (1980): 135–45, 152; Jan Vansina, "The Peoples of the Forest," in *History of Central Africa*, edited by David Birmingham and Phyllis Martin (New York, 1983) I:85; Mumbanza mwa Bawele, "Histoire," 77–154. Many peoples of the equatorial forest have bilateral kinship systems, recognizing both the patrilineage and the matrilineage. However, they have no trouble distinguishing between the two, and one of the systems is usually dominant when it comes to questions of inheritance and succession.

authority in patriarchal terms.[14] Its genealogical calculus served primarily to define hierarchical relationships among males. Although women had a great deal of control over the household economy and domestic life, formal positions of leadership, such as head of the homestead or lineage elder, were monopolized by men. Men also controlled the prestige goods that could be used to pay bridewealth, attract followers, conclude alliances, and enhance the status of the group.[15] Competition among households or among lineages was therefore represented as competition among patriarchs. Although many women exerted a great deal of informal influence over the choices made by their husbands, brothers, and sons, the strategic decisions regarding marriage alliances, warfare, migration, the disposition of lineage resources, and similar issues were portrayed in public and in ideology as male prerogatives.

The lineage model also emphasized generational differences. By portraying the lineage elders as mediators between nature and culture, it attributed ritual power to people whose physical power was diminishing. Thus, when a lineage member got sick or showed other signs of being a victim of witchcraft, it was the elders who decided upon the cure and who were responsible for restoring the natural order of things. The power to protect was double-edged because elders could use the same powers to bewitch members of their own lineage with impunity.[16] Since witchcraft powers were a prerequisite of authority, it followed that only elders could assert leadership in lineage affairs. The

---

[14] The historical origins of this situation remain speculative. For a summary and critique of the major theories, see Gerda Lerner, *The Creation of Patriarchy* (New York, 1986), pp. 15–53. For a detailed study of gender relations in a society dominated by big-man competition, see Maurice Godelier, *The Making of Great Men: Male Domination and Power among the New Guinea Baruya* (New York, 1986). Patriarchy reigned even in societies that followed matrilineal succession. In such societies power passed matrilineally from a man to his sister's son. Women did not hold the formal positions of power.

[15] The strategic considerations involved in a marriage are spelled out in Georges Dupré, *Un Ordre et sa Destruction* (Paris, 1982), 169–87. Similar considerations would have obtained in the Zaire-Ubangi area.

[16] Dupré, *Un Ordre et sa Destruction,* pp. 219–21.

model thus pictured power differentials between the older and younger members of the lineage as a natural outcome of the cycle of birth and death.

Lineage members of the same generation were ranked in a hierarchy based on order of birth. Within a household, the eldest son had the first claim on family aid in accumulating bridewealth for his marriage. He was the person most likely to inherit the family wealth and would be first in line to take over as head of the homestead or lineage after the older generation of leaders had died.[17] The inequality between the eldest brother and his younger brothers was seen as part of the natural order of things and was therefore perceived as just. The ranking could become very complicated when it was extended over several generations: a young descendant of the firstborn son of the lineage founder, for example, would in some cases be considered senior to older descendants of the younger sons.

By focusing on genealogies, the model portrayed the history of the lineage in terms of repeating cycles of birth and death. It therefore pictured inequality as not only natural, but self-correcting as well. At any given moment, elders had power over the younger members of the lineage, but the model held that this situation was merely temporary. Younger brothers would someday replace the firstborn, and new generations would someday replace the old. The inequities that marred everyday life would thus balance out in the long run. The genius of the lineage model lay in the way it justified short-run inequality while holding out a long-term egalitarian hope.

The lineage model clashed with a second ideological construct: the ethos of the "big-man." The goal of an ambitious free male was to become a big-man by gaining a large number of dependents, whether wives, children, slaves, dependent kin, or clients.[18] Vansina has identified a big-man ethos as dominat-

---

[17] On this competition, see Mumbanza mwa Bawele, "Histoire," pp. 125–26, 140–41.

[18] The concept of the big-man was elaborated by Marshall Sahlins in "Poor Man, Rich Man, Big Man, Chief: Political Types in Melanesia and Polynesia," *Comparative Studies in Society and History*, 5 (1963): 285–303. Since then a variety of studies of big-men in the South Pacific have appeared.

ing social competition throughout the equatorial forest. Mumbanza mwa Bawele, who has made a comparative study of the water peoples living between the Zaire and the Ubangi, defines this ethos as characterized by the search for personal liberty and power. An ambitious free man sought to become independent by obtaining ownership of the means of production. He sought to become important by marrying several wives, purchasing slaves, and attracting clients. And he sought to become powerful, both militarily and in controlling supernatural forces. As the Libinza said, "Your friends cannot consider you a man unless they feel that you are as strong as they are."[19]

The organic unity of the lineage model placed severe constraints on the ethos of the big-man. The rigid rules of lineage rank and succession, if strictly applied, left ambitious individuals with little room to maneuver. Moreover, the fortunate few who became lineage headmen held property primarily on behalf of the group, a situation which placed constraints on their capacity to build up personal wealth. They were more like trustees than entrepreneurs. Similarly, the power of a headman was limited by the necessity of gaining the support of the lineage elders before undertaking any sort of collective action.

Instead of simply following the dictates of the lineage model, ambitious people sought to personalize wealth and power by building up what Vansina has called a "house."[20] It consisted of a big-man, his wives, children, kinfolk, non-lineage kin, in-laws, slaves, clients, and any other people under his control or protection. A striking feature of a house was the variety of dependency relationships that bound individuals to the big-man. Although some of the big-man's dependents were members of his lineage, others were tied to him in ways that had more to do with his wealth than with his genealogy.

One of those ties was marriage. In return for paying bridewealth, a man gained certain rights over a woman who was a

---

[19] Vansina, "Peoples of the Forest," pp. 84–5; Mumbanza mwa Bawele, "Histoire," pp. 77–80. For a similar situation farther west, see Philippe Laburthe-Tolra, *Les Seigneurs de la Forêt* (Paris, 1981), pp. 353–75.

[20] Vansina, "Lignage, Idéologie, et Histoire," 145–46; Vansina, "Peoples of the Forest," 84–86.

member of another lineage. In the societies of the Zaire-Ubangi peninsula, this usually included rights over her children, rights to her labor, and rights to a portion of her subsistence production. A wife was not a member of her husband's lineage, but she was an indispensable member of his house.

A second category of dependent people consisted of slaves, both female and male. Equatorial African ideology defined slaves more in terms of their relationship with a kin group than in terms of their relationship with the means of production.[21] A slave, in essence, was a person who, through capture in war, criminal activity, debt, or other means, had become dispossessed of the support and protection of his or her natal lineage.[22] Purchase by an owner provided the slave with the protection of a new group, but not with the rights of a full member of the lineage.

A third type of dependency relation was clientship. It arose when a free person from a weak or poor lineage voluntarily gave up certain personal prerogatives in return for the support and protection of a powerful person. Unlike slaves, clients retained rights in their natal lineages, and they were free to break their ties to the patron if the relationship proved unsatisfactory. In practice, however, clients had few options. They were often in debt to their patron and thus were not free to dissolve the relationship.

A successful house was held together by a mixture of lineage

---

[21] See Bogumil Jewsiewicki and Mumbanza mwa Bawele, "The Social Context of Slavery in Equatorial Africa during the 19th and 20th Centuries," in *The Ideology of Slavery in Africa,* edited by Paul Lovejoy (Beverly Hills, Cal., 1981), pp. 73–79; Suzanne Miers and Igor Kopytoff, "African 'Slavery' as an Institution of Marginality," in *Slavery in Africa,* edited by Suzanne Miers and Igor Kopytoff (Madison, Wis., 1977), pp. 3–81; Pierre Philippe Rey, "L'Esclavage Lignager chez les Tsangui, les Punu et les Kunyi du Congo Brazzaville," in *L'Esclavage en Afrique Précoloniale,* edited by Claude Meillassoux (Paris, 1975), pp. 509–28. The analogy between the exchange of women and the exchange of slaves came out explicitly during my research. Interview: Bomele, 9-29-75, Tape A61.

[22] This is similar to the approach used by Orlando Patterson in *Slavery and Social Death* (Cambridge, Mass., 1982), pp. 17–171.

and extra-lineage ties, and this combination created room for an ambitious man to maneuver. He could draw on lineage resources, especially bridewealth aid and the labor of kin, to attract dependents. Conversely, he could use resources amassed through the labor of his wives, slaves, and clients to strengthen his position within the lineage. By these strategies people who occupied disadvantageous positions in their lineage genealogies could build up houses of their own, and lineage patriarchs could make their houses grow in ways that would not have been possible had the lineage model been strictly applied.

The contradictions between the organic unity of the lineage model and the personal manipulations of the big-man ethos were resolved in daily life by using the metaphor of kinship to link the members of the house together. Slaves and clients thus called the big-man "father," and dependents referred to each other as "brothers" and "sisters." Genealogies were manipulated to make it appear as if the big-man had been the rightful heir to power, even when his position was based on personal wealth and political maneuvering instead of on genealogical reckoning. People talked about relationships and dependence as if the house were a lineage segment, but the realities of daily life contrasted starkly with the lineage model.

Men who sought wives, slaves, and clients were clearly competing for a limited pool of wealth, and this fundamental fact helped to determine the stakes in the competition. If one man had two wives, it increased the probability that another would have none. The competition, in short, was what game theorists call a zero-sum game, in which one person's gain is always offset by another's loss.

This equation was made explicit by witchcraft models that defined relationships between different forms of wealth. The models, which were widespread throughout central Africa, held that in an ideal and equitable world, wealth and happiness would be evenly distributed. The problem was that some people were greedy and wanted more than their share. These people used witchcraft to achieve their ambitions, thereby depriving others of their rightful share. By so doing they caused illness, sterility, dissension, impoverishment, or even death. Members of one's own lineage were the most able and likely to cause harm by trading the well-being of their kinfolk to the spirits in exchange for increased wealth.[23]

Taken together, the lineage model, the big-man ethos, and the model of the zero-sum game defined the parameters of social and economic competition among the forest dwellers in the region of the Zaire-Ubangi peninsula. To use the gaming metaphor referred to in the previous chapter, the ideology defined the players, the goal of the competition, and some of the rules. It was left to the competitors themselves to develop tactics and devise strategies.

THE PRACTICE OF COMPETITION

Success in big-man competition required more than the ability to manipulate human relationships and spiritual forces; it also required material resources. Bècause of this fundamental reality, the natural environment played an important role in shaping the tactics and strategies of the competitors. The specific forms of competition varied over time and space, but some idea of how it operated can be gained by examining the societies of the Ngiri River valley. Van Leynseele's research in that area has provided us with valuable insights as to how ideology and environment combined to influence the actions of individuals.

The Ngiri, a tributary of the Ubangi, bisected the Zaire-Ubangi peninsula. For most of the year, the greater part of the peninsula was flooded. Some of the floodwaters that reached the Ngiri valley came from the Zaire via the numerous channels through the flooded forest, but the dominant influence was the Ubangi, which drew its waters from the northern savanna and which registered a difference of four meters in water level between the highest water periods and the lowest periods.[24]

---

[23] Willy de Craemer, Jan Vansina, and René Fox, "Religious Movements in Central Africa," *Comparative Studies in Society and History*, 18 (1976):458–65; Robert Harms, *River of Wealth, River of Sorrow: The Central Zaire Basin in the Era of the Slave and Ivory Trade, 1500–1891* (New Haven, 1981), pp. 197–215.

[24] Pierre Van Leynseele, "Ecological Stability and Intensive Fish Production: The Case of the Libinza People of the Middle Ngiri (Zaire)," in *Social and Ecological Systems*, edited by P.C. Burnham and R.F. Ellen (New York, 1979), pp. 167–84.

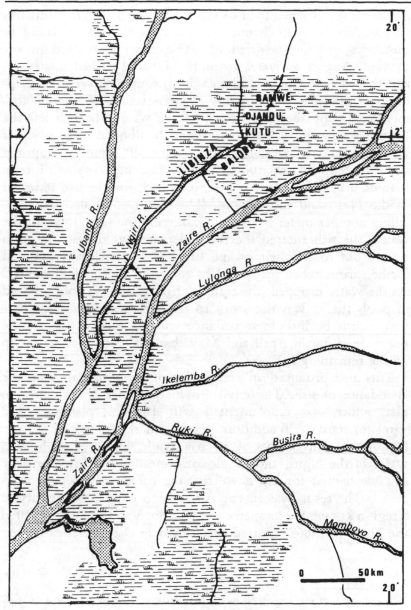

The Ngiri Basin

Source: Pierre Van Leynseele, "Les Transformations des Systèmes de Production et d'Echanges des Populations Ripuaires du Haut-Zaire," *African Economic
History*, 7 (1979):118.

The waters reached their low point in April, when sandbanks appeared in the main channel of the Ngiri, and the surrounding meadows and forests dried up. The water level rose slowly through August as water from the Ubangi rushed upstream, and then it rose rapidly and steadily through November, surging over the banks and flooding the grasslands and adjacent forests. Following the movements of the water, the fish left the Ubangi to go up the Ngiri and enter the flooded meadows that surrounded it. In December the water fell rapidly, dropping about three meters by mid-February. The meadows and forests became dry, the Ngiri retreated to its bed, and the fish returned to the Ngiri and the Ubangi. The water continued to drop, falling another meter by April. Following the movement of the water, the fish entered the flooded meadows during the high water, but found their escape blocked by wicker fences and earthen dams when they tried to return to the main channel.[25] As the water dropped, the trapped fish became so concentrated in pools that it was necessary to feed them as they were harvested little by little in accordance with people's needs. As the pools dried out in April and May, baskets were used to scoop up the remaining fish.

This area produced an abundance of people along with the abundance of fish. The environment provided a high protein diet, which was supplemented with bananas, plantains, and yams for starch.[26] In addition, it was remarkably free of disease. Mosquitoes, the carriers of malaria, could not breed in the acid water of the Ngiri, and the floating meadows did not provide suitable habitat for the tsetse fly, the carrier of sleeping sickness.[27] The result was an enclave of high population density in a region known for its sparse population. Van Gele, who visited the Ngiri in 1886, reported that nowhere else in Africa had he

---

[25] Such a system was described by E. Wilverth, who visited the area in 1896. Cited by Van Leynseele, "Ecological Stability," p. 176.

[26] Mumbanza Mwa Bawele, "La Production Alimentaire dans les Marais de la Haute Ngiri de la XIXe Siècle nos Jours," *African Economic History*, 7 (1979):132.

[27] Van Leynseele, "Ecological Stability," p. 176.

observed such a dense population.[28] Similarly, Lothaire noted in 1893 that the population density was at least double that of the most populous regions along the Zaire, and Wilverth, who visited the area in 1896, wrote of the "immense density of the population."[29]

The extraordinary success of the tactics for extracting resources from nature influenced strategies in the competition among people. People who owned fishing grounds could attract clients and followers and thus become big-men. But as big-men successfully attracted dependent people, they also strained the resources of the area. To prevent depletion of resources, they managed their fisheries with great care to avoid overfishing in general and the capture of young fish in particular.[30] Nevertheless, as population increased, individual catches decreased. Because improved fishing places were owned by small groups of kinsmen but the produce was shared among a larger group of kin, in-laws, slaves, clients, and otherwise attached people, owners responded by restricting participation in the exploitation of the fishing grounds. Sometimes a quarrel would break out among the members of a house, and some members would be forced to leave. In other instances people lacking proprietary rights would recognize that during the low water season they would be without reserves, and they moved elsewhere in anticipation of this grim reality.[31]

The dynamics of population produced a continual spin-off of people from the Ngiri region. Emigrants would explore the frontier areas looking for a similar environment in which to settle. The nearby areas were the first to fill up, and later generations would have to travel farther and farther in search of

---

[28] Alphonse Van Gele, "Exploration de l'Oubangi et de Ses Affluents," *Le Mouvement Géographique*, 4 (1887):40.

[29] "Le Confluent de l'Ubangi et du Congo et la Rivière N'Ghiri," *La Belgique Coloniale*, 1 (1895):52; E. Wilverth, "Au Lac Ibanda et à la Rivière Ngiri," *La Belgique Coloniale*, 1 (1896):575.

[30] Van Leynseele, "Ecological Stability," p. 175.

[31] Van Leynseele, "Ecological Stability," pp. 179–80; Adam Kuper and Pierre Van Leynseele, "Social Anthropology and the Bantu Expansion," *Africa*, 48 (1978):344.

suitable settlement areas. Because canoe travel provided rapid transportation and a way of carrying baggage and children, water people could easily transport entire families over long distances, and hence the migratory movements of water people displayed a pattern very different from the relatively short movements made by people who lived on land.

Evidence in the oral traditions of the Nunu suggests that some of their ancestors left the Zaire-Ubangi peninsula and came to the southern swamps as a result of just such a process. One oral tradition says that Ngeli, the ancestor of the Nunu, lived in a place called Moongo. Ngeli's son was caught sleeping with one of the wives of the local chief. Fearing the vengeance of the chief, Ngeli took his family and fled down the river until he arrived at the southern swamps. This story, a cliché which is told in numerous variants throughout the middle Zaire area, can be interpreted as a metaphor for the process by which people lacking fishing rights of their own posed a threat to the social stability of overcrowded areas and were expelled.[32]

This interpretation is supported by the fact that the name "Moongo," where Ngeli lived, refers to a kind of environment, not a specific place. *Moongo* is a general term for marshlands on the fringes of inundated zones. One informant explained to me that the people currently living in poor fishing areas on the outer fringes of the southern swamps are called Moongo

> . . . because they followed the small streams onto the land. The people of the water are the people of the water, but the people of the land are Moongo.[33]

The statement "We come from Moongo" thus suggests that the immigrants were people from the fringes of swamplands who lacked adequate fishing grounds.

---

[32] The oral tradition was collected by T.J. Deweerd in 1957, and reprinted in J.J.L. Lingwambe "Histoire Banunu-Bobangi" (mimeographed pamphlet: Kinshasa, 1966), p. 7. For details on the interpretation of the tradition, see Robert Harms, "Bobangi Oral Traditions: Indicators of Collective Perceptions," in *The African Past Speaks: Essays on Oral Tradition and History*, edited by Joseph Miller (Hamden, Conn., 1980), pp. 185–86.

[33] Interview: Lila, 7-14-81, Tape 4/2.

Although emigrants from the Ngiri valley and surrounding areas undoubtedly searched for places similar to the ones they had left, the variety of micro-environments in the Zaire basin made it difficult for them to find a perfect match. The settlement of new environments, in turn, affected economic and social competition in unpredictable ways. The emigrants probably arrived in the southern swamps with well-established ideas about the nature of big-man competition and how it was to be played out. However, the environments of the settlement area required new tactics, new strategies, and perhaps even new rules. Emigrants who had left their homelands in hopes of achieving success at a familiar form of big-man competition soon found themselves employing strategies and tactics that were different from anything they had previously imagined.

3. The tactics

A NATURAL ENVIRONMENT, like a playing field, imposes its own rules. Its physical attributes limit the kinds of survival tactics that can be employed, and they favor certain methods over others. The southern swamps, where the ancestors of the Nunu settled, contained a variety of micro-environments, each with its own rules. Environmental adaptation was essentially a process of learning the rules and discovering which tactics would be successful.

In settling the harsh environments of the southern swamps, the ancestors of the Nunu sought to adapt old techniques and develop new ones so that they could not only survive, but also prosper. The early settlers must have done a great deal of experimenting before settling on certain productive techniques. Once the techniques had been perfected, however, the repertory of tactics available in any given micro-environment stabilized. There was little room for further change without a technological breakthrough.[1]

The diverse micro-environments of the southern swamps shared a common subservience to the rise and fall of the Zaire River. The fluctuations of the Zaire, with a difference of only two meters between the highest and lowest points, were less dramatic than those of the Ubangi, which the settlers had previously experienced. This was in part because south of the equator the Zaire had vast floodplains that absorbed much of the excess water. A more important reason was that the Zaire drew water from catchment basins both to the north and to the south of the equator. Because the alternation of rainy seasons and dry seasons in the north was just the opposite of that to the south, the high waters from one climatic zone offset low waters

---

[1] Such a breakthrough occurred in the twentieth century with the introduction of European cord for nets in the 1920s and nylon cord in the 1950s.

from the other. This unusual climatic variation also affected the timing of the ebbs and flows in the southern swamps. Unlike the Ubangi, which has one high-water season and one low-water season per year, the Zaire is bimodal, with two high-water seasons and two low-water seasons per year.[2]

So crucial was the rise and fall of the river to the people who settled the swamps that they reckoned the passage of seasons by the water level instead of following the more common practice of distinguishing rainy and dry seasons. The water reached its greatest height in December, followed by a dramatic drop, known as Mbuwa, through January and February. In March the water leveled off, introducing the season called Mwanga, which lasted until May, when the water began to rise, signaling the beginning of Nzobolo. The waters of Nzobolo reached a height only about half that of the January waters, and they held that height into June, when they dropped to the lowest point. This period of declining water, known as Molengo, lasted until July when the swamps became dry, indicating that Eseu had arrived. In October the water began to rise again, and this gradual rise was called Nzamai. Finally, there was a dramatic rise, called Mpela, in November and December that brought the waters to their highest point.

The regime of ebb and flood created the crucial link between the river and its floodplain, between the fish of the river and food on the land. The Zaire River contained over 500 species of fish, but the food chain that fed them originated on land. Non-predatory species fed mainly on aquatic and terrestrial insects, on fruits and leaves fallen from trees, and on organic matter and bacteria in the mud at the bottom of the water. The channels of the Zaire provided poor habitat for such fish. Many channels had sandy bottoms that rendered them barren of vegetation, and before the nineteenth century there were very few floating plants to provide cover and attract insects. As a result the low water seasons, when the river was more or less confined to its

---

[2] G. Marlier, "Limnology of the Congo and Amazon Rivers," in *Tropical Forest Ecosystems in Africa and South America,* edited by Betty Meggers, Edward Ayensu, and Donald Duckworth (Washington, D.C., 1973), pp. 223–38.

main channels, were times of penury for the non-predatory fish. They were also times of danger because the smaller fish, concentrated in the barren channels, were easy prey for predators.

As the waters rose to inundate the floodplain, the non-predatory fish entered the flooded grasslands and forests in search of food, shelter, and a safe place to spawn.[3] In January the water began to go down, but the fish stayed in this luxurious habitat as long as possible. By April, when they began to return to the river, the water was very low, flowing along the valleys in clearly defined channels that were easily blocked by fishermen. The fish harvest, which began in May, continued until September when the swamps were dry and the remaining fish could be picked up with sharp sticks (much as groundskeepers in public parks pick up pieces of paper).

The ebb and flow of the water constantly altered the landscape of the floodplain.[4] When it was low, it flowed in rivers fed by streams that were in turn fed by small brooks. The courses of these rivers and streams curved tortuously, undercutting the banks and leaving the roots of trees exposed. The soil thus removed was deposited elsewhere, causing a gradual but continuous shifting of the waterways and a redistribution of the kaolin and sand that made up much of the subsoil.[5]

There was also a more general displacement of soil as the incoming floodwaters made deposits in the floodplain and as they later retreated, taking organic matter and suspended soil particles with them. Unlike the valley of the Nile, where the

[3] Tyson R. Roberts, "Ecology of Fishes in the Amazon and Congo Basins," in *Tropical Forest Ecosystems in Africa and South America*, edited by Betty Meggers, Edward Ayensu, and Donald Duckworth (Washington, D.C., 1973), pp. 239–54.

[4] R. Germain, *Les Biotopes Alluvionnaires Herbeux et les Savanes Intercalaires du Congo Equatorial*, ARSOM, Sciences Naturelles et Médicales, n.s., vol. 15 (Brussels, 1965), pp. 103–29.

[5] C. Evrard, *Recherches Ecologiques sur le Peuplement Forestier des Sols Hydromorphes de la Cuvette Centrale Congolaise*, INEAC, Série Scientifique, no. 110 (1968), p. 42; Keith Thompson and Alan C. Hamilton, "Peatlands and Swamps of Africa," in *Mires: Swamp, Bog, Fen, and Moor*, edited by A.J.P. Gore, 2 vols. (New York, 1983), B: 355–57; P.W. Richards, *The Tropical Rain Forest* (London, 1964), pp. 214–15.

annual floods made the soil incredibly fertile, the floods of the Zaire left the soil impoverished. The mineral particles deposited by the floods included limonite (which is a major component of iron ore), mica, and various clays, the major one being kaolin, which is made up largely of aluminum silicate. While the water was bringing in superfluous minerals, it was carrying away organic compost. The trees and bushes of the inundated forest annually deposited tons of organic matter per hectare. Instead of decomposing to form a humus layer, however, much of the organic matter was carried away with the retreating floodwaters. The impact of this loss of humus can be seen from a comparison of soil types: the soils in stagnant swamps have a minimum of 30% organic matter, whereas the alluvial deposits on the floodplains have an organic content of only 2%.[6]

An immediate problem that the regime of ebb and flood posed for settlers was to find a site on which to build a house. Almost all of the land flooded during December and January, and no place could be considered absolutely secure. The settlers solved this problem by constructing mounds of earth three to five feet above the level of the landscape, on which they built their houses. The initial mound–building process required tremendous labor of the early settlers, and each year the mounds had to be repaired after the floodwaters receded. By means of these mounds, however, they transformed an area that had appeared at times as a solid sheet of water into a place that they could call home.

A more difficult problem was how to get food. Protein, in the form of fish, abounded, but starch was harder to obtain. Before the arrival of the cassava plant from the New World around 1700,[7] the main forms of starch were yams and bananas. Banana plants would die when the floodwaters rose, and so they had to be replanted each year with shoots imported from dryland areas. The species of yam most common in equatorial

---

[6] Evrard, *Recherches Ecologiques,* pp. 42–44. See also Germain, *Biotopes Alluvionnaires,* pp. 152–60.

[7] William O. Jones, *Manioc in Africa* (Stanford, 1959), pp. 62–72; Fra Luca da Caltanisetta, *Diaire Congolaise, 1690–1701,* trans. Franois Bontinck (Louvain, 1970), p. 127.

Africa had to grow and be harvested during the dry season. Since most of the fields remained flooded until the end of the dry season, growing it was nearly impossible.[8] There were, however, two forms of yams that could be grown. One was a sweet yam called *epe*; the other was a bitter yam called *liyika*. It is possible that these were water yams, which withstand water better than any other starchy crop.[9]

After 1700, when cassava was adopted as the main starch crop, the situation improved as cassava produces approximately twice as many calories per hectare as yams.[10] Cassava was planted in the grasslands, which were easier to clear than the forest, though the soil was less fertile. It normally takes a year to mature, but even on the highest plateaus a ten-month growing season was the most one could expect before the fields flooded. The cassava had to be harvested before it reached its full size, and thus the yield per hectare was reduced.[11]

The flooded land also presented problems of storage. Bananas cannot be stored once ripe, and the usual technique for surviving on a banana-based diet is to have a variety of banana groves that bear at different times. Since the flood killed all banana plants, however, such a system was impossible.[12] Cassava also presented storage problems. Among dryland farmers, ripe cassava was left in the ground where it was preserved for up to

---

[8] Marvin Miracle, *Agriculture in the Congo Basin* (Madison, Wis., 1967), p. 305. The short dry season in the equatorial forest may have made yam growing difficult even on dry land. Hulstaert notes that the Nkundo to the north of the Nunu grew very few yams in colonial times. Gustave Hulstaert, "L'Evolution de la Production Alimentaire des Nkundo (XIXe–XXe Sicles): Un Bilan Partisant," *African Economic History,* 7 (1979):175.

[9] Interviews: Bampomba, 7-24-81, Tape 13/1, and Lopanza, 7-22-81, Tape 9/2. Neither of these crops is grown today. On water yams (*Dioscorea Alata*), see L.M. Serpenti, *Cultivators in the Swamps* (Assen, Netherlands, 1965), pp. 28–33.

[10] Marvin Miracle, "The Congo Basin as a Habitat for Man," in *Tropical Forest Ecosystems in Africa and South America,* edited by Betty Meggers, Edward Ayensu, and Donald Duckworth (Washington, D.C., 1973), p. 343.

[11] Interview: Longwa, 7-20-81, Tape 8/1.

[12] Interview: Longwa, 7-20-81, Tape 8/1.

two years and eaten a little at a time as needed. The Nunu, in contrast, had to harvest all of it before the floodwaters came. Therefore, they developed a way to store harvested cassava up to four months. Cassava roots were cut into pieces, placed in a basket, and soaked in the river. After three days they were taken out of the water, their skins were removed, and they were returned to the water for one more day. Then, after removal of its inside filaments, the cassava was grated over a wickerwork instrument to form a kind of flour. This wet flour was put in a large, leaf-lined basket that was a meter in diameter and nearly two meters high, and the basket was placed in the river. The flour in the basket was taken out a little at a time, hand milled, and made into small loaves that were steamed, kneaded, and steamed again to make the *engwele* loaves that became the staple of the Nunu diet.

The rising and falling water affected the behavior of the animals who came to raid the gardens when the ground was dry. Antelopes, buffaloes, and elephants ate the tender cassava leaves, and pigs came to uproot the growing cassava. The battle against the animals was continual:

> The elephants and buffaloes ruined a lot of fields. If you had three wives you would put one here, one there, and one there. During the night if an elephant came the husband would shout a warning and the women would get sticks and noisemakers. They would make noise to drive the elephants away. They would shout and sing.[13]

Sometimes people dug pits near the fields to capture the buffaloes who came to maraud in the gardens, but such measures were never completely effective, and the gardens remained in danger until the harvest was over.[14]

The people got their revenge in November when the waters rose. The animals sought refuge on the low hilltops only to find themselves surrounded by water a few days later. They then

---

[13] Interview: Ekando, 7-25-81, Tape 14/2.
[14] Interview: Eyongo, 8-7-81, Tape 17/1.

migrated toward the higher ground thirty kilometers or so to the east, sloshing through water and occasionally swimming. Moving slowly and clumsily, they became easy prey for hunters, who approached by canoe, threw their spears, and then retreated and attacked again. The small canoes used in the flooded forests and grasslands were quick and maneuverable, perfect vehicles for such hunting. Moreover, the meat could be transported back to the village by canoe, a very practical consideration when dealing with elephants and other large animals.[15]

The rising water that plagued the wildlife made it difficult for people to keep domestic animals. Goats and sheep were out of the question, and so people relied mainly on chickens, which could be stored in chicken coops on stilts during the high-water season. Ducks, which liked the water, were introduced to the area in the nineteenth century. The only four-footed domestic animal of any note was the dog, which was allowed to share the homestead with the people.[16]

DOMESTICATING THE LAND

Before the land could be physically transformed, it had to be ritually domesticated. Culture had to dominate nature. A settler had to ensure the prosperity of his settlement by putting himself in harmony with the local spirits. Like their neighbors in other parts of equatorial Africa, the Nunu believed the forests and savannas to be inhabited by a variety of spiritual beings who ultimately determined the success or failure of any settlement.[17]

The task of making peace with the spirits of the land fell to the original settlers. They accomplished it by planting a *nkinda* charm when a new settlement was founded. The most common form of *nkinda* was a wrapped package containing a variety of

---

[15] Interview: Longwa, 7-20-81, Tape 8/1.

[16] Interviews: Bampomba, 7-24-81, Tape 13/1; Longwa, 7-20-81, Tape 8/1.

[17] As Lopanda noted, "When you dig a pond, if you see spirits you try to make them happy. If they are happy, they will attract fish to your pond." Interview: 7-10-81, Tape 1/1.

charms and medicines that was buried in the ground.[18] One oral tradition described the planting of the *nkinda* as follows:

> They took a dog, a chicken, and other items. They dug a deep hole. They cut off the head of the chicken and let the blood flow into the hole. They put the dog in the hole; they put the chicken in the hole; they put in another item called *nkata* [a small, horn-billed bird]. Then they filled the hole. They put a rock over the top of it. Then they planted a palm tree to mark the spot.[19]

The *nkinda* charms symbolically established the dominance of culture over nature. An oral tradition holds that on the day the *nkinda* was consecrated, people planted cassava and banana plants that grew and ripened before nightfall.[20] The symbolism of the story makes it clear that the *nkinda* made nature respon-sive to the wishes of people, not the other way around.

We can only speculate as to how the Nunu adopted this in-stitution. Gaining ritual control of the land by planting the *nkinda* is more common to the southern forest than to the Zaire-Ubangi peninsula.[21] It seems likely that when the ancestors of the Nunu arrived the land was not totally unoccupied, and that *nkinda* had already been planted by the autochthonous inhabi-tants. The Nunu not only had to capture the land physically, but also to capture it ritually by planting their own *nkinda*. This is what they did when they settled in Bolobo in the nineteenth century,[22] and it seems likely that they had followed a similar procedure when settling the swamps.

By planting the *nkinda,* a settler became the guardian of a particular patch of forest or grassland. Future settlers had to ask permission to settle on his patch, but permission was rarely de-

---

[18] Interview: Lopanda, 7-10-81, Tape 1/2.

[19] Interview: Etebe, 8-4-81, Tape 16/1.

[20] Interview: Mangasa, 5-7-75, Tape A7.

[21] Vansina (personal communication) notes that *nkinda* charms are widespread in the southern forest from the Gabon coast to the Kuba. For a reference to *nkinda* among the Kuba, see Jan Vansina, *The Children of Woot* (Madison, Wis., 1978), p. 314. The *nkinda* charm may be the basis for the organization of the Nunu clan, called *likinda*.

[22] Interview: Etebe, 8-4-81, Tape 16/1.

nied.[23] Many settlers meant prestige, and they provided defense against attack. The main task of the guardian of a forest or grassland was to maintain the fertility of the land by regulating the ritual relationship between the people and the spirits. In return he received a leg of any animal killed on his land and a token remuneration for fish caught in his waters. In the nineteenth century, when ivory became valuable, the guardian received the ground tusk of any elephant killed in his territory.

As settlement progressed, hierarchies of *nkinda* developed. The first settler in an area planted the major *nkinda* for the entire area. As other settlers arrived, they planted minor *nkinda* to protect the forest or plain where they established their homesteads. This process was described by Longwa:

> The ancestor Ngeli planted the *nkinda* at Mitima to make the area grow and prosper. Later settlers also planted *nkinda*. Here would be a cluster of six houses; there would be a cluster of seven houses. Each cluster had its *nkinda*.[24]

The hierarchies of charms thus served to humanize the land by organizing geographical space into spheres and subspheres of ritual protection.

Along with the hierarchies of charms went hierarchies of guardianship titles. The highest title was *ngeli,* and it was generally reserved for the guardian of the major *nkinda* charm in any given region. The title itself was almost certainly borrowed from the Boma, who lived to the southeast, even though the Nunu claim that it came down with them from the Ubangi.[25]

---

[23] Interview: Bampomba, 7-24-81, Tape 13/2.

[24] Interview: Longwa, 7-20-81, Tape 9/1.

[25] "Ngeli" is a Boma chiefly title. Boma genealogies collected by Belgian colonial officials in 1930 showed 19 generations between the founding ancestor, Boma Ngeli, and the current chiefs. René Tonnoir, *Giribuma,* MRAC, Archives d'Ethnographie, vol. 14 (Tervuren, Belgium, 1970), pp. 207–17, 268–79. Nunu lists of the *ngeli* who reigned at Mitima are much shorter. Deweerd listed six *ngeli* before the colonial period. See J.J.L. Lingwambe, "Histoire Banunu-Bobangi" (mimeographed pamphlet: Kinshasa, 1966), p. 20. Lila listed nine *ngeli* in the precolonial period. Interview: July 14, 1981, field notes. Both lists are much shorter than the Boma list, suggesting that the title is more recent among the Nunu. For an oral tradition tracing the Nunu *ngeli* title to the Ubangi River, see the interview with Losengo, 12-10-75, Tape A66.

The earliest remembered holder of the *ngeli* title was Ngeli Bokamai, the guardian at Mitima.[26] The number of *ngeli* title-holders in the swamps and their fringes increased over time as new regions were settled. Often it was the first settler in a new region who planted the *nkinda* and took the title of *ngeli*. Nonetheless the number of titleholders remained small. Lila, who was the most knowledgeable informant on this subject, listed only eight locations where holders of the *ngeli* title once sat.[27]

The early *ngeli* are remembered for their ability to dominate nature. Losengo gave some examples:

> When the ancestors arrived here, there were among them people called *ngeli*. They could address all matters of the universe. They would say, "Next year women will bear only male children." After that all the women bore only boys. If he said, "This year you will bear only girls," it was done. Then he would say that for the next five years nobody should die of disease. For the next five years or so, nobody died.[28]

The symbolism of these stories clearly communicates the idea that the office of *ngeli,* like the charm over which it presided, provided a technology by which humans could alter natural processes.

The early *ngeli* were also givers of laws designed to keep human behavior in harmony with the laws of the spirit world and thus to assure peace and prosperity among humans. As Lila explained:

> The ancestors called their great elders *ngeli* because they gave us the laws. . . . In the evenings, they would have all the men sit down, and they would proclaim laws: "I don't want my men to travel to other villages. This is a time of troubles. I want peace." Another time he would say, "Don't do any work on the day of Mpika. The land must rest."[29]

---

[26] See, for example, the tradition told by Losengo, which traces all of the Nunu settlements in the swamplands back to Mitima. Interview: Losengo, 12-10-75, Tape A66.

[27] Interview: Lila, 7-14-81, field notes.

[28] Interview: Losengo, 12-10-75, Tape A66.

[29] Interview: Lila, 7-14-81, Tape 4/2.

The *ngeli* also made pronouncements against men chasing other men's wives, and against stealing.[30]

The *ngeli* had no militia with which to enforce his pronouncements, but this was not necessary because the laws were seen as self-enforcing. People felt that the guardian was not creating laws but rather articulating the laws of the spirit world, the violation of which would bring retribution from the spirits themselves. The fact that the laws also promoted harmony within the society was seen as a happy by-product of harmony with the spirits. If some of the more thoughtful settlers saw the beliefs about spirits as an elaborate metaphor for a certain view of how people should relate to their environment and to each other, they kept such views to themselves.

Beneath the *ngeli* title were lesser titles. One title that is only vaguely remembered today was *miandangoi*. The holders of that title were described as "almost *Ngeli*." As Lila explained: "If an area didn't have an *ngeli*, but had a person of fame, courage, and intelligence who regulated matters on the land, they called him *miandangoi*."[31] The more common lesser title was *mpomb'e mboka*, or "neighborhood elder." The dispersed homesteads that made up a given neighborhood had an elder to oversee the major *nkinda* charm. Some stories describe these elders in terms similar to those used for *ngeli*:

> If the *mpomb'e mboka* said, "This year nobody will die," then nobody died. If he said, "This year we will kill ten elephants," it happened. Then he would say, "Smallpox will not come," and it didn't come. Then he said, "All women will get pregnant and none of the children will die." Then 40 children were born and none of them died.[32]

The *nkinda* charms and their guardians spiritually transformed the landscape. They symbolized the domination of culture over nature. The settlers believed that one of the main differences between people and animals was that people possessed techniques for controlling and manipulating the spirits who, in turn, controlled the processes of nature. As long as people

---

[30] Interview: Longwa, 7-20-81, Tape 9/1.
[31] Interview: Lila, 7-14-81, Tape 4/2.
[32] Interview: Losengo, 12-11-75, Tape A68.

maintained this control, they could successfully exploit the natural resources of the swamp environment. But they also knew that if they ever lost this control, the land would turn against them.

TRANSFORMING THE LANDSCAPE

Once the settlers had ritually domesticated the land, they could physically transform it by constructing dams and ponds to divert the natural flow of the water and by clearing fields for yams and cassava. As modern Nunu see it, differences in individual wealth and landholdings can be traced back to the original settlers. Ekando stated the historical proposition as follows:

> If your ancestors were lazy and did not have strength, then today you won't have many worldly goods. If your ancestors were strong, then today you reap the rewards. If a person was the first to settle a plot of land but did nothing to improve it, he died leaving nothing to prove that he was the owner of the land. If you improve the land by constructing a dam or a pond, then you leave a sign that you were the owner. Later generations will say that you were the first owner of the land.[33]

Because the environment varied greatly from one part of the swamp to another, the types of physical transformations required depended on where one settled. To get a sense of the relationships between environments and productive tactics, it is useful to examine the various micro-environments one at a time.

The mixed environments
The first of the distinct micro-environments settled by the ancestors of the Nunu was dominated by the Nsangasi River, which was little more than an extension of the Zaire. The Nsangasi received most of its water via a channel about ten kilometers long that connected it to the Zaire. Water from this channel entered the Nsangasi, causing it to swell from a small stream to a river whose width reached 200 meters in places. The Nsangasi flowed roughly parallel to the Zaire—never more than eight kilometers away—for about 40 kilometers till it emptied

---

[33] Interview: Ekando, 7-25-81, Tape 14/1.

back into the Zaire. Because the Nsangasi was connected to the
Zaire at both ends, it rose and fell in perfect cadence with the
river. Although the Nsangasi was one of the smallest rivers in
the central Zaire basin, it was nevertheless one of the richest in
fish.[34]

The land between the Nsangasi and the Zaire was grassland
dotted only by a few scattered trees. Inland from the Nsangasi,
the grassland continued for about a mile before giving way to
forest. The sequence of vegetation testified to an alluvial process
common throughout the flooded regions of equatorial Africa.
The banks had been colonized by *vossia cuspidata,* a sturdy grass
which the Nunu called *bikoko.*[35] It had shallow roots that inter-
twined with the roots of neighboring stalks to form large clusters. The roots were only superficially attached to the soil during the low-water season, and during the high water they let go
completely and rose with the water to form a floating meadow.
This phenomenon profoundly affected the visual landscape of
the area because the Nsangasi River was distinct from the surrounding grasslands during both flood and ebb. The difference
was that during the former season the grasses floated on the
water; during the latter they rested on land.

The floating prairies slowed down the current and encouraged sedimentation. As the sediment layer built up, the forest
began to invade, first with bushes and later with trees that were
able to withstand flood conditions. The trees shaded the
ground, causing the original grasses to die. By then the floating
meadows were becoming a flooded forest.[36] This process could

[34] Service des Eaux et Forets, "Aperçu sur la Pêche Lacustre et Fluviale au
Congo Belge et au Ruanda-Urundi," *Bulletin Agricole du Congo Belge,* 50
(1959):1680.

[35] Germain, *Biotopes Alluvionnaires,* pp. 225–29. Some of the floating prairies
may have been made up of *echinochola pyramidalis,* which withstands the
dry season better.

[36] R. Bouillenne, J. Moreau, and P. Deuse, *Esquisse Ecologique des Faciés Forestiers et Marécageuses des Bords du Lac Tumba,* ARSC, Classe des Sciences
Naturelles et Médicales, n.s., vol. 3, no. 1 (Brussels, 1955), pp. 21–27; Van
Leynseele, "Ecological Stability and Intensive Fish Production: The Case of
the Libinza People of the Middle Ngiri (Zaire)," in *Social and Ecological
Systems,* edited by P.C. Burnham and R.F. Ellen (New York, 1979) pp.
169–71.

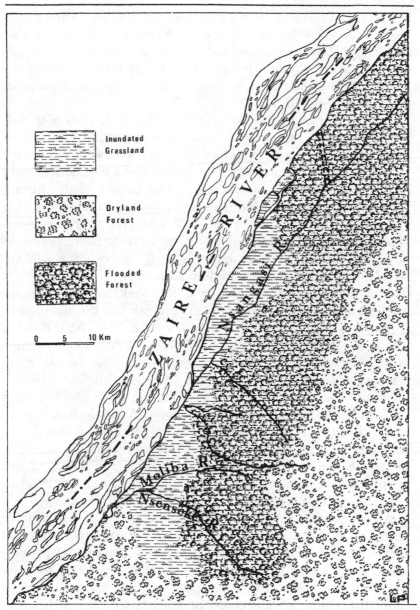

Environments of the Southern Swamps

be arrested and even reversed by human activity. The settlers burned the *bikoko* grass every year during the dry season and thus retarded sedimentation and kept larger plants from invading. Moreover, the fires burned the trees along the edge of the forest, causing the forest to retreat and leaving open spaces to be invaded by grasses.[37]

The major task facing the settlers was devising ways to fish and grow crops in the specialized environment. All fishermen in the area between the Nsangasi and the Ngiri were acquainted with a cluster of fishing methods, but the old techniques could not be used without modification. The timing of the fishing calendar had to be changed, fishing spots had to be picked that would make the best use of the local landscape, and there were new species of fish to be dealt with. All of these problems could be overcome, however, by applying well-known principles and by adapting old techniques to new situations.

One important fishing area was the banks of the Nsangasi itself. When the banks overflowed, the fish left the riverbed to enter the flooded meadows or to go beyond them to the flooded forest. As the water declined, however, the fish sought refuge in the deeper pools of the Nsangasi. To prevent the fish from reaching this shelter, the fishermen stretched fish fences (which looked remarkably like the snow fences found in the American midwest) along the banks of the river. A single fence could stretch for several hundred meters along the riverbank and then turn inland, going up the slope of the riverbank for 40 or 50 meters to make sure that fish encountering the fence did not simply swim around it. Along the fence the fishermen attached a variety of traps with openings parallel to the fence.

As fish sought to return to the river, they encountered the fence and swam along it looking for an opening. In the process they entered the traps and were caught. Because the traps were constructed with funnel-like openings that were easy to enter but difficult to exit from, a single trap could catch a dozen or more fish. This method could be used twice during the year:

---

[37] The *meembe* region of the floodplain, dominated by dead, burnt trees, was created in precisely this fashion.

during the small ebb in January, and again during the large ebb in June. During the dry season the fishermen would cut paths along which to stretch the fence in the grass and bush, making sure that the path was smooth so that the bottom of the fence would nestle snugly against the ground.

After the water went down, the fish were found mostly in the Nsangasi River itself, but they still sought the luxury and comfort of the floating meadows. Under such circumstances, the best way to trap them was to construct artificial floating prairies. The fishermen would bring *bikoko* grass from various places along the riverbank and fix it with stakes in a certain spot along the riverbank. They would enlarge it little by little, and it would grow on its own by capturing small clusters of grass that floated by in the current. The floating prairie provided both vegetal matter and insects for the fish; the stems gave shade and the roots offered hiding places from predators. Thus it attracted small fish as well as predators who wished to eat them.

When the water in the river fell to less than six feet deep at the outer edges of the meadow, the fishermen entered with several canoes loaded with fan-folded fish fences. Starting against the shore at one end of the prairie, they lowered the fence and fixed it solidly with long stakes. In this manner they surrounded the floating prairie with fish fences and trapped the fish under the floating grass. Then they began to remove the floating grass from the enclosed space. When the grass was removed, the fishermen slowly pushed the fish fence toward the bank, concentrating the fish in progressively smaller areas. When all of the fish were in shallow water, the fishermen scooped them up with small baskets or even by hand. This method of fishing, called *ekoko,* was most advantageously used during the periods of lowest water in March and August.

Away from the riverbanks were the beds of numerous small streams that flowed only during the high-water seasons. They flowed away from the Nsangasi when the water was rising, and they flowed toward the Nsangasi when the water was falling. During the highest water they could be detected only by almost imperceptible movements among the grasses that indicated a slight current flowing along the shallow channel. During periods of lower water—either when the water was first rising or when it was in the advanced stages of lowering—these streams became more sharply defined and fish moved along them in their journeys between the Nsangasi and the flooded forest a mile or so inland. Across these temporary streams the fishermen built dams. Some of these were temporary barriers made of sticks and leaves; others consisted of sticks and fish fences. Into holes in the dam would be placed a series of *losongo* traps, which were about a meter long and fifteen centimeters in diameter at the mouth, narrowing to a point at the opposite end. The fish swimming downstream would enter the traps and swim along until they were squeezed by the narrow part. Both the current and the lack of room to turn around prevented the fish from escaping.

Such techniques were based on a subtle understanding of the habits of the fish and the flow of water through the landscape. They were extremely efficient and effective because they were based on the simple principle of letting the fish enter the flooded grasslands and forests and then preventing them from escaping. This was less similar to normal fishing, with its aspects of chance and luck, than it was to fish farming, which has an annual harvest.

The second mixed environment to be settled was located south of the Nsangasi River valley. It was entered by a small stream called Moliba mo Nkubosaka. According to Nunu traditions, the first settlers, Mombinda and Nzumola, entered this stream from the Zaire and founded the village of Nkubosaka near its mouth.[38] They lived off a mixture of river fishing and fishing in the forest-savanna mosaic that characterized the area between the river and the dense, flooded forest. During March through June, they fished in the savanna, and in September they fished in the forest. During the rest of the year, they fished in the river. They placed *ekete* and *etambo* traps in flooded grasses and shrubs. They made circles with fish fences over shallow sandbanks. In the daytime they fished with spears along the edges of floating meadows, while at night they used torches and spears. *Eyiko,* the method of stretching fish fences along the

---

[38] Interview: Lopanza, 7-22-81, Tape 9/2.

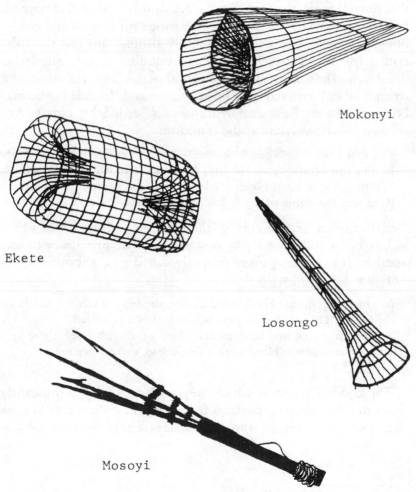

Etambo

Mokonyi

Ekete

Losongo

Mosoyi

Nunn Fishing Equipment

edges of islands, was the only major method they employed along the river that required any improvement of the landscape and therefore entailed permanent ownership of a fishing spot.

The flooded forest

As new settlers arrived and as sons of older settlers sought new places to settle, people moved into more specialized environments. The original settlers along the Nsangasi lived near the river, but future settlers moved farther inland via a small stream that flowed from the east. Both sides of this stream had narrow bands of grassland that provided clearings for houses and fields, but which were too narrow to allow fishing. Instead the fishermen fished exclusively in the surrounding forest. Similarly, those who left the village of Nkubosaka and followed the stream inland entered the great forest and founded Mitima. Nunu traditions hold that Mitima was settled by Ngeli. According to one version of the tradition:

> The first *ngeli* was Ngeli Bokamai. . . . He entered by way of the Moliba mo Nkubosaka. He built Mitima. That village is known as "Liboma limbe Koni Ngeli." Liboma was the name of his wife. Koni was the name of his father. He lived in Mitima.[39]

Like the other settlements in the swamps, Mitima was not a village but a collection of homesteads in close proximity to one another. It is perhaps more properly called a neighborhood. As Longwa described it:

> Mitima was completely flooded during the high water. It was in the forest. There were no grasslands. It was a scattered agglomeration of tiny settlements. Here were six houses; there were seven houses. Here were nine people; there were ten people.[40]

The flooded forest in which they settled differed significantly from the neighboring dryland forests because only tree species that were resistant to the floodwaters could survive. Places

---

39 Interview: Lila, 7-12-81, Tape 3/1.
40 Interview: Longwa, 7-20-81, Tape 8/1.

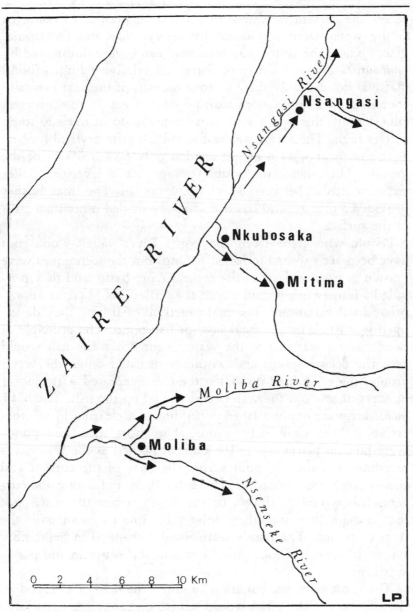

Settlement Routes and Sites

where the current flowed strongly during periods of rising or falling water were dominated by *Scytopetalum* and *Oubanguia*. Places where the water was relatively calm were dominated by *Guibourtia*. Stands of mature forest on relatively high ground that was flooded only three to four months of the year typically contained an upper canopy composed of trees 35 to 40 meters tall. Beneath this was a second layer made up of trees 20 to 25 meters high. The forest was not as thick as the dryland forests, as the two canopies together shaded only 60% to 90% of the ground. Underneath the double canopy was a layer of smaller trees and bushes between 8 and 15 meters tall. The small bushes provided a thin ground cover that rarely shaded more than 30% of the surface.[41]

People who came from the Ngiri River valley would not have been accustomed to forest fishing, but the techniques were known in various parts of the central Zaire basin, and they provided a framework within which the settlers could create appropriate local variations. The main method of fishing they developed was based on the *monsongo,* or fish pond. The principle of pond fishing was that as the water went down the fish would seek the deepest pools and would be isolated when the water around the pool dried up. Then the fishers entered with wicker buckets, threw out the water, and picked up the fish. The basic *monsongo* was simply a large pond dug in a clearing in the forest, but there were elaborations. The most successful ponds were built in places where the current flowed as the water was receding. A dam was built across the flow of the current and then a large pond was dug behind the dam. Following the current, fish would be drawn to this pond; when the water got low enough they would no longer be able to swim over the dam to escape. The ponds were usually emptied in September when the land had long dried out and the water in the ponds was low.

The most elaborate variation required the help of a crocodile. The diggers of the pond would situate one edge against a large

---

[41] Evrard, *Recherches Ecologiques,* pp. 121-30. See also J. Lebrun, "La Forêt Equatoriale Congolaise," *Bulletin Agricole du Congo Belge,* 27 (1936):183-84.

tree whose roots stabilized the soil along the embankment. A crocodile would enter the pond and construct a den by tunneling between the roots of the tree, as these held the soil in place and kept the ground from caving in. When the pond was being emptied, the fish would flee into the crocodile's cave. The fishers would then block the entrance to the cave, dig into it from the top, and take out the fish.

Pond-fishing techniques were based on knowledge of the habits of the fish. The fishermen knew that the lush vegetation and insect life of the flooded forest made a more desirable habitat for many species of fish than did the relatively barren channels of the Zaire. The ponds lulled the fish into complacency as the waters around them dried up and isolated them. Because the fishers emptied the ponds with buckets, every fish that sought the lush depths of the ponds would ultimately be caught. Pond fishing became the basic fishing method of the forest people because it was efficient and thorough. The people did not have to seek the fish; the fish simply congregated in ponds and remained there until they were harvested.

The reliance on ponds as the major method of fishing influenced patterns of land settlement and land claims. The ponds were usually dug in natural clearings because the work of clearing trees and roots from a patch of mature rain forest would have been daunting.[42] Because suitable clearings were scarce and scattered, the desirable parcels of land were spread thinly over the landscape. Moreover, because a pond was designed to attract all the fish in the surrounding drainage area, its owner tried to prevent other settlers from constructing ponds too close to his own. It therefore seems certain that the most desirable patches of land were settled first, leaving large stretches of undesirable and often unproductive forest for the latecomers.

The forest dwellers supplemented their diet with products from gardens and fields. Although they often cleared tiny patches of forest near their homes to make small gardens and plant bananas, they did not make large forest clearings for yam

---

[42] Interview: Longwa, 7-20-81, Tape 9/1. For descriptions of such clearings, see Evrard, *Recherches Ecologiques,* pp. 122–23.

or cassava fields. Instead, they sought the nearest grassland areas, which were easier to clear though less fertile. People living along the tributaries of the Nsangasi made their fields in the small strips of grassland that paralleled the streams. Those living at places such as Mitima in the center of the forest traveled about ten kilometers to the south to make fields in the grasslands. These fields had to be watched to protect them from animals, so people built huts near the fields where they stayed throughout the growing season. Because fields were made in grassland, the women could clear them by themselves, and so the customary division of labor in equatorial Africa, in which men cut the forest and women planted the crops, did not exist there.

Some crops could be grown in the forest itself. Mitima and Masaa became centers of palm oil and palm wine production, the products coming from small clusters of palm trees planted near the homesteads. Because palms require sunlight, they grew best on land cleared for human habitation. Even today clusters of palm trees mark the locations of long-abandoned settlements. A variety of foods with names such as *lokolele, lipambu, maloke, ekomu, lomba, longungutu, losango* and *mpeke* grew wild in the forest.[43] The forest also provided a variety of building materials. The *ndele* leaves used to cover houses came from there, as did the *ngoli* vine used to make fish traps. From the raffia palms came palm fronds called *mbanzi* used to make sleeping mats and fish fences. *Nkinga,* the string used to tie together the various fish traps and fences, and *elonga,* a string made from the bark of the *makongi* bush, also came from the forest.

The floating prairies
South of the forest lay the great floating prairies of the Moliba and Nsenseke. Except for scattered clumps of trees, the land was covered by *bikoko* grass as far as the eye could see. During the high-water seasons, the grass would turn a lush green and the hollow stems would float upward as the water rose. So

---

[43] Interview: Lopanda, 7-10-81, Tape 1/1. There are no English equivalents to these names.

dense was the grass that the water under it was often completely hidden. Because the surface of the water remained perfectly level, hiding the undulations and valleys in the earth's surface, the landscape had the appearance of being absolutely flat and monotonous. When the water departed and the ground dried out, the grass turned a pale yellow, lying on the earth in twisted clumps ready to be burned by the inhabitants.[44] It was only then that the low hills and shallow valleys of the true landscape became visible.

The only pathway from the Zaire into this strange world was the Moliba, a stream that a few kilometers inland from its mouth narrowed to nothing more than a channel through the grass kept open by the constant passage of canoes. The further one went into the prairies, the narrower the channel became until finally it disappeared altogether. Fishermen forced their small canoes through the grasses, poling with long, forked sticks that would not stick in the mud. The major tributary of the Moliba was the Nsenseke, another small channel in the grass that would have been covered over by the floating prairies, had not canoemen kept it open.

According to oral tradition, the first settler along the Moliba was a certain Malingatoli, who came from up the Zaire. As the person who planted the first *nkinda* charm, he is remembered as its first guardian. The tradition lists a total of eight guardians of the charm before the coming of the Europeans.[45] Assuming that each person on the list held the position for twenty years, the list would go back to the mid-eighteenth century. It is highly likely, however, that the list is telescoped, and that the settlers arrived much earlier. The first remembered settler to branch out and settle along the Nsenseke was a certain Mwele who founded a settlement at the place where the Nsenseke branches off from the Moliba.[46]

The major method of fishing was based on dams made of wooden poles and filled with earth. In areas where the terrain was uneven, they constructed levees to guide the water into the

---

[44] Germain, *Biotopes Alluvionnaires,* pp. 225–29.
[45] Interview: Ekando, 7-23-81, Tape 12/1.
[46] Interview: Bampomba, 7-18-81, Tape 7/1.

proper channels. The earthen dams had holes into which long, narrow *losongo* traps were placed. The dams were built low so that when the water was rising the fish could get behind them simply by swimming over them. When the waters began to recede, the fish did not leave right away because they preferred the shaded waters under the grasses, with their abundance of insects and vegetal nutrients, to the barren sands of the Zaire River. By the time they began to head for the river, water no longer covered the entire landscape. It flowed toward the Zaire in channels that became increasingly well defined as the hilltops and higher ground became visible. By this time the water had dropped below the level of the dams, and it flowed through the holes in them. The fish swimming with the flow got caught in the traps that the fishermen had inserted into the holes.

Dam fishing was extremely efficient. Once the water was low enough to flow in clearly defined channels that were blocked by dams, every fish in those channels could be caught. As the population spread out, more and more channels were dammed up; therefore, a very high percentage of the fish that entered the flooded grasslands every year failed to return to the river. However, this highly efficient harvest did not permanently endanger the fish population because of two factors. First, many of the fish spawned during January, and the minnows were small enough to get through the holes in the traps and make it back to the Zaire. Second, swamp fishing depended on the annual influx of fish from the Zaire as the waters rose. As long as there were fish in the Zaire, there would be fish in the flooded grasslands.

This dominant method of fishing influenced the way people settled the land. Each person sought to lay claim to a stretch of a small stream and the land on both sides of it.[47] The streams designated the paths by which the floodwaters drained as they receded and thus indicated where the dams should be placed. The size of a given plot of land was determined by the length of stream it encompassed. The width of the plot was relatively unimportant because nobody wished to settle the areas not

---

[47] Interview: Bampomba, 7-18-81, Tape 7/1.

drained by streams. What was important was that nobody else should settle too nearby along the same stream. Modern Nunu claim that dams should be about two kilometers apart, but at the time of the early settlers the distances were probably much greater. Bampomba explained the general pattern of settlement:

> In the time of the ancestors, if they came to settle an area, an ancestor would pick a spot and then go and cut boundary markers. He would say, "This piece of land is for me and my family. The next person who comes has to settle beyond me."[48]

Although dams were the single most important method of fishing, their production was supplemented by methods that captured fish at other times of the year. During the high water, fishermen would put *mokonyi* traps beneath the floating grasses. After the water had begun to recede, fishermen often used a method called *nkala li mimboko*. They used a fish fence to block off an open channel, and they slowly drew the fence toward the shallow water. The fish were then scooped up in baskets or speared. As the water receded, shallow pools or coves were often left in low-lying areas. The fishermen would stretch a fish fence across one end of the pool and slowly push it toward the other end, trapping the fish in the shallow water at the far end of the pool. They then scooped up the fish with fish baskets. After the dam harvest ended and the grasslands were dry, people would burn the grass and probe the parched ground with spears in search of male *nzombo* (*protopterus*) fish which would dig holes in the mud and construct mud houses for themselves as the females fled with the falling water.

The distinct terrain of the grasslands influenced other aspects of food production as well. The absence of trees made it relatively easy for women to clear fields for growing crops. As in other areas of the swamp, crops had to be grown on high ground and the harvest had to be completed before the high waters turned the entire area into a floating prairie. It is difficult to know just what the early settlers planted, but in the nineteenth century the women planted mostly cassava, which they

---

[48] Interview: Bampomba, 7-18-81, Tape 7/1.

supplemented with a yam called *epe,* sweet potatoes, and plantains.[49] The absence of trees made it difficult for the women to get firewood for cooking. There were a few small forests scattered here and there, and the women would travel to them in canoes. They would cut wood and bring it back by the canoeload. They would also search for the *nsange* tree, which grew in the grasslands, and cut off the bark near the ground. After about four months the tree died and could be used for firewood.[50]

CONCLUSION

Much of the writing about peoples in small-scale, pre-industrial societies has emphasized their almost unconscious ecological wisdom. They are pictured as natural conservationists, desiring above all to live in harmony with nature. Writing about the peoples of the Amazon basin, a region environmentally similar to the Zaire basin, Betty Meggers stated the proposition in its most extreme form:

> Primitive peoples regard themselves as part of nature, neither superior nor inferior to other creatures (although often superior to other groups of men). The souls of human beings are believed to be capable of entering the bodies of animals and vice versa, and animal spirits are often thought to exercise control over human destiny. Such supernatural concepts are a translation into cultural terms of checks and balances that exist on a biological level to maintain the equilibrium of an ecosystem. Since unrestricted use of increasingly efficient hunting techniques would cause rapid exhaustion of the very resource they were designed to make accessible, supernatural sanctions develop to limit or channel their use. This kind of functional relationship between a religious belief and a tool is one example of the infinite number of links that serve both to bind a cultural system together and to make it a compatible part of an ecosystem as a whole.[51]

[49] Interview: Bampomba, 7-24-81, Tape 13/1. The cultivation of *epe* was abandoned during the colonial period.
[50] Interview: Bampomba, 7-22-81, Tape 11/2.
[51] Betty Meggers, *Amazonia* (Chicago, 1971), p. 2.

The actions of the settlers in the southern swamps did not fit into this neat scheme. They devised tactics for exploiting the environment with great skill and deadly seriousness. In the first place, they planted *nkinda* charms and recognized guardians of the land in order to establish symbolically the dominance of culture over nature. In the second place, the settlers maximized their production. They cleared forest patches, dug ponds, built dams, strung fish fences, and created artificial islands of floating grasses. Their fishing techniques were designed to ensure that the vast majority of the fish that entered the swamps with the floodwaters would never leave.

The settlers did, however, make some attempts to manage their environment to assure long-term productivity. The *losongo* traps that they inserted into the holes in their dams were made of strips of raffia palm set from one to two centimeters apart so that the fingerlings born during the high water could escape to the river. Likewise, the fish fences left about two centimeters between strips of palm frond through which minnows could escape. On the other hand, the ponds trapped fish of all sizes that sought refuge in their depths.

Like people the world over, the settlers in the southern swamps were interested in conservation only to the extent that they felt their resource base threatened. Because their dams and ponds gave high yields of fish year after year, they saw no need to alter their tactics. The sustained high yields can be explained by two factors. First, the Zaire River, which was nearly ten kilometers wide as it flowed past the swamplands, provided a new supply of fish each year. The fishermen were not living off the produce of their immediate environment, but were harvesting fish that had been nurtured and sustained in neighboring environmental zones. Second, the population density of the swamps remained low. Because each settler wished to maximize his fish production, he claimed as large a drainage area as possible for his dam or pond. By the reckoning of some, two kilometers was the minimum allowable distance between dams. Such large claims kept population densities low and allowed each landowner to produce more fish than he needed to feed his family. In short, the competition among people kept population densities low, which reduced the need to regulate the human impact on the land.

The choice of tactics for exploiting the environment had clear social consequences. As the settlers built dams and ponds, they were also building up vested interests in the ownership of certain plots of ground. By developing ways of producing far more fish per year than their immediate families needed, they implicitly raised the issue of distribution of surplus. By using harvesting techniques that required a considerable labor force, they laid the groundwork for social inequality. The tactics developed in the struggle against nature helped to define and shape the strategies in the competition among people.

4. The strategies

WHILE THE SETTLERS were developing methods for surviving in the new environments of the southern swamps, they were also devising strategies for turning production into wealth and wealth into power. It is no longer possible to reconstruct the strategies of the earliest settlers, but it seems reasonable to assume that at first they followed practices common in their former homelands. The frontier situation in the southern swamps, however, gave them freedom to experiment and to innovate. They developed new strategies, and over time the most successful strategies became institutionalized, forming a new framework of action.

MOBILIZING LABOR

A major problem for the earliest settlers was to mobilize labor to construct ponds and dams. Nunu say that it takes about 20 workers to dig a small pond with any efficiency because a smaller number of people working during the dry season can make only a shallow pond that will become partially filled with silt during the coming flood.[1] In a similar way, dams have to be made large enough during the dry season so that the floodwaters do not wash them away. Because of these requirements, it was difficult for an individual or his immediate family to construct a dam or a pond a little at a time over a period of years.[2]

---

[1] Interview: Longwa, 7-20-81, Tape 9/1.

[2] The pond of Mbonge Botele was dug by three brothers who worked with their children and the children of their sister. This would represent the minimum number of workers necessary. Interview: Mbonge Botele, July, 1975, Nkolo-Lingamba field notes.

The more labor one had, the easier to dig a pond or construct a dam.

The key to building up an estate, therefore, lay in mobilizing labor. One way to accomplish this was through cooperative arrangements. Many immigrants had probably come to the southern swamps in groups of brothers or other kinfolk, and such people would have worked cooperatively to dig successive ponds over a period of years. Similar cooperative groups may have been formed by people who lacked kinsmen. Voluntary teams have long been a common institution among river fishermen, and it is not difficult to imagine that early Nunu formed such teams as well.

Another way to gain labor was to procure it from the neighboring populations. As a group, the Nunu were richer than the neighboring Sengele and Mpama because of the unequal distribution of resources between the swamps and the surrounding inland regions. The region as a whole contained much more farmland than swampland. Fish were therefore scarcer and commanded a much higher value than yams or bananas. The fishermen were thus in an excellent position to barter valued commodities for bridewealth. The early settlers were probably men who had left their upriver homelands precisely because they were poor and unable to obtain spouses. Armed with their newfound wealth, they turned to neighboring groups as sources of wives.

They also bought slaves. In normal times they could purchase criminals, debtors, people caught in adultery, or people accused of witchcraft. It was during times of famine, however, that fishermen could best take advantage of the valuable commodities they possessed. There were times when the agricultural peoples suffered crop failures resulting from local factors such as too little rain, too much rain, or crop disease. These factors did not affect fishing in the swamps because the rise and fall of the river were controlled by climatic elements as far away as the upper Ubangi and the upper Zaire. Although there is no way to document famines for the early period, Nunu oral traditions recount that when famine reigned along the Alima River in the late nineteenth century, starving families would sell some of their children to obtain food to feed the others.[3] According to the traditions, the situation was so desperate that the Mboshi would sell a slave for a small basket of fish. The Nunu then put the slaves to work building mounds of earth for houses and digging fish ponds. It is highly probable that there were famines in earlier times that presented the settlers with similar opportunities.

While absorbing wives and slaves from the surrounding areas, the settlers were also adopting the customs and institutions of the southern forest peoples. They added matrilineal inheritance and succession onto the predominantly patrilineal kinship system that they had brought down from the Zaire-Ubangi peninsula. The form of marriage they adopted resembled that of the Sengele and was probably borrowed from them. The iron and copper prestige goods used for social transactions along the Ubangi were replaced by the shell money typical of the lower Zaire.

FINDING LAND

By the eighteenth century, the time of the farthest reaches of Nunu genealogies, the situation in the core settlement areas had reversed itself. Shortage of land, not shortage of labor, became the major problem. This new reality gave rise to a new set of strategies.

The increase in population had taken place gradually, perhaps over centuries. Contrary to the schematic genealogical charts that show population increasing geometrically as if in accordance with Malthus' law, the actual population of the swamps most likely grew in irregular and fitful ways. Nunu genealogies show that in some families the children would die before they

---

[3] Interviews: Lopanda, 7-10-81, Tape 1/2, and 7-15-81, Tape 6/2; Ekando, 7-25-81, Tape 14/2; Etebe, 8-4-81, Tape 16/2. Jacques de Brazza in 1883 noted the contrast between the robust river peoples and the emaciated inland peoples who looked like "skeletons." Catherine Coquery-Vidrovitch, *Brazza et la Prise de Possession du Congo* (Paris, 1969), p. 304.

could procreate, or the grandchildren would die, or the family would have sons but no daughters, or vice versa.

Disease was the main enemy of population growth. A deadly constraint on population came from the mosquitoes that bred in the stagnant floodwaters. Unlike the black waters of the Ngiri, which were loaded with humic acids that kept mosquitoes from breeding, the brown waters of the Zaire were neutral (pH above seven), in part because the high calcium content of the water neutralized the acid water flowing in from the tributaries.[4] The neutral waters provided an ideal habitat for malaria-bearing mosquitoes that would swarm about in the evenings. Malarial fevers, called *mowewe* by the Nunu, are common today and probably have been so for a long time.

Early settlers from the Ngiri valley would likely have had lower-than-normal resistance to malaria for two reasons. First, they lacked the resistance that children born in malarial areas develop during the first three years of their lives. Because children in malarial areas who failed to develop resistance generally died at a young age, most adults were relatively immune to the effects of the disease. People from non-malarial areas who had not built up such resistance, however, would have been more susceptible to the disease. Second, immigrants from the Ngiri valley probably had a lower-than-normal rate of sickle-cell carriers in their population. The sickle cell, which is found in the blood of roughly half the people living in malarial areas of central Africa, gives people a greater chance of surviving malaria.[5]

---

[4] Pierre Van Leynseele, "Ecological Stability and Intensive Fish Production: The Case of the Libinza People of the Middle Ngiri (Zaire)," in *Social and Ecological Systems,* edited by P.C. Burnham and R.F. Ellen (New York, 1979), p. 176; G. Marlier, "Limnology of the Congo and Amazon Rivers," in *Tropical Forest Ecosystems in Africa and Latin America,* edited by Betty Meggers, Edward Ayensu, and Donald Duckworth (Washington, D.C., 1973), p. 230; J.P. Gosse, *Le Milieu Aquatique et l'Ecologie des Poissons dans la Région de Yangambie,* MRAC, Sciences Zoologiques, no. 116 (Tervuren, Belgium, 1963), p. 138.

[5] See A.C. Allison, "Malaria in Carriers of the Sickle-Cell Trait and in Newborn Children," *Experimental Parasitology,* 6 (1957):418–46; Arno Motulsky, "Hereditary Red Cell Traits and Malaria," *Supplement to the American Journal of Tropical Medicine and Hygiene,* 13 (1964):147–61.

In malarial areas, people with sickle cells survived childhood bouts of malaria at higher rates than people without them, and thus the percentage of sickle-cell carriers in the population remained high. In a mosquito-free area such as the Ngiri valley, however, people lacking the sickle cell would survive childhood at higher-than-normal rates, and thus the percentage of sickle-cell carriers in the population would drop. If a population group with a low percentage of sickle-cell carriers moved to the southern swamps, they probably experienced higher-than-normal death rates, as did their children.[6]

Sleeping sickness was another danger. The forested portions of the swamps provided ideal habitat for the tsetse fly, *G. palpalis Rob. Desu.* This fly, which thrived in wooded waters, was a vector of the *Trypanosoma gambiense,* which caused sleeping sickness.[7] Because of the flies, sleeping sickness, which the Nunu called *ewo,* was endemic in the forested parts of the floodplain, and it was occasionally caught by grassland dwellers who ventured into the forest to collect firewood, to hunt, or to gather leaves for covering the roofs of houses and vines for making fish traps. These people would sometimes bring the flies back to the grassland villages with them.[8]

Despite the disease factor, settlement and migration patterns indicate an expansion of population over the long term. Some of this was due to continued immigration, but there were factors that favored natural increase as well. Although the early settlers from the mosquito-free Ngiri valley probably died at a

---

[6] The experience of mine workers in Katanga illustrates this phenomenon. Workers who came to the mosquito-infested mining areas from the mosquito-free mountains of Rwanda and Burundi not only suffered from malaria in much higher proportions than other groups of workers, but also, many of them had to be treated for malaria two or three times a year. A. Duren, *Un Essai d'Etude d'Ensemble du Paludisme au Congo Belge* (Brussels, 1937), pp. 13–14.

[7] C.L. Henrard, *Notice de la Carte des Tsé-Tsé au Congo Belge et au Ruanda-Urundi,* Institut Royal Colonial Belge, Atlas Générale du Congo (Brussels, 1952); Ian S. Acres, "A Study of Sleeping Sickness in an Endemic Area of the Belgian Congo over a Period of Ten Years," *Transactions of the Royal Society of Tropical Medicine and Hygiene,* 44 (1950):77–92.

[8] Interview: Bampomba, 7-24-81, Tape 13/2.

high rate due to their diminished resistance against malaria, later generations were more resistant. Because babies with sickle cells survived their first exposures to malaria at a higher rate than babies who lacked them, the percentage of sickle-cell carriers in the population gradually increased over several generations.

As the population grew, fishing grounds became scarce. Given the extensive methods of fishing that made it possible for a single dam to trap fish from an area several kilometers square, it did not take a very large population to overcrowd a portion of the swamps. Owners of dams or ponds did not want others to build too close-by to them. Ekando explained the principle involved:

> If you have a dam here, the fish come to it from this area. Over there is another dam that draws fish from that region. If somebody tries to build a dam in between, he won't get permission because he would divert fish from our dams.[9]

This was not absolute overpopulation in the ecological sense of exceeding the carrying capacity of the land. It was relative overpopulation in the legal sense that there were men who lacked rights to fishing grounds near their homesteads. We can get an idea of the legal carrying capacity of the swamp by recognizing that in 1909 the population of a two-hundred-square-kilometer portion of the swamps was less than one person per square kilometer.[10] This figure is probably low as a result of the epidemics in the 1890s, but even if the nineteenth century figure was three times as high, the population still would have been low in absolute terms. Yet the area had long been considered overpopulated, as attested by the numerous people who had left the swamps to seek their fortunes in less prosperous environments.

---

[9] Interview: Ekando, 7-25-81, Tape 14/1. An example of the effect of having dams too close together comes from the area of Malebo Pool. In the early part of the century a single dam produced 500–1000 kilograms of fish. By 1958, after a considerable increase in the number of dams, the catch per dam had dropped to 50–100 kilograms. Service des Eaux et Forêts, "Aperçu sur la Pêche Lacustre et Fluviale au Congo et au Ruanda-Urundi," *Bulletin Agricole du Congo Belge,* 50 (1959):1678–79.

[10] See the 1909 statistical tables for the chiefdoms of Makongo, Bongamba, and Moliba-Mitsange in DCMS.

Population increases had special social consequences in the southern swamps because dams and ponds were owned by individuals, not by lineages. In the Nunu language a landowner was called *momene nce,* "the owner of the land." The terminology of landholding was not a mere figure of speech referring to a figurehead who held communal land on behalf of a lineage. Had that been the case, dams and ponds would have been handed down within a single matrilineage over several generations. The histories of Nunu dams and ponds, however, reveal a far more chaotic pattern indicative of individual ownership. The dam built by Bokota, for example, went to his sister's husband, then to her son Botuka, and then to his son Nsamonie. In effect, it passed down matrilineally in one generation and patrilineally in the next. The dam constructed by Epatia, however, went to his son Nkobonda, and then to Nkobonda's son Lopanda, a straight patrilineal succession in an area characterized by matrilineal kinship. Over three generations the dam was in the possession of three different matrilineages.[11]

The system of individual inheritance engendered fierce competition for dams and ponds. Although in theory fishing grounds were passed down matrilineally from a man to his sister's son, in practice candidates from all sides of the family staked their claims. Sons and nephews alike tried to curry favor with the owner and demonstrate that they had both the intelligence to manage the estate and the witchcraft power to make it prosper. The details of such competition have disappeared from the historical record because winners claimed legitimate ownership and losers often moved away. But the chaotic histories of individual dams and ponds hint at the power struggles that surely took place.

Because of the vicissitudes of inheritance, some people ended up with several dams or ponds. Mongemba, to take a modern example, inherited three dams. The first dam passed from the builder, Bokonongo, to his brother Libwa, who left it to his maternal nephew Molilu. Then it went to the husband of Molilu's sister, who left it to Mongemba, his son. Here the succession followed a straight matrilineal line. The second dam came

---

[11] Interviews: Nsamonie, 7-8-81, field notes; Lopanda, 7-8-81, field notes.

to Mongemba from a man who left it to his daughter, who left it to her son, who left it to his son Mongemba. This succession alternated from patrilineal in one generation to matrilineal in the next. The third dam came to him as a result of several complicated changes of ownership, the details of which even he did not remember clearly. The confusion suggests that it did not pass down within a single lineage.[12]

The competition in the swamps thus contained a fundamental contradiction. Each person's goal was to become a water lord who controlled fishing grounds and attracted a following. Yet the control of fishing grounds by one person meant fewer fishing grounds for his sons and nephews. The result was a division of the swamp society into landed and landless, water lord and client. Each type of person pursued different strategies for gaining wealth and power. Landowners sought to use their resources to procure wives, purchase slaves, and attract clients. Shrewd use of resources could make a landowner into a water lord. The landless sought to find new settlement areas and to mobilize the resources to construct dams and ponds.

Both groups worked within a larger framework of institutionalized rules. By the eighteenth century, the farthest reaches of the genealogies, people were already leaving the core settlement areas and moving toward the fringes of the swamps. By this time the basic institutions that structured the water lord competition had almost certainly been established. The evidence for this is comparative. My reconstruction of basic institutions such as kin-group organization and land tenure in the late nineteenth century showed great uniformity throughout the swamps and the fringe settlement areas.[13] It therefore seems probable that these institutions had been established well before people started leaving the swamps in the early nineteenth century. Whereas the early settlers had enjoyed great flexibility to experiment with institutionalized rules, later generations inherited an institutional framework within which they developed

---

[12] Interview: Mongemba, 7-7-81, field notes.
[13] The reconstruction of kin group organization was based on oral testimony and supported by family genealogies. The reconstruction of land tenure was based on the histories of dams, ponds, and fields.

their strategies. They had less latitude for making further changes, and it seems likely that the institutionalized rules remained relatively stable.

STRATEGIES FOR ESTATE OWNERS

In an environment where everybody lived in biodegradable huts, wore raffia or bark cloth, and cooked in pots made from local clay, a rich person enjoyed few material goods that were not equally available to the poor. Wealth was instead measured in terms of control of people. This attitude is clearly illustrated by the Nunu terms for poverty and wealth. The Nunu word for a poor person was *moyoko,* a person alone. The opposite was *mokuli,* a person who had acquired and was presumably no longer alone.[14] The most socially desirable goal for a Nunu male was to move from being a person alone to being a water lord who controlled a large number of people, whether kinfolk, wives, friends, clients, or slaves.

Estates as wealth

The best way to attract people was to control an estate, which included a homestead and fishing grounds. The precise strategy varied according to whether the fishing grounds included ponds or dams. In the flooded forest, where fishing was normally done in ponds, the major problem was attracting laborers. A large pond required over a hundred people to empty it, a task which would last up to a week. As harvest time neared, the owner would look for workers. As Etebe described the process:

> The owner of the fish pond goes around asking, "Do you have a pond to fish now?" If the answer is no, he tells the person to be ready on a certain day. [When the day comes] men come with their wives. They empty the pond and get the fish. Then they build smoking racks. The women gather a lot of firewood. The men stand on one side of the racks and turn the fish; the women, on the other side, add wood to the fire. Then the owner marks a

---

[14] The root of *moyoko* is *oko,* meaning "one" or "alone." The root of *mokuli* is *kula,* meaning "to get" or "to acquire."

spot along the rack. He takes all the fish on one side; the fish on the other side are divided among the workers. Men and women get equal shares.[15]

The payment given to each worker varied from owner to owner and from year to year. It was arrived at by a tacit bargaining process. People who were unsatisfied with their payment might seek another patron the following year. Because all of the ponds were harvested at approximately the same time, a single worker could work at only a few of them in a given year. A shortage of workers led to competition among pond owners, with each trying to prove himself a generous patron, whereas an abundance of labor forced workers to beg for the right to participate in a harvest. The bargaining between owners and clients fluctuated over time as demographic changes or the construction of new ponds tilted the labor market in favor of owners or toward workers.[16]

In dividing the spoils, the owner often gave away a considerable portion of his fish, but he gained clients and he gained the prestige that came from being the bounteous provider to other members of the community. Clients would avoid displeasing him in other social contexts. Fish were thus traded for social prestige. Still, patrons could never be sure of the loyalty of their clients. Although clients normally emptied ponds for the same owner year after year, some would search for the best deal, switching loyalties from patron to patron. Moreover, many clients had divided loyalties, working for more than one pond owner in a given year.

The relationship between owners of fishing grounds and clients was very different in the floating meadows, where estate owners used dams to trap fish. Here the bargaining power was on the side of the owner, as a dam could be worked by one or two people. Etebe recalls how he fished with his father:

---

[15] Interview: Etebe, 8-3-81, Tape 15/2.

[16] Informants gave widely differing estimates of the owner's share of a pond harvest. The highest estimate came from Bomboko, who said that his father, Nkoto, had received 50% of the harvest from his dam. Field notes for Nkubosaka, July, 1981.

My father's dams were not close together. My father and I would leave the homestead together in separate canoes. At a certain point we would separate. I would fish one dam, he would fish another. Later, we would meet to go home.[17]

In areas where dam fishing predominated, there were far fewer opportunities for people who did not own land. Bampomba explained the system of clientship:

A dam must be built on your own land. It cannot be built on the land of another person. If a landless person comes along, he must beg: "I don't have a place to work. Divide your dams with me." If the owner agrees, the stranger will work that dam for that year. At the end of the season, the stranger will pay the owner a fee called *mbando*. The amount depends on the relationship between the two people.[18]

The emphasis on personal relations reflected the fact that having a client who was reliable was often more important than the exact quantity of fish the owner received. Dishonest clients disguised the true value of the harvest, or they simply absconded with the proceeds and left nothing to the owner. Other clients plotted to steal the dam from its owners. In the face of these challenges, dam owners took precautions to assure that they got trustworthy and loyal clients. A new client usually received permission to fish a certain dam for only one year. If the owner was satisfied with his performance, permission would be renewed for a second year. If he returned for the third year, the owner would grant him permission in front of three witnesses so that nobody would think that the client had become the owner of the dam.

Even after a client had established himself, the patron still retained the power over him in the form of *mokake,* a charm that guaranteed a bountiful fish harvest. It was made from the *mosasangi* plant, which had an orchid-like flower. Its symbolism was powerful. If two friends formally broke off their friendship, for example, they drank a juice made from this flower to

---

[17] Interview: Etebe, 8-3-81, Tape 15/2.
[18] Interview: Bampomba, 7-18-81, Tape 7/1.

symbolize the broken relationship. When a father sent his son out on his first hunting trip, he would give him the *mokake* charm to assure his success. If it was given to a client, it assured him prosperity in fishing his patron's dam. Thus, it was not given out until the patron was sure of the client's reliability.[19]

Money as wealth

An estate not only attracted clients directly, but also generated money which could be used to attract clients. The currency used by the Nunu prior to the arrival of brass rods in the nineteenth century was *nsi,* a small shell. Because this shell was not found locally, but was passed up from the Malebo Pool area from market to market along the Zaire, the quantity of currency in circulation increased only as trade increased. This factor limited the quantity of *nsi* in circulation and assured that its value was always high.

The best way to build up a supply of *nsi* shells was through the production of fish. The fishing methods used in the swamps encouraged the marketing of fish by producing large catches all at once. Because smoking techniques could not preserve the fish for more than a couple of months, the surplus was best bartered for cassava or sold. One potential market was the inland villages, but more lucrative opportunities for gaining money lay in the villages along the Zaire River.[20] Before the introduction of modern nets in the twentieth century, the low-water season when fish were being harvested in the swamps was the hungry season for river fishermen.[21] This differential in the fishing calendars of the two areas created a market for fish in the river villages, where *nsi* shells were most readily available.

There was no simple correspondence between access to fish and access to *nsi* shells, but it is certain that without fish to sell the shells were very difficult to obtain. It was the surplus in fish that distinguished the owner of the fishing grounds from the client. Even if a pond owner took only 25% of the catch for himself, the remaining 75% was divided among a sizable group

---

[19] Interviews: Bampomba, 7-24-81, Tape 13/2; Ekando, 7-25-81, Tape 14/2.
[20] Interview: Bampomba, 7-22-81, Tape 11/2.
[21] Interview: Bokanza Ece, 6-2-75, field notes.

of people. Although clientship may have sufficed to feed a family, it could not provide enough surplus to obtain *nsi* shells.

Although any item from a loaf of cassava to a marriage could be purchased with *nsi* shells, people who possessed them tended to save them for important transactions and carry out the more mundane economic activities by barter. Currency was indispensable for obtaining capital goods such as fishing grounds and canoes. Fishing grounds could not ordinarily be bought and sold for the simple reason that their owners were loathe to part with them, but they could be purchased in exceptional cases, such as when the owner of a dam was charged a fine that he could not pay. The creditor would sometimes take the dam in lieu of payment, or sometimes a benefactor would pay the fine and take the dam in return, thus, in effect, buying the dam. Canoes, also, could be purchased only with currency. By requiring money to obtain the means of production, existing owners of fishing grounds had erected a formidable barrier against newcomers who wished to break into the system.

A common use of *nsi* shells was for bridewealth payments. There is no way of knowing just what types of bridewealth payments the early settlers used, but by the nineteenth century they had long been abandoned for a system that was very similar to the one used by the neighboring Sengele. The most plausible explanation of this switch is that the original immigrants were poor men who often lacked wives. Once they settled in the swamps, they obtained wealth in the form of fish that could be used to obtain wives from the inland Sengele. The form of payments followed Sengele rules, and thus the aboriginal form of marriage was replaced by the Sengele form.

In the nineteenth century, marriage required a series of payments which added up to a considerable amount of money.[22] The payments increased as the marriage came closer to fruition.

---

[22] This account of marriage is based on J.J.L. Lingwambe, "Histoire Banunu-Bobangi" (mimeographed pamphlet, Kinshasa, 1966), pp. 23–29. That similar payments were made in the nineteenth century is attested by the fact that Lopanda could recite typical prices of the various payments in *nsi*, a currency that was no longer used in the late nineteenth century. Interview: Lopanda, 7-15-81, Tape 6/2.

The initial payment could take two forms, depending on the situation. If a man saw a young girl that he liked, he would approach her parents and pay *bosimbisela bampele,* a reservation fee that gave him first refusal when the girl reached marriage-able age. In cases where this was not done, the marriage arrangements would start when the young man approached the girl and gave her a gift of money, called *botamunya*. If the girl accepted, the two arranged to meet the girl's father. On this occasion the boy brought a much larger payment, called *botombomwene,* along with several gourds of palm wine. The boy would give the money to the girl, who would turn it over to the father to show her consent.

If the payment was accepted, no further steps could be taken until any grievances by the boy's family against the girl's family had been compensated. This compensation was called *epoto*. Once the suitor had obtained the consent of the girl's father, he also had to obtain the consent of her maternal uncles. This entailed a similar payment of money and wine. Then came another series of payments of money and wine to the paternal and maternal families of the girl. These were called *bosombandoko, liboko, lombonzo,* and *bolongola mwene*. After the completion of all these payments, the two were properly engaged, but not yet married. A young man who was engaged was obligated to give his fiancée and her sisters a series of gifts of cloth and beads, according to his means.

The marriage itself consisted of a new series of payments. There was *nkamba,* a blanket for both the father and the mother of the bride, and a money payment, *ekumani,* which was divided equally among the father and the maternal uncles. Then a feast was prepared and enjoyed, but before the boy could leave with his bride he had to pay *liboko* to the mother of the bride and *ebongo* to the father. After he went off with his bride, there was a honeymoon fee, *botungwampwa,* which the husband paid to the bride.

Finalizing the marriage did not put an end to payments. When a child was born, the husband made a payment, *boonga,* to the bride's father and a gift of wine to her maternal uncles. A few months later the bride's family demanded that the husband come and bring the child and pay *meesu,* which was divided equally among the paternal and maternal families. This payment was the largest single payment of any in the series.

The use of bridewealth as a means of gaining control of people was laced with irony because it gave a man only nominal control over his children. In addition to adopting the Sengele form of marriage, the Nunu had also adopted the matrilineal kinship system common along the southern fringes of the forest.[23] Primary control over a man's children lay with his wife's brothers, and therefore marrying many wives did not bring a man control over many children.

Another use of money to control people was to obtain pawns: people who were left with a creditor as collateral on a debt. The pawn, usually a child, worked for the creditor, who often assigned the pawn the harshest and least desirable tasks.[24] If the debtor failed to repay the debt, the pawn would eventually become a slave of the creditor.

Greater control over people could be gained by buying slaves. The available slaves were usually people who had gotten into debt or people who had been convicted of a crime and lacked the money to pay the fine. In such circumstances a rich person would pay the fine and take the person in exchange. Such slaves were often well treated because they were destined to become permanent members of the owner's family. Children of slaves were usually considered free people and full members of the lineage that claimed them.

Rich people could also use their money to attract clients. Young men borrowed money from estate owners to get mar-

---

[23] Changing from patrilineal to matrilineal kinship is not unknown in this part of Africa. The Bobangi are patrilineal in their homeland along the lower Ubangi, but switched to a matrilineal system when they migrated to the middle Zaire. For another example of a switch to matrilinearity, see Mumbanza mwa Bawele, "Fondaments Economiques de l'Evolution des Systèmes de Filiation dans les Sociétés de la Haute-Ngiri et de la Moeko, du XIXe Siècle à nos Jours," Enquêtes et Documents d'Histoire Africaine, 2 (1977):1–30. Wyatt MacGaffey has suggested a reason why such shifts are possible by arguing that kinship systems in equatorial Africa are essentially bilateral. Wyatt MacGaffey, "Lineage Structure, Marriage, and the Family amongst the Central Bantu," Journal of African History, 24 (1983):184–85.

[24] Interview: Bampomba, 7-24-81, Tape 13/2.

ried, to pay fines, to buy food, or to get treatment from a
healer. The exact obligations entailed by clientship varied according to the individuals and circumstances, but clients helped
out their patrons in a variety of ways. The following accounts
give a sense of the obligations involved:

> In the days of *ngele* [brass rod] currency, a marriage cost between
> 4000 and 8000 *ngele*. That was a lot of money. If a man didn't
> have it, he had to go to a rich man and ask for it. The rich man
> gave him a loan. He had to work very hard to repay it.[25]

> If a young man's father was dead, or if he lacked money, the
> young man went to a rich man to borrow money. He then
> married the wife, and he worked, worked, and worked to repay
> the loan.[26]

In addition to creating dependents, money helped one keep
up the social contacts necessary for maintaining high social
standing. A death in the family, for example, required the purchase of a dog to be eaten. Dogs could be purchased only with
nsi shells, as were chickens and ducks, the domestic animals eaten at feasts. Similarly, people who did not make their own
palm wine had to purchase it with *nsi* for marriages and other
ceremonial occasions. Wine was outside of the barter circuit.
The death of a friend or an important elder required special gifts
that could be purchased only with money. Rich people also created special social networks by throwing expensive feasts for
their friends and by concluding blood brotherhood agreements
with powerful men in distant villages. Blood brother relationships were maintained by a continual exchange of gifts. As Lopanda noted, "Rich people had many blood brothers. If you
had no money, you had no blood brothers."[27] The essence of
the competition, in short, was manipulating land and money to
build up a social network and thus become a water lord.

---

[25] Interview: Yasi, 7-13-81, Tape 3/1.
[26] Interview: Longwa, 7-20-81, Tape 6/2.
[27] Interviews: Etebe, 8-4-81, Tape 16/2; Ekando, 7-25-81, Tape 14/1; Bampomba, 7-22-81, Tape 11/2; Longwa, 7-22-81, Tape 9/1; Lopanda, 7-10-
81, Tape 1/2.

Successful water lords stood a chance of gaining a guardianship title as the ultimate symbol of success.[28] Although succession to the guardianship of a specific patch of ground stayed
within the family that owned it, the higher guardian titles, such
as *ngeli, mpomb'e mboka,* and *miandangoi,* passed to the "most
worthy person."[29] In listing qualities that made a candidate attractive, informants listed intelligence, witchcraft power, and
good judgment. It goes almost without saying that a successful
water lord could make a strong claim to all of those qualities.
The reigning titleholder usually chose his own successor in consultation with other powerful elders. We can only speculate as
to the wheeling and dealing that went on behind the scenes
when a new titleholder was being chosen, but it seems certain
that powerful allies enhanced a person's candidacy.

STRATEGIES FOR THE LANDLESS

For those without estates, significant quantities of money were
very difficult to obtain. The social circuit was one way by
which one could obtain money, but it had severe limitations.
As mentioned above, many of the payments in marriage and
even at feasts and ceremonies were in the form of wine or food
that was consumed on the spot, leaving the receiver with no
monetary gain. Even when payments were made in money,

---

[28] The guardianship titles of the Nunu may have had something in common
with the famous *nkumu* title among the Tumba peoples living to the north-
east of the Nunu. The *nkumu* title was literally purchased because the person chosen had to pay for his own installation ceremonies. On *nkumu,* see
H.D. Brown, "The Nkumu of the Tumba," *Africa,* 14 (1943–44):431–47.
The Nunu titles were clearly distinct from the *nkumu* titles, but there were
nevertheless some connections. Booto, a nineteenth century *ngeli* titleholder, wore a hat similar to those worn by the *nkumu.* Interview: Eyongo,
12-19-75, Tape A72.

[29] In 1957 Deweerd listed six *ngeli* guardians who had held office at Mitima.
They represented five different clans. Lingwambe, "Histoire Banunu-Bobangi," p. 10. Losengo emphasized that guardianship titles passed from family to family. Interview: Losengo, 12-10-75, Tape A66.

they ended up being distributed among a large number of people, with no single person gaining a large share. The bride-wealth paid at a wedding was divided into two equal parts: one for the father of the bride, and one for the maternal uncle. Each of these people then divided the money among their own paternal and maternal families, giving each adult a small portion.[30] The matrimonial calculus in the swamps was thus very different from that in many parts of Africa, where a father would marry off a daughter to gain bridewealth which would allow his son to get married, or where a father would marry off a daughter to gain money to marry a second wife. Among the Nunu, the marriage of a daughter brought little direct gain to either her father or her maternal uncle.

The advantage of such a system was that a man would get a portion of bridewealth payments for nieces as well as for daughters, and for more distant kinfolk as well. But most of this was out of his control because it depended upon the reproductive powers of others, and therefore gain or loss on the matrimonial circuit was largely a matter of chance. The matrimonial circuit tended, in the long run, to distribute *nsi* shells throughout the population. But it did not lend itself to concentrating money in the hands of any one person.

The egalitarian tendencies of the social circuit reinforced the importance of fishing as a means of gaining wealth. One way for a landless young person to earn money was by fishing with an estate owner: a father, uncle, or patron. The stories of twentieth century informants reveal strategies of apprenticeship that were surely attempted in earlier periods as well. Here is the story of Longwa:

> My father taught me [to fish]. I went with him to the forest to
> fish his dam. It took two or three people to work the dam because
> it was very long. It stretched from one clearing to another, going
> through forest. My father fished it with help from me and my
> younger brother. My father's brothers did not fish there. My
> father gave the money to his wife, who used it to buy cassava

---

30 See field notes of the marriage ceremony observed at Nkolo-Lingamba in July, 1975. The elders at the ceremony assured me that the same principles had applied at their own weddings early in the century.

from Nkuboko. When I was a little older, he gave me some cloth at the end of the fishing season. When I was a little older I made a *ngobe* trap and I caught fish which I sold. I made 500 brass rods which I used to buy a canoe. It was a small canoe for one person.[31]

Nsamonie had a similar experience.

I started going to fish with my father at the age of 12. I didn't do any work; I just ate and left. When I was fifteen I started working little by little. By the time I was eighteen I was working together with my father. We fished at the dam, caught fish, and sold them in the village. He gave me food and cloth. When I was old enough to pay tax, I started to work for myself. My father, my brother, and I all fished together, but I got my own share of the catch. My father got the biggest share. When I married a wife the money for the bridewealth came from my fishing. My father gave me a hand, but most of the money was mine. By then I had a canoe. I bought it myself for twenty francs. It was very small.[32]

These stories refer to the early 1920s, when the market for fish in the region was growing and currency was plentiful. While similar strategies were probably followed in the eighteenth and nineteenth centuries, the results were certainly more meager. The opportunities to gain wealth by being a good client were in all cases limited. Although hard work in a subordinate role helped one achieve a form of independence, it was a minimal strategy designed more to ensure survival than to gain wealth and control over people.

The migratory strategy

For those who did not inherit estates, migration offered the only real hope for upward mobility. Although the necessity for movement placed burdens on the young, these burdens fit comfortably within the cultural framework of the swamps. Movement was seen as part of the normal life cycle, part of the process of establishing oneself as an independent adult. So deeply were the notions of movement and independence ingrained in

---

[31] Interview: Longwa, 7-23-81, Tape 12/1.
[32] Interview: Nsamonie, 7-14-81, Tape 5/1.

swamp culture that even males who inherited fishing sites shifted their homesteads after the deaths of their fathers in order to establish new ones with themselves at the head.[33] A typical male moved homesteads twice during his lifetime. The first time was when his grandfather died and he moved with his father to a new site. The second move came when his own father died and he could at last set up his own homestead.

If short-distance migration was common for men, it was equally common for women. The predominant marriage pattern called for the woman to live in the homestead of her husband, and therefore a typical woman would move once with her father when she was young, once upon marriage, and usually a third time when her father-in-law died and her husband moved to establish a new homestead. If she was divorced or widowed, she would move again as the household split up.

Even though the *idea* of migration was an accepted feature of life in the swamplands, the specific act of a young man leaving his natal homestead was nevertheless fraught with tension and potential conflict. Leaving the homestead deprived it of labor, and, perhaps more importantly, reduced the number of warriors to defend it. Fathers therefore resisted the emigration of their sons, and this fact explains why Nunu family histories stress that the sons moved only *after* the deaths of their fathers. In the few remembered cases in which sons moved before the father had died, they sneaked away at night.[34]

Maternal uncles also had claims on the labor and fighting capabilities of young men. If a maternal uncle had contributed bridewealth to his nephew's marriage, he could claim the young man's services when the father died. In cases where the father had provided the bridewealth for the young man's marriage, the maternal uncles sometimes provided bridewealth for a second wife so that he would settle with them after his father had died. Such circumstances meant that becoming independent took place in two stages: a move away from the father's homestead to live with a maternal relative, and then a second move

---

[33] Interview: Nsamonie, 7-15-81, Tape 6/1.
[34] Interviews: Eyongo, 8-3-81, Tape 15/1; Etebe, 8-4-81, Tape 15/2.

to set up an independent homestead. Botuka, in the nineteenth century, for example, left his father's village upon the elder's death and went to live with his maternal uncle. Only after the uncle died did he set up an independent homestead. He was later joined by Longyangi, his wife's brother, who had left his own father's homestead upon the elder's death and come to live with his sister. Thus Botuka became the head of a small estate.[35]

The motivations for striking out on one's own came from a combination of a pull factor (desire for independence) and a push factor (lack of opportunity at home). The impact of these two factors can be illustrated by reference to the experiences of two Nunu. Likwabela, who lived in the nineteenth century, lived with his maternal uncle until the uncle died. Then he said to his brother, "Our maternal uncle has died. Let us leave this village and go to live in one where we are the owners."[36] This illustrates the pull of a new homestead site. The push of poverty is illustrated by Manzanga, who was born in the village of Bomiondo during the middle third of the nineteenth century. When he became an adult, he went to live in the village of Bosongo, because there were no places to work, either as an independent fisherman or as a client, in his natal village.[37]

These types of individual movements were the motivating forces behind the settling of the frontier. A young man living in a crowded zone and seeing no hope of gaining wealth in his homestead would move to an unsettled region, perhaps with his brothers, and construct fish dams and ponds. If the move was successful, he would be joined by cousins, nephews, and in-laws who were willing to work in constructing the dams and ponds in order to gain a foothold in the frontier region. Thus the homesteads of pioneers became the stepping stones for the next wave of immigrants.

Immigrants could quickly form networks and alliances in the frontier regions by utilizing clan ties. The clan had few visible functions in normal life. There was no recognized head of a clan, and there were no clan reunions or clan councils. Yet in a

---

[35] Interview: Nsamonie, 7-15-81, Tape 6/1.
[36] Interview: Etebe, 8-3-81, Tape 15/2.
[37] Interview: Ekando, 7-23-81, Tape 12/1.

highly mobile society it served as an "old boy" network, a way
that strangers could establish common ground and trust. When
a person moved into a new area, he could look for people
whose ancestors had shared a *nkinda* charm with his own, and
thus a bond would be established. As Bampomba explained it:

> My ancestors settled in the village of Mobembo. They had an oath
> in that place. The people of Nsenseke have the oath of their
> ancestor there. If you are far from your home village and you tell
> someone where you come from, he is obligated to help you if his
> ancestors came from the same place because the two of you share a
> single oath.[38]

Settlement proceeded by a leapfrog action as each established
frontier settlement became a stepping stone for the next group.
A sense of this process comes from Enzimba's family history,
which sees the key events in terms of the construction of dams
or ponds by successive generations of settlers. It is hard to say
how many generations this description includes.

> Our ancestors came from the village of Bokaa. They went to build
> at Liombo, then at Lilebu. They built six dams at Mecamenzel and
> Bibuka, and they dug six ponds. They went to Masaa, and there
> they built six dams. They left Masaa and came to build three dams
> at Bokungu. After that they went to build at Mboma.[39]

In a frontier situation, the character of individuals was crucial. Moving to the frontier was a strategy that carried high
risks as well as potential rewards. It meant not only hard work,
but also separation from kinship and support networks. There
was danger of attack, and a man could build a dam only to have
it seized by someone else. The lazy, the fearful, and the merely
cautious adopted minimal strategies, staying at home to work
as a junior partner of an older brother or an uncle. As long as
most people moved on, those who stayed behind could antici-
pate a reasonably comfortable life. Thus, during the frontier period, there were inequalities in wealth, and there were patrons
and clients, but the mixture was not explosive, nor were the
burdens of clientship oppressive.

---

[38] Interview: Bampomba, 7-24-81, Tape 13/2.
[39] Enzimba, manuscript family history, n.d.

Even during the frontier period, there were pockets of overcrowding while less desirable areas remained underpopulated. Perhaps the most overcrowded area of all was Mitima, a village in which many families now living on the eastern edge of the swamp claim ancestry. The many testimonies of people whose families had left Mitima indicate its overcrowded condition. As Longwa noted, "A long time ago there were a lot of people at Mitima who had no place to work."[40] Although the early emigrants from Mitima, such as Enzimba's family, moved relatively short distances, the leapfrogging got longer and longer. By the late nineteenth century, Mitima was still overcrowded, and emigrants would move all the way to the dry land on the eastern edge of the swamp, passing over the settled areas in-between.

CONCLUSION

Unlike the productive tactics of the settlers, which were designed to maximize efficiency, their social strategies were based on more complex considerations.[41] Estate owners gave up much of their wealth in order to ensure the loyalty of their clients. Landless people had to make complex choices between

---

[40] Interview: Longwa, 7-20-81, Tape 9/1. See also interviews with Ekanda, 7-23-81, Tape 12/1, and Nsamonie, 7-14-81, Tape 5/1.

[41] The difference between the two can be stated in formal terms by using the game theorists' distinction between a game against nature, which poses a simple maximization problem, and a game between people, which poses a cross-purposes optimization problem. This distinction was first made, without using those terms, in John Von Neumann and Oskar Morgenstern, *Theory of Games and Economic Behavior* (Princeton, 1944), pp. 9–12. The first person to apply this distinction to human societies was Daniel Bell. In *The Coming of Post-Industrial Society* (New York, 1973), he distinguished (p. 116) between pre-industrial societies, which are characterized by a game against nature, industrial societies characterized by a game against fabricated nature, and post-industrial societies, characterized by a game between persons. Whereas Bell sees a single type of game as characterizing an entire society, the analysis here would picture the game against nature and the game between people as going on simultaneously in any society. The two games interact in complex ways, and this interaction is a vital source of social dynamics.

minimal strategies that assured survival but did not bring wealth, and migratory strategies that promised wealth but also carried great risk.

Individuals possessed different resources and perceived different opportunities, and they accordingly chose different strategies. The combined effect of the various strategies created a complex dynamic throughout the swamplands as a whole. Water lord strategies could not succeed unless other people were pursuing clientship strategies, and vice versa. The result of the conflicting strategies was a symbiotic stability in the core settlement areas and dynamism in the frontier regions.

Because the landed and the landless were bound together in a variety of ways, strategic choices often had contradictory effects. A young person leaving his father's estate for the frontier, for example, was diminishing his father's capacity to sustain the life-style to which the young man himself aspired. And the young man who eschewed a life of clientship could not himself become a water lord unless he attracted clients.

The dynamic of contradictory strategies that dominated the eighteenth century swamplands could be maintained only as long as open land remained on the frontier. As the swamplands began to fill up, people would be forced to make new and more difficult choices.

5. The drylands

B Y THE EARLY nineteenth century, the scarcity of un-
claimed fishing grounds in the swamps was creating a
class of landless people. Because the southern swamps
marked the southernmost extension of the great equatorial African marsh, such people could not replicate the actions of their
ancestors and move to new swamplands. Their only hope for
gaining an independent livelihood was to leave the swamp and
seek their fortunes in the surrounding environments. One
choice was the dryland region called Nkuboko, located just beyond the eastern fringe of the swamps. The new micro-environment would impose its own rules and force the settlers to
adopt new tactics, new strategies, and even new goals. It would
turn fishermen into farmers, and in the process it would gen-
erate a new form of big-man competition.

SETTLING THE DRYLANDS

In the eastern portion of the flooded forest, the spillover of emigrants from Mitima resulted in a series of settlements along the
channel that led to the east. Beyond Masaa the channel divided. One branch continued eastward to the edge of the
swamp. The other turned to the southeast, where settlers
founded the village of Minsange. Nsamonie described the process:

> Our ancestors came from upriver and built Nkubosaka. From
> Nkubosaka they went to Mitima. From Mitima they went to
> Minsange. To build Minsange they built mounds of earth for the
> houses so they wouldn't flood during the high water. Minsange
> was a large settlement area. When the Mitima area was too
> crowded, many people came to settle at Minsange.[1]

---

[1] Interview: Nsamonie, 7-14-81, Tape 5/1.

From there, some people moved southward to found other villages along the eastern edge of the swamplands. Eventually there were no further swamplands left to settle, and those who got squeezed out of the family fish ponds or dams had no place to go.

Life on the eastern fringes of the floodwaters differed significantly from that nearer to the river. The inland fringes of the swamps were at the end of the migration routes of the fish. They were the last places the fish entered and the first that they left. Fish harvests were not as abundant as they were in other parts of the swamps.[2] A similar pattern could be seen in the circulation of money. The farther one went into the swamps the scarcer *nsi* currency became. This was because the *nsi* shells came to the swamps from the Malebo Pool area via the Zaire River trade. The villages close to the Zaire had relatively easy access to *nsi* because they traded directly with river villages. The people who had *nsi* wanted to keep them for social expenditures and not squander them on cassava or pots. They tried as much as possible to procure ordinary goods from farther inland by barter. The result was that *nsi* were scarce in the inland areas, and this situation produced hardship because people who lacked the little shells were excluded from important social transactions.[3]

The tension and conflict engendered by the relative poverty of the overcrowded villages on the fringe of the swamps are reflected in the apocryphal stories told about the people of Minsange.[4] One story tells about a man who caught a *nzombo* fish, which was normally kept alive in a clay pot until it was ready to be eaten or sold. The fish died in the pot, and the owner, full of sorrow, set out on the path to his village. On the road he met another man who was crying. "Why are you crying?" he asked. "My wife has just died," the friend replied. "Well," said the man, "let us sit down and mourn together, for we have

---

[2] Interviews: Bomboko, July, 1981, Nkubosaka field notes; Nsamonie, 7-15-81, Tape 5/1.

[3] Interviews: Lopanda, 7-10-81, Tape 1/2; Bampomba, 7-22-81, Tape 11/2.

[4] Interview: Lila, 7-14-81, field notes.

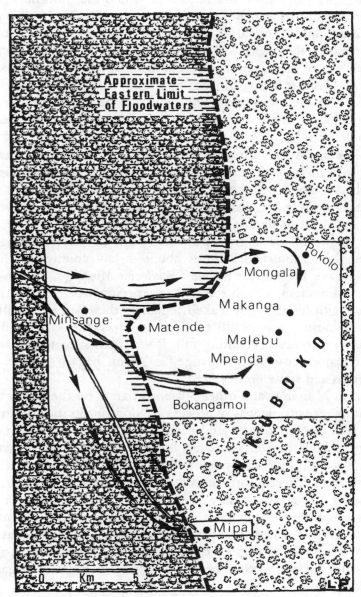

The Settlement of Nkuboko

both suffered great losses. You have lost your wife, but I have lost my fish."

Another story tells of a funeral at which the mourners came upon a man sitting behind the house of the deceased and crying his heart out. "You must have loved him very much to be so distressed," they said. "No," he replied, "I am crying because when I came to the back of the house I spied his large baskets of dried fish. It is not fair that he should have fish while I have none." So the mourners gave the man a basket of fish so that he could put aside his jealousy and mourn for his deceased friend.

Minsange stories also concentrate on relations between people and their in-laws. One story tells of a woman who was visited by her brother while her husband was away on a trip. She would not give her visiting brother any fish to eat, nor would she eat any fish herself while the husband was away, for fear that he would be angry upon his return to find his stock of dried fish diminished. Stories about in-law conflicts in Minsange gave rise to the phrase *"bokilo bo Minsange"* (an in-law from Minsange), which referred to a person who was not generous with his in-laws. Taken together, these stories testify to the jealousies and conflicts that arose as the last available swamplands were becoming full. It was such situations that led to a major eco-cultural change, as Nunu began to leave the swamps and settle on dry land.

From Minsange and other settlement areas on the edge of the swamp, expansion was a process of slow infiltration onto the dry land of Nkuboko, a landscape dotted with seasonal and permanent bogs and crisscrossed by a network of small creeks and streams. Like the swamps into which these streams fed, they ran in different directions at different times of the year, depending on whether they were feeding the swamps or the swamps were feeding them. These streams could be dammed up or even widened to create ponds. But the prospect was not very attractive, as attested by the fact that Minsange was overcrowded for a long time before the excess population began to seek dry land.

All along the eastern edge of the swamp similar transitions were made. Some emigrants from Minsange pushed southward to the region of Mipa, where they became dryland farmers and stream fishermen. Other settlers from the heartland region of Mitima kept to the main channel that continued eastward directly to the Nkuboko drylands. North of that was a channel that went eastward from the village of Nsangasi. As the settlement sites along this channel filled, emigrants began to spill over onto dry land.

Because the dryland region was settled relatively recently, the names of the settlers who planted the original *nkinda* charms are still remembered. The following account refers to subdivisions of the area collectively known as Bokangamoi:

> These are the ancestors who first settled the land of Bokangamoi: Manzau built Bonyeke. Moyenge built Nziku. Likamba also built Nziku. Esangu built Bongyangia. Mongonga built Biobo. Nzanga built near Makasu. Monkonongo built at Bongyangia. Montoko was at Bongyangia. Litupa went down to the plains of Makasu. Bompinda built at Libata. Mpentenya built Bosolibata, then moved to Bozunguzungu. These are the names of the ancestors who built up this land.[5]

Later immigrants to the area had to seek permission to settle from the guardians of the *nkinda*. Lopanda explained the process:

> When an immigrant arrived, he had to get permission to settle from the owner of the land. He brought beer to the owner to ask permission. The first settler was the owner.[6]

FISHING AND HUNTING

Fishing sites were at a premium. There were three creeks that drained Nkuboko, and each of them had numerous small tributaries. The early settlers claimed the best sites by building dams or ponds along the streams. Eyongo explained:

> Each person worked with his own hands to take possession of a site. If you constructed a dam, then that place became yours. Your

---

[5] Interview: Lila, 7-12-81, Tape 3/1.
[6] Interview: Lopanda, 7-10-81, Tape 1/2.

ownership began the day you constructed the dam and continues until now, when your grandchildren fish there.[7]

The settlers adapted the methods of the swamps to the task of fishing in the creeks. Using wooden poles, they built barricades across the streams and left openings in them for fish traps. When the water in the swamps was high, the current in the streams ran toward the inland area. When the water level in the swamps diminished, the streams flowed the other way. During both seasons fishermen placed traps on the appropriate side of the dam openings to catch the fish. In some places people dug ponds beside a stream and made channels to guide fish into them. In the dry season the stream would dry up and leave the fish isolated in the ponds. People also placed traps and weirs in the bogs that dotted the landscape during the high-water season.[8]

Latecomers had fewer options. Some of them got permission to fish in streams claimed by earlier settlers. Others worked as clients to help empty the small dams and ponds.[9] Still others returned to the swamps during peak fishing seasons to help their kinsmen or patrons drain their dams or empty their ponds. The settlements of Nkuboko were all located near the farthest reaches of the swamp, and the settlers had easy access to the swamplands by canoe when the water was high. By June, when most of the water was gone, people of Nkuboko went in large numbers to an area of the swampland called *meembe*. This was a formerly forested area of blackened, burnt-out trees that was being reclaimed by grasses. There, in grasslands claimed by no particular owner, they speared the *nzombo* and other fish that flopped in the few centimeters of remaining water.

For the men of Nkuboko, the rhythms of life could be much the same as those of their counterparts in the swamps. The ma-

---

[7] Interview: Eyongo, 12-12-75, Tape A70.

[8] On fishing methods, see the annual report to the Commissaire de District du Lac Léopold II, written by T.J. Deweerd in 1957, reprinted in J.J.L. Lingwambe, "Histoire Banunu-Bobangi" (mimeographed pamphlet, Kinshasa, 1966). Interview: Nsamonie, 7-8-81, Tape 1/1.

[9] For example: Yasi, 1975 field notes.

jor difference was that the yields were less. The streams and bogs on the land could not produce anywhere near the quantity of fish as the flooded forest or grassland, and clientship to swampland water lords was not very remunerative.

One way that men compensated for their diminished capacity to catch fish was by hunting. Because the lands of Nkuboko were not inundated, animals could be hunted during all periods of the year. One of the best times was during August, when the patches of grassland were burned to allow the women to collect mushrooms. Animals fled ahead of the fire and were vulnerable to the hunters. Most men also set traps in the forest near their houses or their fields in order to catch small animals, and they hung nets in trees to catch monkeys.[10]

Large animals such as elephants were hunted only by specialists. A man who wished to learn to hunt apprenticed himself to a hunter, much as some young men apprenticed themselves to blacksmiths. The Nunu used two methods to hunt elephants. One was a pit dug along a path. They put branches over the top of the pit and covered them with grass. When an elephant fell into the pit, the hunters killed it with spears. The other method required a trap which consisted of a large spear inserted into a heavy log that was suspended between two trees over a path through the forest. The vine holding up the device was attached to a trigger cord stretched across the path. When the elephant tripped the cord, the spear dropped onto the base of its neck. Then the hunters tracked the elephant for up to a month until the wound forced it to lie down.[11] The killing of an elephant caused great excitement, and crowds of people quickly materialized to buy the meat. The hunter gave a front leg to the guardian of the patch of forest on which the elephant had died, and he sold the meat for *nsi* shell currency. One informant recalled that 40 or 50 *nsi* would buy an entire elephant.[12] The tusks were divided, with the ground tusk going to the guardian of the forest and the other tusk going to the hunter.

---

[10] Interview: Mongomo and Mosengo, 12-13-75, Tape A72.
[11] Interview: Yasi, 12-10-75, Tape A-67.
[12] Interview: Lopanda, 7-10-81, Tape 1/1.

The other way by which men produced meat was by keeping domestic animals. In the late nineteenth century, they kept chickens, ducks, goats, and pigs, animals which were difficult to keep in the swamplands. Despite this innovation, the men still thought of themselves primarily as fishermen, and the domestic animal herds were never large enough to compensate for the paucity of fish.

AGRICULTURE

The major compensation for the inadequate supply of fish lay in the abundance of agriculture. Because Nkuboko was on solid ground, the settlers enjoyed the luxury of planning their agricultural calendar according to the rains instead of the rise and fall of the river. The growing season began in late August, when the rains returned after a two-month absence. Abundant rainfall, averaging around 200 millimeters per month, could be counted on until late January, when the rains diminished for two to three weeks before intensifying again. After that, rainfall was plentiful until mid-June, when the two-month dry season began.[13] The climate thus permitted two plantings a year of certain crops.

Most of the land was covered with a type of dryland forest that was striking for the complexity and variability of its floral composition. The upper canopy, which was up to 45 meters high, was made up of such a variety of trees that as many as 40 species have been identified in a single quarter of a hectare. The canopy was therefore highly irregular, not only because of the varying heights of the trees, but also because of their different shapes. Sunlight filtered through the seams in the canopy, creating a mosaic of lighted spots on the dark undergrowth. The layer of medium-sized trees underneath the canopy was more uniform, although its exact composition varied according to the quality of the light that filtered down. Closer to the ground were small trees ranging from five to twelve meters in height.

---

[13] Franz Bultot, *Atlas Climatique du Bassin Congolais,* 3 vols., INEAC (Kinshasa, 1971), vol 2, maps 9.1–9.12.

Under that layer was a variety of bushes.[14]   Despite the luxu-
riant vegetation, the soils of the forest bed were actually very
poor. The vegetation itself counteracted the poverty of the soil
by creating a closed cycle of plant nutrients, as follows. The
deep roots of the larger trees absorbed nutrients that had been
liberated by the decomposition of the bedrock and which were
then distributed throughout the plant. Eventually, all of these
nutrients returned to the soil after the death and decomposition
of the tree or its parts. Since the movement of water in tropical
soils is predominantly downward, these nutrients were in danger of being washed down into the deeper layers of soil and
removed in the drainage water. Instead, the smaller bushes and
plants with shallow roots absorbed them almost immediately
and used them for further growth. The supply of plant nutrients was therefore stored mainly in the living plants, not in
the soil itself.[15]

Selecting a site for a field required a great deal of skill. The
forests of Nkuboko, like all tropical rain forests, exhibited an
astonishing range of tree, bush, and vine species. Botanical surveys have so far identified over 3000 plant species in a single
sector of the Zaire forest.[16] The floristic composition of one potential field site was often very different from that of another
only a short distance away. Ecologists do not yet agree on how
to account for such variation, but it seems to be related to elevation, soil type, the availability of water, drainage, and the
impact of flooding, all factors that a farmer would consider in
choosing a field.[17] The key to successful farming was to choose
the site with just the right combination of plants. Curiously, it
was not the fertility of the soil that made the right plants grow
in a certain spot; rather, the soil was fertile because the plants
had made it that way.

---

[14] C. Evrard, *Recherches Ecologiques sur le Peuplement Forestier des Sols Hydromorphes de la Cuvette Centrale Congolais,* INEAC, Série Scientifique, no. 110
(1968), pp. 86–96.

[15] Paul W. Richards, *The Tropical Rain Forest* (London, 1964), pp. 219–20.

[16] Evrard, *Recherches Ecologiques,* p. 47.

[17] See Patrick S. Bourgeron, "Spatial Aspects of Vegetation Structure," in
Tropical Rain Forest Ecosystems, edited by F.B. Golley (New York, 1983),
pp. 29–47.

The standard method of creating fields from virgin forest was to clear the brush, cut the trees, let the slash dry, and then burn the clearing to get rid of the debris and to create a layer of ash that fertilized the soil. This process violently disrupted the intricate web of floral associations that had given the patch its appearance of fertility, and it caused an immediate impoverishment of the soil.[18] Clearing the vegetation removed many nutrients and set others free to sink back into the deeper layers of the soil. The humus layer was destroyed by burning and exposure to the sun. The remaining nutrients were absorbed by the crops and the fertility of the soil declined rapidly. Even with crop rotation, the Nunu could use a field no longer than three years before leaving it to regenerate.

The abandoning of a field initiated a natural process of forest regeneration. The ground was first invaded by rapid-growing grasses that completed their life cycle in a few weeks. This was quickly followed by a second stage dominated by perennial herbaceous and woody climbing plants. After some months, the third stage began. Bushes and small trees, growing both from seeds and from stumps which had survived in the soil, became dominant and quickly formed a canopy that shaded the soil from the sun. This first tree stage lasted up to 30 years. As larger trees crowded out some of the smaller ones, the patch entered the second tree stage, which lasted up to 50 years. Some 60 to 100 years after the regeneration began, the species characteristic of primary forest began to dominate, and the patch began to approximate its original state.[19]

A key decision for the owner of the plot was when to interrupt this process and clear the field again. There were good reasons for making the fallow period as long as possible. First, although a thick humus layer built up rather quickly, the organic composition of this layer became more favorable over time. As new successions of plants grew up and decomposed, the percentage of the organic matter that was stable and did not precipitate humic acids increased. As the composition of the organic matter changed, so did the chemical composition of the

---

[18] Richards, *Tropical Rain Forest*, pp. 219–20.
[19] Richards, *Tropical Rain Forest*, pp. 390–91.

soil, and fertility increased.[20] A more pragmatic reason for waiting was that long fallow permitted a thick, multilayered canopy
of trees to grow up. It shaded the ground, killed the under-
brush, and reduced the need for brush clearance. It also killed
the weeds and grasses and negated the need for extensive hoeing
after the field was cleared.

But clearing thick forest in Nkuboko presented two special
problems. First, it was difficult to get a patch of mature forest
cleared and burned during the dry season. Cutting the trees
took two full months,[21] and the resulting slash required two to
three months to dry properly before it could be burned.[22] Yet
the dry season averaged only 65–70 days in this area, which was
less than two degrees south of the equator.[23] It was very difficult to get the fields burned properly before the rains came. The
second problem was that the dry season, when the men cleared
the fields, was also the season when they harvested the fish
from their dams and the ponds in the streams.[24] Forest clearing
thus carried high opportunity costs, and men were reluctant to

[20] Evrard, *Recherches Ecologiques,* p. 39.

[21] Interview: Boyili, 7-15-81, Tape 6/2.

[22] Harold Conklin found a similar phenomenon in the Philippines. He wrote,
"Second-growth forests are preferred because the clearing of primary forest
requires much more manpower for a given area and demands a longer
drying time before burning can take place than can profitably be allocated
to such tasks." Harold Conklin, "An Ethnoecological Approach to Shifting
Agriculture," in *Environment and Cultural Behavior,* edited by Andrew P.
Vayda (Garden City, New York, 1969), p. 225. Burning works best if the
slash has two or three months to dry before it is burned. See Allen Johnson,
"Machiguenga Gardens," and Robert Carneiro, "Cultivation of Manioc
among the Kuikuru," in *Adaptive Responses of Native Amazonians,* edited by
Raymond B. Hames and William T. Vickers (New York, 1983), pp. 39,
72–73.

[23] The dry season usually started about June 15 and ended about August 20.
June averages 50 mm. of rainfall, July averages 25 mm., and August averages 50 mm. Franz Bultot, *Atlas Climatique,* vol. 2, maps 9.6–9.8, 11.1–
11.3.

[24] Georges Dupré found a similar situation among the Nzabi of Congo. He
argued that this situation discouraged polygyny because a man could not
easily clear enough fields for several wives. The ratio of married men to
married women among the Nzabi was 1:1.4, much lower than in the savanna areas to the south. Georges Dupré, *Un Ordre et sa Destruction* (Paris,
1982), p. 116.

invest time in cutting trees when the more lucrative task of fishing was available.

People therefore avoided long fallow periods as much as possible. They sometimes returned to abandoned fields after as little as five years of regeneration. The small trees and bushes cleared from regenerating fields dried out rather quickly, and the fields could easily be burned clean before the rains returned. Moreover, women as well as men worked at the task of brush clearing. They began in June, at the beginning of the dry season. The clearing process could take up to a month. They would leave the slash to dry for a month and then burn it. Although the relatively short fallow periods saved the men considerable time during the crucial weeks of the dry season, this efficiency came at a price. The fertility of the fields was reduced, and the hoeing and weeding required of the women increased.

Although most of the land in Nkuboko was covered with forest, there were also patches of natural grassland that could be cultivated. Most families had fields in both grassland and forest, planting slightly different crops in each. They planted two varieties of peanuts, for example. The *nzoku li mosenze* were planted in grassland fields, while the *nzoku li mombote* were planted in forest fields.[25] The forest peanut was thought to taste better and was therefore more valuable. Although forest fields were generally deemed to be more productive than savanna fields, the cultivation of grasslands had two distinct advantages. First, the risk of a crop failure was spread between two microenvironments, and the chances of a food shortage were reduced. Second, fields in the grasslands could be easily cleared by women alone, whereas fields in the forest required the labor of men.

In both forest and grassland fields, women prepared the mounds and planted the crops in August in anticipation of the heavy September rains. By the time the Nunu settled this area

---

[25] Note that peanuts, like cassava and corn, were crops that had come from the Americas as a result of the slave and ivory trade. The agricultural techniques involved in their cultivation were relatively recent, probably dating back to the eighteenth century.

around the beginning of the nineteenth century, cassava and peanuts, two staple crops imported from the Americas, were already well known. In March the peanuts were ready to be harvested. Because the fragile soil would not support two peanut crops in a row, the women planted cassava when they returned to the field in May. Between the hills of cassava they planted corn and sweet potatoes. The cassava required a full year to mature. After it was harvested, the field was replanted with a different variety of cassava. After this second cassava crop was harvested, the woman would leave the field fallow for about five years before her husband cleared it again for a new crop of peanuts.[26]

Most women alternated among several fields. Because peanuts could not be planted two years in a row on the same field, a woman planted each new peanut crop in a fresh field. If each peanut field then produced two crops of cassava and lay fallow for five years, there were seven years between peanut crops on a single field. A woman therefore needed eight fields in order to plant a new peanut crop every year.

Because the task of clearing virgin forest was so difficult and carried such high opportunity costs, previously cleared patches became valuable possessions. Like improved fishing sites, field sites were handed down over generations. Normally, fields were handed down from mother to daughter, but the practice of women moving to live with their husbands complicated the inheritance arrangements. If a young woman married a man who lived nearby, she could inherit her mother's fields. If she moved away, a family member who still lived near the old homestead would claim them. Since sons often settled initially in their natal homestead while daughters moved to live with their husbands, men often gained possession of the family field sites.[27] Those people who did not inherit sites were forced to cut new ones from virgin forest. Sometimes, however, they simply cleared a regenerating plot belonging to someone else. In the nineteenth century such appropriation was a major cause of feuds between families.[28]

---

[26] Interview: Boyelima, 7-10-81, field notes.
[27] Interview: Boyelima, 7-10-81, field notes.
[28] Interview: Lopanda, 7-10-81, Tape 2/1.

Bananas were the only crop reserved for men. They would make a clearing in the forest and plant the bananas during September. The first bananas would be ready for harvest the following June or July. Thereafter, the man would replant shoots to ensure a continual supply.

The shift from fishing to agriculture carried with it the potential to revolutionize social and economic competition. In the first place, it made Nkuboko the "breadbasket" of the entire swampland area. People from all over the swamps flocked to the markets of Nkuboko, usually located at the edge of the swamps so that people could come in canoes to trade their fish for cassava and other crops from Nkuboko. But this development did not alter the balance of economic power in the region. Cassava remained a low-value crop in relation to fish, and although cassava production partially compensated for the paucity of fishing, it was not in itself a source of wealth.

The second potential for change came from the altered balance between men's production and women's production in the domestic economy. A woman owned the entire product of grassland fields that she had cleared herself, and she kept most of the harvest from forest fields that had been cleared by her husband.[29] The woman used the production primarily to feed her own family, but she bartered the surplus at the market for household goods and fish.

Gender roles in food production were nearly the opposite of what they had been in the swamps. In the swamplands men produced the fish, and traded the surplus for cassava. Men were therefore providers of both meat and starch. In the drylands of Nkuboko women produced much of the starch and also much of the fish through barter trade. Such a shift undoubtedly affected relations between husbands and wives, and it altered the balance of production within the household. However, the impact of these changes was too subtle to be detected by an outside researcher.

One reaction of men was to make sure that the surplus cassava was bartered at marketplaces and not sold for money. At

---

[29] Interview: Boyelima, 7-10-81, field notes.

the marketplace men came with raffia cloth, camwood, fish, animal meat, and baskets, all of which could be sold for currency. The women's section of the market was always conducted by barter, a practice that served to keep women from accumulating money that would give them social power. As Lopanda noted:

> Women didn't buy with money; they bartered with cassava. Only men used money at the market. Women didn't have any money.[30]

There is no evidence of any structural shift in kinship systems or marriage customs as a result of the gender shift in production. The Nunu of Nkuboko do not differ noticeably from their counterparts in the swamps on these matters. Still, it seems likely that the shift in productive relations between men and women created great tensions within the households, and for a time some women may have dreamed of accumulating wealth in a manner similar to men. It is equally evident that such a revolution never took place, and that men continued to monopolize social power despite their dependence on the production of women.

Although men managed to retain dominance over their homesteads, they could not aspire to a status analogous to that of water lords in the swamps. Ownership of streams and bogs gave men access to resources, but the fish production was often insufficient to feed the household and seldom sufficient to support clients. Landowners enjoyed the title of *momene mai,* or "owner of water," but the title carried with it little power over other people. Aspiring big-men had to content themselves with tiny increments of status earned by owning waters or even by owning fields. By moving to the land, they had altered the nature of the competition. Aspiring big-men in Nkuboko pursued different goals, devised different strategies, and followed different tactics than their counterparts in the swamps.

The settling of the inland regions opened up a new frontier that served, for a while, as an outlet for landless people from the swamps, but eventually it, too, became a region rife with

---

[30] Interview: Lopanda, 7-10-81, Tape 1/2.

inequality. Men could be divided into three classes. There were the descendants of early settlers who had claimed good fishing spots in streams. There were men who returned to the swamps during the fishing season to work as clients. And there were men whose households were fed mainly by the agricultural production of women who sold their surplus cassava for fish to maintain the protein balance in the household diet.

Yet inequality in Nkuboko was of a different magnitude than that in the swamps. The wealthiest people were less wealthy, and the poor people were less poor. Because the fields of the women produced agricultural products that could be traded for fish, even families lacking access to fishing grounds could support themselves primarily from the produce of their own land.

CONCLUSION

The movement from the water to the dry land brought about very little change in the formal structures of Nunu society. The kinship system of Nkuboko remained the same as it had been in the swamps. *Nkinda* charms continued to be planted, and the hierarchy of guardians was similar to that found in the swamplands. Society remained politically decentralized, and even the rules of ownership and clientship remained the same on both land and water.

Within the stable framework of structures and institutions, however, patterns of life changed drastically. Men cut fields during the dry season, and women produced the foodstuffs that fed the household. Ownership of waters became a small-scale affair, and would-be patrons could support few clients. Fields became points of pride for families who controlled no waters. The rules had changed, and with them the tactics and the strategies. The settlers in Nkuboko had achieved the independence they sought, but at the same time they had developed a form of big-man competition that was but a pale reflection of the water lord competition in the adjacent swamps.

6. The river

THE ZAIRE RIVER provided a second possible solution to the problem of overcrowding in the swamps. This choice appealed to many landless people who found their other options distasteful. Movement to Nkuboko, with its small streams and agricultural way of life, held little appeal for those who regarded fishing as superior to agriculture. But remaining in the swamps as a client or junior partner was stifling. For people who saw their situation in these terms, the river offered the best and last hope for becoming an independent person and perhaps even a big-man.

Just as the swamps marked the extreme southward limit of the Zaire's floodplain, the river south of the swamps was the southern extremity of the riverine fishing grounds. At the point where the river passed the swamps, it was approximately ten kilometers across and dotted with islands.[1] The water was relatively shallow and moved fairly slowly. All of these features made this stretch of river attractive to fish and fishermen alike. This basic pattern continued as the river flowed southward for another 130 kilometers. Then the Zaire entered a long, narrow stretch called the channel, which was seldom more than one kilometer across yet carried as many cubic yards of water per second as the much wider stretches upstream. Therefore, as the shallow, meandering waters of the middle Zaire entered the channel they became fast and deep. The channel was almost barren of islands and the riverbanks were abrupt, rising to form the golden and purple hills of the Bateke Plateau. These waters were attractive to neither fish nor fishermen.

---

[1] Egide Devroey, *Le Bassin Hydrographique Congolais,* IRCB, Sciences Techniques, vol. 3, no. 3 (Brussels, 1941), pp. 25–6; George Grenfell, "A Map of the Congo River between Leopoldville and Stanley Falls, 1884–89" (London: Royal Geographical Society).

Settlers along the stretch of river above the channel sought an optimum combination of access to fishing grounds and a permanent site for their homestead. Such a combination was best found on the east bank along the fifty-kilometer stretch beginning at the southern extremity of the swamps. Here the soil changed abruptly from the black clay of the swamps to the Kalahari sands of the Bateke Plateau, which formed high bluffs plunging steeply down into the Zaire River. This is the Bolobo-Yumbi Strip. The downstream limit of this strip is delineated by the modern town of Bolobo. South of Bolobo the bluffs veer inland, too far to give convenient access to the water. North of Yumbi the bluffs disappear entirely, giving way to the swamplands that the Nunu called home. But from Bolobo to Yumbi the bluffs run right along the edge of the river and provide both escape from the high waters of May and December and easy access to the great waterway. It was these bluffs that attracted emigrants from the swamps, refugees of failed dreams in other environments.

By the late eighteenth or early nineteenth centuries when, according to genealogical evidence, Nunu immigrants began to settle along the river in considerable numbers, most of the desirable sites had long been inhabited by people claiming a river heritage. Oral traditions collected in these villages refer to founding ancestors who came down the river from the lower Ubangi.[2] The most famous of these ancestors was Ngobila, who founded the village of Makotempoko on the west bank of the Zaire. His followers gradually spread out along the west bank and acquired the ethnic name Moyi. As time passed, many of them moved across the river to the bluffs of the Bolobo-Yumbi Strip and mingled with other river peoples who had already settled there.[3]

---

[2] Interviews: Mobongi, 5-10-75, Tape A65; Bokembe, 5-10-75, Tape A65; Bonko, 8-8-75, Tape A39.

[3] This mingling helps to explain the confusion of early missionaries and colonial officers as to the ethnic identity of the peoples of the Bolobo-Yumbi

Linguistic evidence supports the oral traditions. The inhabitants of the fishing villages south of the swamps form an intru-
sive sliver of northern Zaire language-speaking populations in
an area dominated on both sides by people using Lualaba-Atlantic languages.[4] This linguistic configuration clearly indicates that
the settlers came from somewhere up the Zaire. Moreover, linguistic data collected from both sides of the river show three
separate dialects that have less than 80% correspondence to one
another.[5] This situation could indicate divergence from a common linguistic stock beginning well before 1700, but it could
also reflect the impact of different settler groups on different
localities.

Although small numbers of swampland dwellers had probably infiltrated the river settlements throughout the eighteenth
century, it was not until the land shortages in the swamps became acute in the late eighteenth or early nineteenth centuries
that a considerable outward migration developed.[6] By then the
only remaining settlement sites along the riverbank were at Bolobo, at the southern extremity of the high bluffs. The reason
that Bolobo had remained unsettled was probably related to the
fact that there the river narrows and the current temporarily

---

Strip. George Grenfell identified them as Bobangi in "A Map of the Congo
River, 1884–1889." In 1924 F. Gustin identified the Moyi as the original
inhabitants of the Bolobo-Yumbi Strip and reported that Nunu immigrants
had intermingled with the Moyi to the extent that the terms Nunu and
Moyi had become interchangeable along the riverbank. F. Gustin, "Les
Populations du Territoire de la Pama Kasai," 1924, MRAC-E, Prov. Equateur, Dist. Equateur, Terr. Bikoro, 5.

[4] The linguistic classifications are those of Vansina. See Jan Vansina, "Western
Bantu Expansion," *Journal of African History* 25 (1984):129–45.

[5] Jan Vansina (personal communication) discovered these data on a February,
1986, computer printout from the linguistic section of the Musée Royal de
l'Afrique Centrale, Tervuren, Belgium. They have not yet been published.

[6] Using genealogical evidence, Reynaert placed the founding of Bolobo at
around 1840. L. Reynaert, "Histoire Succincte des Populations Constituant
l'Actuelle Sous-Chefferie de Bolobo," 1934, Dossier Politique: Bolobo,
MZA. This would represent the latest possible date. The actual settlement
probably occurred somewhat earlier.

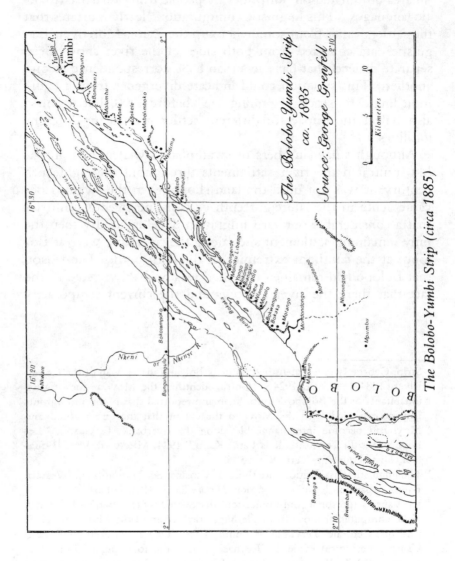

The Bolobo-Yumbi Strip (circa 1885)

Yumbi

The Bolobo-Yumbi Strip
ca. 1885
Source: George Grenfell

BOLOBO

speeds up. As a result, few islands had formed and the fishing was poor. Anyone living in Bolobo had to travel several miles to find a good fishing spot.

According to tradition, the founder of Bolobo was Monyongo, who came from Bokaka, a village in the flooded forest the only outlet of which was to the Zaire. The story focuses on the events that led to the planting of the *nkinda* charm. After coming down the river, Monyongo established a fishing camp on the sandy island of Nkenge, about a kilometer offshore from the present site of Bolobo. Fishing was good and soon the sandbank became crowded with immigrants, causing Monyongo to worry about what would happen when the waters rose and the island flooded. He looked to the east and saw the high bluffs of the riverbanks. He sent some scouts to explore the land, and they reported that it was empty of people. Moving to the riverbank posed a major problem, however, because the people had no canoes with which to cross over.[7] Here is how Etebe described the crossing:

> So on that day he gathered all of his people. He, Monyongo, and all of his people: tappers of palm wine, singers of songs. He called those people to sing [to give courage to the others]. He called people of all professions. The singers strengthened them, they sang the songs and beat the clapperless bells. Then they took a sleeping mat and spread it out on the water. When they finished spreading it out on the water, all the people got onto the sleeping mat. . . . Monyongo took two rats. They were his rats that lived in his house. He brought them to the beach of the island of Nkenge and released them saying, "Now go to the land." The rats swam and swam and swam till they reached the shore. Monyongo said, "Let's push off and go." They didn't paddle, but little by little the sleeping mat moved toward the shore, traveling under its own

---

[7] There is clearly a contradiction in the story, for how could people settle on the island if they had no canoes? The story of crossing the river on sleeping mats is a cliché that is also known in lower Zaire. The Nunu adapted the cliché to local circumstances, thus creating the contradiction.

power. They crossed that channel until they touched the land here. So the village where they settled was called Lonyoku.[8]

The story emphasizes that Monyongo was a powerful magician. In the tradition told by Mangasa the miracles continued:

> After they began living there [at Bolobo] they prepared for the day of *Mpika*. They planted a *lokenya* tree, they planted a banana shoot, they planted cassava stalks. They planted all these things on the same day. These plants grew and ripened on that very day. They planted the *nkinda* so that the village would never die. When they did the *nkinda* rituals they prepared a monument, a tree so tall that it could be seen from afar so that the village would remember forever its fame and so that it would never die. It was their own village. Then they buried a man and a woman alive. When they had buried them the banana plant grew and ripened that very day. The cassava grew and matured that same day. The tree flowered on that day. They had a large feast.[9]

Monyongo was keeper of the *nkinda*. He could therefore proclaim laws that would regulate relationships among people, relationships between people and the water, and relationships between people and the spirits. According to tradition, Monyongo proclaimed four laws.[10] First, no one should die on the water. Such deaths were attributed to crocodiles, which were thought to be under the control of witches. Indeed, in the nineteenth century a crocodile attack on a person could cause war between the village of the victim and the village held responsible for the attack.[11] The law, in effect, banned witchcraft from the water. The second law was that no woman should die in childbirth. Like death on the water, death in childbirth was seen as a sure sign of witchcraft, and Monyongo was, in effect, banning witchcraft from the land. The third law was that no one should quarrel on the day of Mpika. Respect for Mpika not only let the land rest, but let people rest from the quarrels of

---

[8] Interview: Etebe, 5-22-75, Tape A4.
[9] Interview: Mangasa, 5-7-75, Tape A7.
[10] Interview: Etebe and Ngamakala, 5-27-75, Tape A6.
[11] Charles Liebrechts, *Souvenirs d'Afrique: Congo, Léopoldville, Bolobo, Equateur (1883–1889)* (Brussels, 1909), pp. 81—83.

daily life. The fourth law was more straightforward. No man should chase the wife of another. Such extramarital affairs were said to be a major cause of strife in river villages. Having thus regulated affairs on the water, on the land, and among the settler families, Monyongo had completed his work as the founder of Bolobo.

The second wave of settlement in Bolobo is associated with Mampwabe, who came from the Nsangasi River valley. Oral tradition holds that there was a close relationship between Monyongo and Mampwabe. One version holds that the two had the same father, but different mothers; another holds that Mampwabe was the illegitimate son of Monyongo.[12] The story is that Mampwabe had to pay a fine in Nsangasi, but lacked the money, so he came down to borrow it from Monyongo. Seeing that there were open fishing grounds, he decided to settle and went back home to gather up his wives and children. They came down to settle with Monyongo at Lonyoko. Soon they decided that if they lived in the same village there would be trouble, so Mampwabe moved and founded Bonzongo, which was to become the largest of all the villages of Bolobo.

Because emigrants from the swamps preferred to settle in places where they had kin who could help them get started, Bolobo at first attracted mostly people from Bokaka, the home of Monyongo, or from the Nsangasi region, the home of Mampwabe. Thus the villages of Ponzo and Mabwa were founded by settlers from Bokaka, and the villages of Mondanga, Bombongo, and Bosanga were founded by people from Nsangasi. As time passed, however, people from all parts of the swamps began to move toward the river and found settlements at Bolobo. The village of Nkubosaka at Bolobo, for example, was founded by immigrants from Nkubosaka in the swamps. When people from the farmlands of Nkuboko began to settle along the river, they found the high bluffs of Bolobo already occupied, so they moved south of them to the low flooded banks and formed the settlement of Ngabenge.[13] Thus, gradu-

---

[12] Reynaert, "Histoire Succincte"; Interview: Etebe and Ngamakala, 5-22-75, Tape A4.

[13] Interview: Mbolo, 8-5-81, Tape 17/1.

ally, each area of the swamps came to have a counterpart along the river.

As more settlers arrived, the villages began to display a dense settlement pattern that was very different from those in the swamps. Everybody settled near the riverbank. Sons settled near their fathers, but no longer moved their homesteads upon their fathers' deaths, as there was essentially no place to go. Gradually, a series of houses would form a cluster as an old man, his sons, and his grandsons all settled in the same place. These clusters did not have a distinct name; they were called simply *etomb'e mboka,* a piece of the village. The old man who presided over the cluster was simply called *mpomba,* an elder.

The concentrated villages developed a political structure that was more formal than that found in the swamps. Each village had a chief who bore the title *mpomb'e mboka,* the village elder. The original chief of each village was its founder, the person who had planted the *nkinda.* The chief was the keeper of the *nkinda.* If he had a reputation for being strong, his village attracted immigrants. No strict rules governed succession. The village wanted the most powerful man, the one who could best assure the prosperity of the village. Generally, such a man would serve as the chief's assistant and counselor and would be named by the chief as his successor. When the chief died and a respectable mourning period had been observed, the heads of the residential clusters gathered to choose the new chief. Then they called the elders and chiefs of the neighboring villages to dance, feast, and drink palm wine so that the status of the new chief would be recognized among all of the villages.

The most powerful chief among the Nunu villages of Bolobo was recognized as the senior chief, or *mokonzi monene.* His main job was to keep peace among villages and settle quarrels. The first such chief was Monyongo, the founder of Bolobo. After his death, Mampwabe, chief of Bonzongo, was recognized as the senior chief of the Nunu villages. After Mampwabe died, no consensus could be reached as to who was the senior chief, and the task of mediating disputes among the component villages fell to whomever was in the best position to handle the case.

This tighter structuring of relationships among political units should not be seen as a stepping-stone toward centralized urbanism. Rather, it was a necessary compromise between the desire for autonomy of the individual elders and the need for orderly methods of conflict resolution among a dense population. The centralization remained very limited. The chiefs never became administrators, and they are best remembered for ritual pronouncements rather than for administrative or legal innovations. Moreover, when there was conflict between two component villages of Bolobo, the chief did not have the power to stop it. Somewhat like the modern Secretary General of the United Nations, the senior chief could only plead for peace and offer his mediation when both sides tired of war.

The Nunu of Bolobo thus developed what appeared to be an urban situation, with densely packed settlements and ranked chiefs, without developing the centralized hierarchy and functional interdependence that anthropologists usually associate with urbanism. The Nunu villages of Bolobo were, in essence, the homesteads of the swamps concentrated in one place.

THE RIVER ENVIRONMENT

Although the river was, so to speak, the mother of the swamps, its environment differed in fundamental ways. It imposed its own rules on the fishermen, and it forced them to adopt tactics for exploiting natural resources that were radically different from anything they had known in their previous home.

The people of the middle Zaire have long recognized the uniqueness of the river environment. They referred to the Zaire River simply as *"ebale,"* the river, a term that distinguished it from *moliba, mosolo, mokele,* and a variety of other words that designated creeks, streams, and other small waterways. As the river that moves more cubic meters of water per minute than any other river in the world except the Amazon, it clearly merits a category by itself. To the Nunu, the river provided the water that formed the swamps, and it provided the fish. It regulated the seasons and the rhythm of life. Its power was awesome, its influence pervasive.

The most striking feature of this environment was that the wide river channels, with their sandy bottoms and moving currents, were relatively barren of food for fish and therefore did not make for good fishing. The most fruitful areas were the riverbanks and the islands, but these features constantly changed as banks eroded and islands arose.

The creation of islands was the fundamental natural process in the river environment.[14] The first step was the formation of a sandbank. Although a sandbank could grow up around any obstacle such as a boulder or a fallen tree, a more common cause was a slowing of the current at a place where the river widened. As the current slowed, the suspended sand particles would settle. Because the current slowed gradually, more sand would be deposited at the downstream end of the sandbank, and this end would appear first. During the low-water season, the sandbank appeared above the surface and would be colonized by grasses. During the high water, the grasses caused a further slowing of the current and provoked the sedimentation of finer particles of earth. Gradually, a layer of limonite soil began to build up. During the next low-water period, the tall *echinochloa* grasses that made up floating prairies sank their roots into the fertile soil. The floating prairies slowed down the current even more, and the layer of limonite steadily became thicker as the years passed.

As the soil built up, *alchornea cordata* bushes, which the Nunu called *mabonzi,* took root, contributing to the further sedimentation of the island. Gradually, various species of trees typical of flooded forests took root. If sedimentation continued long enough, the soil became so thick that the island only rarely flooded during the high water. In such situations, vines and species of trees less resistant to water would eventually spring up. Even at this stage, however, the island was not permanently fixed. The current constantly eroded the head of the island and carried the sediments around the sides to be deposited at the tail. Thus one could find dense vegetation at the head and sandbanks at the rear. Each island thus exhibited various stages of its continuing development simultaneously.

Each stage of island development provided a different kind of

---

[14] J.P. Gosse, *Le Milieu Aquatique et l'Ecologie des Poissons dans la Région de Yangambi*, MRAC, Annales, Sciences Zoologiques, no. 116 (Tervuren, 1963), pp. 123–42.

habitat for fish. The sandbanks, although sterile, attracted minnows and other small fish to the shallow, overheated waters
along the edges. The calm, deep waters situated downstream
from the sandbanks were richer in organic debris and attracted
fish of the species *Labeo, Citharinus, Tilapia,* and *Tylochromis*.[15]
The most attractive habitat for fish was the flooded islands during the high water. Certain types of fish would enter the floating meadows; others sought the *mabonzi* bushes, while still others preferred the shade of the mature forest. The vegetation
attracted insects and larvae, which the fish ate, and gave shade
from the glaring sun.

The most common way of fishing on the islands was with
traps similar to those used in the swamps.[16] *Ekete,* the large
trap, was placed either in the aquatic grasses or among the inundated bushes on the fringes of an island. It was made of *ngoli,*
a vine about one centimeter thick. Fishing with the *ekete* could
be done by a single person, but it was accomplished generally
by two people; one to hold the canoe steady and the other to
check the trap. The trap was best checked daily, but two or
three times a week was more common. Often a single fisherman would have up to twenty *ekete* traps in different spots. He
would check out his traps in one area one day, another area the
next day, and so forth. Since the holes in the *ekete* were approximately ten centimeters square, only large fish were caught.[17]

Mokonyi, the smaller trap, was used for smaller fish.[18] It had
a double cone-like entrance, so that fish could easily swim in
but had difficulty getting out. There was a small trap door in
the back which could be opened to remove the fish. The trap
was made of strips from raffia fronds tied together with *nkinga*
(a stringy substance found in raffia palm trees). Cassava skins
were often put in the trap to attract fish. Like the *ekete,* this trap
was best worked by two people in a canoe.

---

[15] The Nunu names are respectively: *mpopo, mayanga, mabondu,* and *nyende.*

[16] The major sources on fishing were Etebe and Ngamakala, 6-2-75, Tapes
A8 and A9.

[17] Mainly *mboto, milolu* (L. *Nasus*), *mayanga* (*Citharinus*), *nsinga* (*Ophiocephialus*), *nyumi* (*Clarias*), and *nsembe* (*Protopollol*).

[18] Mainly *nsinga* (*Ophiocephialus*), *ngolo* (*Clarias*), *binkaba* (L. *Brevis*), *milombi,
mabundu* (*Tilipia*), and *nzombo* (*Protopterus*).

The *etambo,* or trigger trap, was less popular than the other two. It had an open mouth to which a trap door was hinged. The trap door was attached to a trigger mechanism that pulled the door shut when the trigger was disturbed. Like the *ekete* and the *mokonyi,* this trap was placed in the bushes of flooded islands with fruit or cassava inside as bait. When the fish tried to eat the bait, they triggered the mechanism and were caught. The *etambo* could thus catch only one fish at a time.

To catch large fish, fishermen would go out with harpoons, which often had four detachable heads. Two people would fish together, one paddling, the other waiting with the harpoon poised and looking for the large fish that swam near the surface.[19] They paddled along the edges of floating prairies or drifted with the current, the paddler using his paddle as a rudder to keep the canoe on a steady course.

As the waters went down, the submerged islands gradually protruded above the surface and the fish left for the deeper and more barren channels. Often, however, there were pools left in the low-lying grassy areas in the middle of the younger islands, a result of the fact that limonite deposits built up most rapidly around the edges of the islands. Fishing in these pools required two or more people. Beginning work on the fringes of a pool, they cut the grass and packed it down to fill the edges. They added dirt and trampled down the mixture. Slowly they filled the pool so only a small center was left. Then they entered the diminished pool with *bosolo* fish baskets. Making noise, they herded the fish into shallow water and scooped them up.[20]

Most fishing during the low-water season, however, was done in the shallow water near sandbanks. One of these methods was *nkombo*. It required fish fences. It was carried out toward noon on a sunny day, when the *milolu* and *mapiti* fish came into the clear, shallow water to sun themselves.[21] They often swam single file, their backs sometimes breaking the surface. When the fishermen spotted the fish, they beached the

---

[19] This method was used mainly for *mboto, milolu* (L. *Nasus*), *nyumi* (*Clarias*), and *mayanga,* (*Citharinus*).

[20] This method yielded *nsinga, ngolo, malembi, milombi,* and *enkaba*.

[21] The latin names are, respectively, *L. Nasus* and *Parauchenoglanis macrostoma*.

canoe and took out the fence, which had been folded in accordion pleats. Each of the ten or twelve men involved carried a section on his head, walked out into chest-deep water, and spread the fence roughly parallel to the shore with the ends curved toward the sandbank. Thus, they blocked the fish from escaping to deeper water. Then one man with a long stick began to hit the shallow water near the shore and make loud noises. The frightened fish fled toward the deeper water and ran into the fence. The men at the extreme ends of the fence rushed toward the shore and toward each other, bringing the fence into a circle with the fish inside. Then three men got inside the fence and scooped out the fish with their hands or with fish baskets, handing them to the men in the canoe. If a large school of fish was found, the men could capture up to two hundred fish at a time.

With the fish in the open channels, the low-water season was ideal for net fishing. The most common nets were the *maya* net, which had openings about four centimeters square, and the *malota* net, which had larger openings. These nets, made from the supple bark of the *nkosa* plant, were neither long enough nor strong enough to be strung out in the manner of the modern seine nets. Each net was designed for a specific type of fishing. The *malota* net was stretched around *bikoko* grasses near the shore. Then the fishermen beat the water near the shore with sticks to make the fish flee into the net. The *maya* net, which had smaller holes, was stretched between two canoes and maneuvered into a closed circle, trapping the fish inside. Because of the limitations of the nets, the low-water season was considered the poorest season for fishing.[22]

RIVER NOMADS

In settling along the banks of the Zaire, the Nunu were less developing a new way of life than they were discovering an old one. The riverbanks of the Bolobo-Yumbi Strip had first been

---

[22] Interviews: Etebe and Ngamakala, 7-1-75, Tape A27; Etebe, 8-4-41, Tape 16/1; Lobwaka, 8-5-81, Tape 17/1; Bokanza Ece, 6-2-75, field notes.

settled during the stone age,[23] and over the millennia a riverine mode of life had developed that was remarkably uniform all along the middle Zaire, no matter what the ethnic identity of the people involved. All along the river, different ethnic groups responded in roughly similar ways to the rise and fall of the water and the seasonal movements of the fish.[24] It was this ancient pattern of life that the Nunu immigrants had to discover anew.

Unlike swamp fishing, which was very much like farming, river fishing was more like hunting. One set traps and waited, or one searched for fish and then stalked them. River fishing was very much a game of chance, especially in the open water where the fish were constantly on the move. Unlike the swamps, where a family fished the same dam or pond year after year, generation after generation, river fishermen were ready to shift spots from day to day depending on where the fishing was said to be good. Despite this extraordinary effort, the yield of nets and traps was never as high as the yield of dams in the swamplands.[25]

The most significant movement was seasonal. During the two high-water seasons (May to June and December to January), fishermen mostly fished near the village, as camping sites were scarce on the flooded islands. They made day trips to check traps, or they stayed in the village to make traps, fish fences, and nets. During the low-water season (July to August), the islands and sandbanks appeared. They made excellent spots for camping, and the fishermen along with their wives and children headed for a fishing camp as the water went down.

---

[23] Maurice Bequaert, "Contribution à la Connaissance de l'Age de la Pierre dans la Région de Bolobo," *Bulletin de la Société Royale Belge d'Anthropologie et de Préhistoire* 60 (1949):95–115.

[24] In 1887 Froment wrote that to describe one of the ethnic groups along the middle Zaire was to describe them all. E. Froment, "Trois Affluents Français du Congo: Rivières Alima, Likouala, Sanga," *Bulletin de la Société de Géographie de Lille* 7 (1887):469–70.

[25] Service des Eaux et Forêts, "Aperçu sur la Pêche Lacustre et Fluviale au Congo Belge et au Ruanda-Urundi," *Bulletin Agricole du Congo Belge,* 50 (1959):1682.

As each new fishing season approached, a fisherman had to make three choices: where to fish, which methods to use, and with whom to fish. All three choices were open to wide variation from season to season and from year to year. The choice of a new place could entail the choice of a new method, and both could force the fisherman to look for new partners. Although the most common fishing teams were composed of a father and his sons or an uncle and his nephews, not all kinsmen fished together, and not all fishing teams were composed of kin. Indeed, the family was more secure if different family members were fishing in different places, for then if one had bad luck, another might make up for it with good luck.

Once a team was formed, the members went to the chosen area and sought a site for a fishing camp. They often picked a sandbank, where there was no brush to be cleared, as a temporary campsite, but if the fishermen hoped to return to the area in future years, they sought the higher ground provided by a mature island. Having chosen a spot, they built huts of sticks covered with thatch. Sometimes they built permanent huts on stilts to which they could return during the high water. If the fishing proved to be good, the word spread, and other fishermen came to join them. The arrival of newcomers did not threaten them; the river was vast enough to provide fishing sites for everyone. Some of the newcomers built their own fishing camps on vacant sites, but others joined the existing camp. Little by little it grew.

If the fishing continued to be good and the fishermen returned there several seasons in a row, the camp acquired a name and it became a landmark for people travelling along the river. It also acquired a political structure. The founder became its "owner," or headman. The Nunu did not plant *nkinda* charms on islands because the island itself could not be owned. The headman was primarily a mediator of disputes between members. Serious decisions, such as whether to banish a member from the camp, were made in consultation with the senior members of the camp. The headman also served as spokesman for his camp in negotiations and disputes with other camps.

The membership of the camp changed constantly. Members were free to leave if they wanted to try their luck someplace else, and newcomers were welcome to join. Although some people returned to the same camp year after year, others changed camps several times during a single fishing season. If a man left, he retained rights in his hut, though not in the island itself. A newcomer would have to get his permission to use the abandoned hut. Once the high waters had washed the hut away, however, the builder lost his claim. Sometimes the head-man left, and the remaining members would gather to designate a successor, often the oldest man in the group. Just as new camps were continually being created, old ones were often abandoned. The key characteristic of river fishing was its un-predictability, and the best strategy was to be ready to move to where the fishing was best.

The frequent absence of men from the villages left agriculture to the women. The hinterlands of the river towns were a mo-saic of forest and savanna, with savanna dominating. Because the men were often away at fishing camps during the dry sea-son, they made little attempt to clear fields. This task was left to women, who found open spots in the savanna that they burned during the dry season and cleared. By clearing their own fields, the women freed themselves from dependence on men. They could make their fields as big as they wished, and they could leave them for longer fallow periods. Because clear-ing a spot for a field was relatively easy, fields were not consid-ered valuable commodities, as they were in Nkuboko. More-over, the Nunu were reluctant to assert ownership claims to the land they cultivated because the hinterland of the river villages was claimed by the inland Tio and Tiene. In these fields the women planted mostly cassava, but also peanuts, corn, and sweet potatoes. Plantains and bananas were grown in clusters behind the houses.

The major constraint on agricultural production was the time women spent at the fishing camps, where they occupied them-selves with smoking the fish caught by the men. The freshly caught fish were placed on smoking racks and smoked for up to seven days. During this time the fire had to be watched to keep it at the right temperature, and the fish had to be turned periodically. If the fire got too hot, it charred the skin of the fish and prevented subsequent smoke from penetrating the

meat. A second constraint was the time it took women to travel
to their fields. As the populations of the towns increased, people had to travel farther and farther from the town to find good
agricultural land. Time spent by women at the fishing camps
and in travel to and from their fields may have severely limited
agricultural development, as attested by the fact that Bolobo
was by no means self-sufficient in cassava. A series of markets
arose between the riverine Nunu and the inland Tiene and Tio
to facilitate the exchange of river fish for inland agricultural
products.

Like the river itself, river society was highly fluid. River people, with no ties to an estate, moved frequently from one river
town to another. In so doing, they often lost contact with their
more distant kinsmen. In contrast to genealogies collected in the
swamps, which went back as far as seven generations, river genealogies were generally shallow, sometimes going back only
two generations.[26] In the swamps, genealogical knowledge was
important for defending claims to dams and ponds. Along the
river there were few claims to be defended, and such knowledge often seemed irrelevant to the concerns of everyday life.

RIVER BIG-MEN

The nomadic lives of the fishermen led to a more egalitarian
version of competition among people. In contrast to the
swamps, where people fought over space and property, there
was little property of significance to be had along the river.
There were no dams or ponds that were passed down from
generation to generation. Fishing was mostly done in open waters, which had no owners. Similarly, the islands had no owners. Even fields were planted on land that belonged to nobody
and to everybody.

There was, however, one substantial piece of property that

---

[26] For swamp genealogies, see those of Ekando and Mongemba, 1981 field
notes. For river genealogies, see Miluka, 5-5-75 and 5-6-75, field notes, and
Lobwaka, 8-5-81, Tape 17.

was necessary for success as a fisherman. That was a canoe. The trees in the Bolobo area were not suitable for making canoes, so canoes had to be purchased from upriver traders. The cheaper canoes were about three meters long and were made of soft wood that would rot in about three years. The more expensive canoes were made of mahogany and would last ten to fifteen years with proper care.

The most common method of accumulating money toward the purchase of a canoe was to work for one's father or one's uncle, or for any prosperous fisherman who needed assistance. For activities such as spear fishing or checking traps, the assistant, called *mpende,* paddled in back while the owner, called *ntange,* checked the traps or wielded the harpoon. Sometimes each man had his own traps and they would check both sets during the day. The fish would be placed on a common pile, with the owner of the canoe getting the bulk of the fish and the assistant getting perhaps a tenth. If a child was working for his father or his uncle, he would often get even less, but work throughout his teenage years would sometimes be rewarded with a gift of a small canoe. Once he had his own canoe, he would be in a position to attract a client to work for him.

Unlike the dams and ponds in the swamps, ownership of canoes did not divide river society into two visible classes. Most canoeless people were young, and they would eventually find the means to strike out on their own. The cost of buying a small canoe was not prohibitive. Although there were probably some who remained clients all their lives, these were often people who lacked the ambition necessary to make their own way.

River society in the early nineteenth century was more egalitarian than swamp society. There were few men who could command a large group of dependents, but there were also few men who depended on others for their survival. While the river economy provided little aid toward the old ideal of power over others, it provided ideal conditions for reaching the goal of personal independence. Unlike the swamps, which had an abundance of fish but a shortage of agricultural products, and unlike Nkuboko, which had a surplus of cassava but a shortage of fish, the river provided a good balance of both. The savanna fields behind Bolobo resolved the old conflict between time spent fishing and time spent clearing fields, and therefore a family could attain relative self-sufficiency in both protein and starch.

River society was competitive, though within a narrower range than swampland society. The difference between rich and poor was determined less by ownership of the means of production than by hard work and skill in fishing. Life in the fishing camps was arduous, and the unambitious often lounged in the towns while their more ambitious neighbors were fishing at distant camps. The reward for hard work was money. Currencies such as *nsi* shells and even copper rods circulated widely along the river. Because river fishermen did not have to trade large quantities of their fish for cassava as did people in the swamps, a fisherman could produce a net surplus even though his total catch was smaller than the swampland catches. The surplus could then be sold for currency.

Surplus fish and currency could be used in several ways to gain dependents and status. First, a successful fisherman could acquire more than one wife. Second, he could purchase a slave or two. Third, he could purchase a second canoe, and thus attract clients. Fourth, he could lend money to people in need, and thus build up a group of people who had obligations to him. Finally, a man with a surplus of smoked fish could give them away to friends and kinsmen and thus create reciprocal obligations. By all of these means, a fisherman could gain status and power, and thus he could become a riverine big-man.

CONCLUSION

The river environment created a strange contradiction in everyday life. On the one hand, the settlers crowded into densely settled towns and brought the old cycle of generational migration to an end. On the other hand, they led a nomadic existence, moving from fishing camp to fishing camp, with the river towns as the only fixed points in their wanderings. Both patterns were radically different from life in the swamps.

New forms of competition developed as men tried to earn money for bridewealth and sought to attract junior fishing partners. Gradations of wealth were visible in the size and quantity of a man's canoes and the size of his household. Still, the tactics, strategies, and even the goals of big-man competition were very different from the water lord competition in the swamps. The distinction between landed and landless had become meaningless. Because everybody who could obtain a canoe had access to the means of production, there was neither a class of the very poor nor a class of the very rich. People competed over small increments of wealth and status. Like the drylands of Nkuboko, the Zaire River had forced people to create a mutant of the water lord competition.

7. The Core

A T THE SAME TIME that people on the frontiers were developing innovative strategies to exploit new micro-environments, the water lords in the older core regions
were using defensive strategies to try to hold on to their estates.
Until the early nineteenth century, the core areas of the swamps
had maintained a precarious stability as excess people were
thrown off toward the periphery. This practice had allowed the
water lords to maintain control of their land and had provided
the remaining landless people with the possibility of making
their livelihoods as clients. The filling up of the prime fishing
grounds rendered possibility of moving to open land less and
less feasible.

The limit of eastward expansion was marked by the villages
of Nkuboko, located on dry land just beyond the farthest extension of the floodwaters. Further movement to the east would
have required abandoning fishing altogether, a prospect that
Nunu males found unpalatable. Power over people was related
to power over fish, and even the poorest fisherman in the
swamps participated in the ethos of the fishing life. When the
limits of the inundated zone were reached, expansion came to
an end. No new villages were established inland. In time the
best fishing grounds along the streams were claimed, and Nkuboko began to suffer the same types of inequalities found in the
swamps. The other option, expansion along the river, allowed
emigrants to continue fishing as their major occupation, but the
rewards were limited. River fishermen did not have any means
to build up estates in the manner common in the swamps. They
were far from their kinsmen in the swamps, and so gaining an
independent existence along the river required giving up collective security.

Because movement to the fringe areas had clear drawbacks,
many poor people who in earlier periods would have left their

homesteads now chose to stay, and their presence threatened the precarious equilibrium of the core areas. The end of expansion did not provoke an ecological crisis because the land became *legally* full long before its ecological carrying capacity was reached. A single dam holder could catch far more fish than his immediate family could eat, and this fundamental economic fact created a situation in which the fishing spots controlled by the water lords provided the food for the landed and the landless alike.

The continuing growth of population nevertheless created new tensions that exacerbated inequalities that had long been present in Nunu society. The discussion which follows will distinguish between forms of inequality that created conflict within the domestic group and those that created wider juro-political conflicts.

INEQUALITY AND DOMESTIC CONFLICT

Inequality between women and men was a pervasive feature of swampland society. The very terms used in discussing gender relationships illustrate how Nunu ideology pictured this situation as natural. The Nunu term for "right hand" was literally "the hand of the husband." The left hand was the hand of the wife.

In the household economy women were responsible for agriculture, while the men were responsible for fishing and other activities which aided the amassing of wealth. Moreover, women had primary responsibility for feeding the household, and much of their production went toward this end. Even women who traded pots and foodstuffs in the marketplace were doing so primarily to assure the survival of the household. They usually had little left over for themselves. The subsistence responsibility of women was reinforced by the fact that women's markets generally operated by barter and kept women segregated from the cash economy. As one informant put it, "Women sold their cassava in the marketplace, but for no price."[1] In a similar manner, production of pottery or palm oil

---

[1] Interview: Nsamonie, 7-15-81, Tape 6/1.

provided women with trading commodities that served mainly to purchase cassava for their households.

Still, male and female economic roles sometimes overlapped. Although women were primarily responsible for agriculture, men cut the fields in virgin forest and they cleared the bush again after an abandoned field had regenerated. During the growing season when the cassava was in flower, men shared the task of keeping animals away. They built rude shelters resembling those in fishing camps near the field, where they spent the nights scaring off marauding buffaloes, elephants, antelopes, and wild pigs. Despite these efforts, the produce of the fields normally belonged to the women.

Then again, women sometimes fished. One common form of female fishing was emptying the ponds. The women entered the partially desiccated pond with tightly woven buckets and threw out the water. Then both men and women picked up the fish. In the drying process the men and women performed complementary tasks, with the women stoking the fires while the men turned the fish on the rack. In the end, both men and women laborers got equal shares of the fish. The other common form of fishing for women took place in August and September, when the water had disappeared from the flooded grasslands. Shallow pools and flooded gullies remained in which women could scoop up fish with oblong baskets. While the women were involved in this task, the men were burning the grasslands and walking through the grass with spears to find the *nzombo* fish which had burrowed into the mud. In this way men and women cooperated to squeeze the largest number of fish out of the grasslands. In the end, the fish were divided, and men and women got roughly equal amounts.[2] Women's fish, however, normally went to feed the household, and their excess would be bartered for cassava at the markets of Nkuboko.

Despite barriers to female participation in the cash economy, women were never completely excluded. Money transactions sometimes took place even in markets that operated predominantly by barter because women did not always have items to

---

[2] Interview: Ekando, 7-23-81, Tape 12/2.

barter when they needed fish or cassava to feed their households. They therefore purchased items with money and created
a cash profit for the woman doing the selling. As Nsamonie
noted, "Women sometimes sold things for money, but the accumulation of money progressed only little by little."[3]

A few women managed to accumulate significant amounts of
material wealth. Women involved in craft production sometimes purchased their own canoes to make the trips to the Nkuboko markets or to the villages along the Zaire River. Women
with money were often older women whose children were
grown up and who therefore needed little to maintain the
household. Some women purchased slaves to assist them in
their work. At Nkubosaka, a well-known pottery producing
village, women were the largest buyers of slaves in the nineteenth century.[4] Although many women who owned slaves
held them together with their husbands,[5] other women were
the sole owners. If a female slave owned by a woman married,
her female master collected the bride-price. Even when women
acquired money, however, their social power was limited because they did not own dams or ponds. The history of Mongemba's fishing dam shows that after the death of a former
owner who had no heirs the dam went to the husband of his
niece, not to the niece herself.[6]

The second structural inequality in swampland society was
between slave and free. The slave population had to be constantly renewed through active recruitment because slaves were
rapidly assimilated into the family. As Lopanda noted, "After a
few years a slave is just like any other member of the family."
When he fished, he got a share equal to that of a free person.[7]
The children of slaves were usually full members of the household. Nevertheless, the life of a slave was not easy, as slaves
usually were assigned the most difficult tasks. The life of a slave
was also risky. Slaves could be sold at any time, and they had
no legal protection against abuse by their masters.

---

[3] Interview: Nsamonie, 7-16-81, Tape 6/1.
[4] Interview: Lopanza, 7-22-81, Tape 9/2.
[5] Interview: Lopanda, 7-16-81, Tape 6/2.
[6] Interview: Mongemba, 7-8-81, field notes.
[7] Interview: Lopanda, 7-10-81, Tape 1/2.

Tensions between men and women, free and slave, were felt most often within the homestead itself. It was there that tasks were assigned and income was distributed. The inequalities in work and in rewards were repeated on a day-to-day basis until they became a monotonous drone. Like the inequalities themselves, the conflicts they provoked were so pervasive as to be almost invisible. The victims employed well-known weapons of the weak: they argued, they dragged their feet, they sought to carve out separate lives for themselves, they gossiped.[8] The result was everyday strife, bickering, and jealousy within the homestead. These conflicts were the background to the more visible conflicts that shaped political action in the society.

The major institution mitigating the tension within the homestead was based on the concept of the moral economy. All members of the household had the right to eat the food that was available. When fish were harvested, a certain quantity was set aside for the household members to eat, and only the surplus was sold. Even so, all people did not have equal access to food. At mealtime free men ate first, and then the women, slaves, and children ate what was left. The second means of control came from the very pervasiveness of the structural inequalities. They made the cleavages seem natural, part of the order of things. They also gave the victims of inequalities few options. A slave who ran away from one household would find himself a slave in another; a wife who ran away would find herself as a wife or as a daughter in another.

A third sphere of inequality within the household concerned relations between father and son, uncle and nephew, or older brother and younger brother. Being free males, these people were all potential water lords, but the younger members were not yet water lords, and that distinction was a major source of tension within the household. Etebe captured the ambivalence of this relationship when he mentioned that outwardly nephews acted as if they loved their maternal uncles, but inwardly they were afraid of them.[9] The dominant lineage ideology held that these inequalities would balance out over the long run as the

---

[8] See James Scott, *Weapons of the Weak* (New Haven, 1985).
[9] Interview: Etebe, 9-19-76, Tape A147.

elders died and their juniors replaced them. Junior members of
the household, in short, were encouraged to support their elders
instead of competing with them.

Yet in the short run, the inequalities were great indeed, and
young, free males chafed at the denial of full participation. As
young men learned to fish they gradually did more and more
of the upkeep on the ponds and dams of their uncles and fathers, and they gradually took over fishing the dams or super-
vising the emptying of the ponds. Yet they received only token
rewards. Elder sons or nephews could do little more than patiently wait until they inherited the fishing grounds that they
had been working.

Younger siblings had even less to look forward to. The opposition between *moyebi* and *molimi,* the older and the younger
brother, influenced inheritance of property and position in the
matrilineage. Although in some cases a strong younger brother
would inherit the property instead of his weaker older brother,
the elder had a clear edge in the competition. It was theoreti-
cally possible that each brother would get his turn—histories of
dams and ponds show that they often passed from older to
younger brother—but the younger brothers nevertheless chafed
under the control of the elder brother. In earlier periods, these
younger siblings would have left to found their own estates, but
now more of them stayed home, and their presence created tensions in the family.

In the face of such tensions, the elders relied on various
mechanisms to uphold their privileges in a political system that
had no civil authorities to enforce property rights. Because the
inheritance and distribution of wealth were carried out primarily within the extended matrilineal family, the matrilineage was
a major arena of conflict between uncles and their nephews, and
between elder brothers and their siblings. It was simultaneously
an important institution for the suppression and resolution of
conflict. A matrilineage usually encompassed a number of
homesteads in scattered parts of the swamps because the
women who formed the genealogical links between generations
left home upon marriage to settle with their husbands.

Studies in other parts of Africa have argued that the power of
the lineage headmen often derived from their control of bride-

wealth, with which they provided wives for the junior males in the lineage. Control over bridewealth, according to this argument, gave them control over the biological and social reproduction of the lineage.[10] In the southern swamps, however, circumstances and institutional arrangements made it difficult for lineage headmen to control bridewealth. First, lineage control of bridewealth usually required a type of currency that was good only for social transactions and that could not be obtained through the actions of the marketplace. There were no such specialized currencies among the swamp dwellers, who used *nsi* shells for bridewealth as well as for marketplace transactions. In the absence of specialized currencies for social transactions, it was difficult for elders to monopolize bridewealth.

Moreover, bridewealth could potentially come from a variety of sources inside and outside the lineage. In accordance with the prevailing ethos of independence, a young man tried to finance his own marriage in order to begin married life as independently as possible. If he could not finance the whole bride-price himself, he could seek aid either from his father or from his maternal uncles. The father wanted to be the one to help because his aid would assure that the son would settle with him in the family homestead. If the father did not have money, he tried to raise it from among his kinsmen. If he was unsuccessful, then the young man would turn to his maternal uncles for help and would probably settle near one of them. In cases where the father successfully provided aid in procuring a wife, the maternal uncles would sometimes gather resources to aid the young man in procuring a second wife. In this way they might convince the young man to settle with one of them upon the death of the father, or they could solidify patron–client ties in case they needed labor.

A more powerful form of control within the matrilineage derived from the uncles' power to bewitch their nephews. According to prevailing witchcraft beliefs, after a magical spirit had helped a person become wealthy, it came to collect pay-

---

[10] See Claude Meillassoux, "Essai d'Interprétation du Phénomène Economique dans les Sociétés Traditionnelles d'Auto-Subsistance," *Cahiers d'Etudes Africaines* 4 (1960):38–67.

ment, usually the soul of a member of the rich man's family. The rich man would usually designate a nephew, who would later die of accident or disease. The trade-off here was between two forms of wealth: wealth in the form of money or goods, and wealth in the form of kinsmen.

Because maternal uncles claimed such powers, they had direct control over the treatment of disease. If a child got sick, initial responsibility for treatment lay with the father, but if the illness persisted, the child's matrilineage was called in. If the father failed to call in the matrilineage and the child died, he would have to pay them a substantial sum of money. If he refused to pay, it was cause for war, and the matrilineage might unite to seize his house, his pond, or his dam.

The father went to the eldest of the child's maternal uncles, who called a conference of all the maternal uncles.[11] The father supplied beer and explained the problem. The maternal uncles then gave the beer to their own children, who went off by themselves to drink part of it. These cousins, being related to the heads of the matrilineage through paternal links, were not part of the lineage itself, but they played an important role in the healing process.

While the cousins were off drinking beer, the maternal uncles discussed the possible causes of the illness. They weighed the merits of various healers and chose a general course of treatment. The Nunu had a variety of medical specialists, and thus the key decisions were which type of specialist to use and which individual specialist to consult. This responsibility was given to the maternal uncles for a very sound reason: the sickness may well have been the result of witchcraft, and the bewitcher may well have been the maternal uncle himself. The meeting thus created an occasion for reconciling whatever conflicts lay behind the bewitchment, and it allowed the uncle to withdraw the curse without an open confrontation.

When the uncles had made their plan, they summoned the cousins and sent them with a jar of beer to the diviner. They

---

[11] This description comes from interviews with Bampomba, 7-24-81, Tape 13/1, and Ekando, 7-25-81, Tape 14/1.

told the diviner, "Heal this child, and when the sickness is gone, call us and we will pay the fee." If the child did not respond to the treatment, the uncles would gather again to make a new plan. If the treatment succeeded, the cousins would return the child to the maternal uncles, who called the father. Bringing more beer, the father met with the uncles to discuss the diviner's fees.

The father had originally left a sum of money with the uncles, and now it was time to square the accounts. If the fees were more than the original sum, the uncles called upon the father to make up the difference. The father would either pay or ask the uncles for help. He would say, "I rejoice that the child is healed, but I have paid all the expenses and you have paid nothing." Then would begin a process of bargaining that could result, if relations between father and uncles were good, in the uncles and the father splitting the costs. In any case, the father provided beer to the uncles as an acknowledgment of their services. The treatment process thus gave both the father and the maternal uncles power to provide healing or to withhold it.

INEQUALITY AND JURO-POLITICAL CONFLICT

The most politically volatile inequalities were those among people who considered themselves to be in economic and social competition with one another. One persistent source of conflict was over inequalities in landholdings. At the extremes, there were homesteads that possessed fishing grounds and those that did not, but there were also significant gradations in between. Large landholders had more wealth and power than small landholders. Among the landless there was a distinction between those who enjoyed regular rights as clients and those who scrounged for work on dams or ponds.

The seriousness of poverty for those lacking fishing grounds can be seen in the fact that there were men who never married because they could not pay bridewealth. Longwa stated the proposition succinctly:

Before the whites came there were people who never married because they couldn't find the money. If you didn't have a pond or a dam, it was difficult to get money. Rich people were the ones who had dams and ponds.[12]

Whereas the structural inequalities between men and women, slave and free, and old and young were seen as part of the normal order of things, the visible inequalities among free people were explained in terms that sound almost like social Darwinism. The ideology of the swamps placed a heavy emphasis on individual initiative and hard work. During the days of open land, a combination of initiative and hard work could lead to prosperity, but as fishing grounds and high ground for fields became scarce, individuals had less control over their fates. The frontier ideologies remained, however, and poverty continued to be blamed on the poor themselves. "Hunger," Ekando explained, came about because "some people didn't work hard and therefore they couldn't feed their own children."[13]

The unequal distribution of wealth engendered jealousy and conflict. The most common expression of this conflict was witchcraft accusations. The witchcraft model common among the Nunu pictured economic activity as a sort of zero-sum exchange in which one person's gain was always offset by another person's loss. Such a view corresponded to reality in two important ways. First, if wealth was measured in terms of wives and land, both were in finite supply. The fact that some men owned two dams or had two wives while others had none was a perfect illustration of the zero-sum character of the competition.

In the metaphor of the middle Zaire, if a person wanted to get rich, he obtained a magical agent to work for him. This agent, often the spirit of an animal, would preemptively steal money destined to be earned by others and bring this money to its master. Thus, if one fisherman had good luck and another using similar methods had bad luck, it was assumed that the one was stealing fish from the other. Longwa explained:

---

[12] Interview: Longwa, 7-20-81, Tape 9/1. A similar statement was made by Lopanda, 7-15-81, Tape 6/2.
[13] Interview: Ekando, 7-25-81, Tape 14/1.

> If your pond got a lot of fish and the neighboring ones did not, people would say, "He has an *edzo* [a spirit agent]. If you are rich, people will say, "He has an *edzo* which gives him his money. Now he will finish people off."[14]

Another manifestation of witchcraft was seen in the *nsi* shells that served as currency. Sometimes the animal inside the shell was not dead, and if the shell was put in a pot of water, it would multiply. As a result, everybody kept their shells in water pots and hoped that their wealth would increase. Most people were disappointed. Yasi explained the situation:

> If you put *nsi* money in a pot of water, the shell would give birth. But that didn't happen to everybody, only to rich people. The *nsi* of the rich gave birth; those of the poor did not.[15]

People who saw themselves as victims of such manipulations sought to retaliate by bringing witchcraft accusations against the wealthy, obtaining charms to neutralize the power of the rich, or even going to war. In the dominant cosmology of the area, there was little room for the notion of accident. Misfortune had causes, and the root of these causes lay in human greed.

Witchcraft accusations were the flip side of the stress on individual achievement, and they reveal the tension inherent in a society that tried to balance individual initiative with collective security. This tension is mirrored in Nunu proverbial wisdom. There are proverbs about the importance of hard work and strength, but there are also proverbs warning of the dangers of wealth and inequality. One proverb says that wealth is a curse that leads to death. Lila's explanation was that wealth gives a man the desire for women. It also makes a man impose upon his friends. It makes him want to reduce his friends to slavery.

---

[14] Interview: Longwa, 7-20-81, Tape 9/1. In 1981 I met Likinda, who had just finished fishing his dam and had gotten almost nothing, while the dams above and below his were full of fish. He believed such a situation could only be the result of witchcraft.

[15] Interview: Yasi, 7-13-81, Tape 3/1.

It causes one thing after another, and eventually leads to the death of the wealthy man.[16]

A similar proverb holds that if you clamor for wealth, wealth will clamor for your throat. Lila explained that there were three ways in which this could happen. First, people would say that the man's wealth did not come from work, but from an *edzo* (a spirit agent), or from a *likundu* (a growth in the intestine that was held to be the seat of spiritual powers). Because supernatural agents required payment in the form of human souls for their services, people would fear that the rich man's *edzo* or *likundu* wanted to finish them off. To defend themselves, they would go to the charm maker and purchase charms to kill him. Second, when a rich man traveled with his sack full of money, his enemies would ambush him along the trail and steal his money. Or else they would invite him to drink with them and put poison in his beer. The third danger of wealth was that a rich man would be tempted to have affairs with his neighbors' wives, who were attracted by his wealth. Alternatively, if he married a large number of wives, there were fewer wives to go around among the rest of the male population. In either case, the other men became jealous and searched for charms to kill him.[17]

Another form of conflict arose when a poor person would steal fish from the dam of a rich man. Since this crime attacked the basis of inequality—an individual's right to the produce of a certain dam—it was considered a very serious offense, and the offender was charged a large fine. If he could not pay, he could be sold into slavery.[18] In other cases, a poor man would try to steal from a rich one by being an unfaithful client. He would cheat on the shares he gave to the owner of the dam, or, after many years of working a dam, he would claim that it belonged to him. The practice of taking clientship oaths in front of witnesses, which was designed to prevent such takeovers, was a

---

[16] Interview: Lila, 7-14-81, Tape 4/1.
[17] Interview: Lila, 7-14-81, Tape 4/1.
[18] Interview: Mbonge Botele, July, 1975, Nkolo-Lingamba field notes.

tacit acknowledgment of the conflict inherent in patron-client relations.[19]

More serious conflicts arose when poor families would try to seize a dam or pond by force, or, alternatively, when a greedy rich man would try to seize fishing grounds from a poor family. The seizure of a fishing ground sometimes resulted from a quarrel. Boketa's family, for instance, had been wronged, and the wrongdoer refused to pay a fine. So they made war on him and seized the dam as payment. Similar cases existed in the Nsenseke area, where people would demand fines and seize dams in lieu of payment. Other dams, however, were simply seized by force. Lila's family had a dam near Mongala, which they remember as simply taking by force from the owner. A more complex situation is remembered along the Moliba. There, a family lost its dam to another family; in retaliation they stole a different dam from the family that had wronged them. The two families, in effect, exchanged dams. The seizure of fishing grounds usually led to war, so the real difficulty was to hold a stolen dam or pond after it was taken.[20]

Competition over wives was another source of conflict. Many a young man who could not afford bride-price simply kidnapped a wife from a distant village. Such episodes sometimes led to small wars in which five or six people were killed. Several wars between the villages of Bokangamoi and Mipa are believed to have been triggered by the kidnapping of women.[21]

In addition to the competition among free males, there was also competition among free women. Although women could not legitimately compete with men, they could and did compete with each other. Some women had large fields which they worked with the aid of daughters or slave girls. Other women had small fields, and thus a large share of the fish caught by their husbands went to purchase cassava at the market. Like

---

[19] Interviews: Longwa, 7-20-81, Tape 9/1; Ekando, 7-25-81, Tape 14/1.

[20] Interviews: Bampomba, 7-18-81, Tape 7/1; Lila, 7-14-81, Tape 4/1; Moliba field notes.

[21] Interviews: Lopanda, 7-10-81, Tape 2/1; Lila, 7-10-81, Tape 2/2; Ekando, 7-23-81, Tape 12/1.

sites for dams and ponds, field sites were at a premium. In the swamps, where women cleared their own fields in the grass-lands, the best sites were on raised ground, the last places to be inundated by the rising water. The early settlers picked the best sites, and latecomers had to plant on more vulnerable terrain. In the dryland forests of Nkuboko, fields were at a premium because of the difficulties in clearing and drying them during the short dry season. Thus, not everybody had equal access to fields. In accordance with their dominant ideology, modern Nunu explain these inequalities by reference to individual char-acter:

> The size of a woman's field depended on her strength. A strong woman would have a large field; a weak woman would have a small one. Most fields came from the ancestors. If your ancestors were strong, you will inherit many fields; if they were weak, you won't inherit many fields.[22]

Although the standard way for a woman to get fields was to inherit them from her mother, women who left to marry men in distant villages had to depend on their husbands. Boyili, who lived in the drylands of Nkuboko, did not inherit any fields. Her husband, Lopanda, cut them from virgin forest, a task re-quiring about two months of labor for each field. He cut the trees with an ax and burned the brush and the stumps. In this way he cut three fields. She planted cassava and corn.[23] Boye-lima was more fortunate because her husband had inherited seven fields from his mother, who had no daughters.[24]

Other women were not as fortunate. Whether through mis-fortune or otherwise, there were some women who did not grow enough food to feed their children. Sometimes the chil-dren would steal food from other houses. If they got caught and the parents had no money to pay the fine, they were sold into slavery. In other cases, women were caught stealing food for their children. A child would be sold into slavery to pay the

[22] Interview: Ekando, 7-25-81, Tape 14/2.
[23] Interview: Lopanda, 7-15-81, Tape 6/2.
[24] Interview: Boyelima, 7-8-81, field notes.

fine.[25] Some women who lacked fields of their own simply cleared and planted fallow fields belonging to others. This was a primary cause of feuds in the dryland forests of Nkuboko.[26]

CONFLICT RESOLUTION AND SOCIAL CONTROL

Conflict between households having no kinship or affinal ties posed special problems. Nunu society, with its emphasis on the autonomy of the homestead, had no centralized authorities to suppress local conflicts and to uphold the power of the landowners. Instead, it relied on a delicate balance between institutions designed to prevent conflict and those designed to resolve it.

There were a variety of mutually reinforcing institutions that provided a safety net for the poor and thus served to prevent inequality from turning into conflict. The shared ideology that underlay these institutions was that of the moral economy.[27] In simplest terms, it was the proposition that everyone had the right to survive. As Bampomba said, "There are a lot of people who don't have any land. They have to eat, too."[28] Nunu society therefore had rules and institutions that mitigated the circumstances of the landless. All waters were open for fishing with traps, but this form of fishing depended upon the luck of the individual and gave yields that were paltry in comparison with the annual fish harvests of a dam or a pond. For landowners, trap fishing was a way of keeping the family in food while waiting for the large harvest. For the landless, it was the sole independent source of fish.

Whenever possible, landowners allowed clients to work on their dams or ponds. Although maintaining clients was sometimes costly, it gave the patron prestige, and it reduced the potential for conflict. If the client developed a long record of de-

---

[25] Interview: Ekando, 7-25-81, Tape 14/1.

[26] Interview: Lopanda, 7-10-81, Tape 2/1.

[27] The term "moral economy" is borrowed from James Scott, *The Moral Economy of the Peasant* (New Haven, 1976).

[28] Interview: Bampomba, 7-18-81, Tape 7/1.

voted service to his patron, he could expect a generous share of the harvest and might feed his family well. Yet clientship carried with it two costs. First, it was difficult for the man to accumulate *nsi* shells for bridewealth or other social transactions. Second, the very fact of being a client made his social status lower than that of a patron. His position violated the prime objective of the competition, which was to establish himself as an independent producer who built up a large following and attracted clients.

Institutions that allowed the poor to survive were not in themselves adequate to diffuse conflict, and so the estate owners invested a portion of their profits in creating and maintaining alliances in case their holdings were challenged. The most common way to create an alliance was through marriage. Since a rich man generally had several wives and a number of marriageable children, he also had the strongest network of marriage alliances.

To supplement lineage and clan ties, kinship-like obligations could be created through the institution of blood brotherhood. Two men made a blood-brother pact at a public ceremony in which each man made an incision in his arm just below the elbow. Then the two men rubbed their punctured arms together, allowing the blood to mingle. The men then took oaths promising to uphold the other in times of sickness, war, or material need.[29] After the ceremony the two were as members of one family. The relationship was maintained through the regular exchange of gifts. People with such relationships would often go on visits for the purpose of exchanging gifts and renewing the relationship. The gifts were often expensive, consisting of wine or cloth.[30]

Attendance at special ceremonies was important for keeping one's network of alliances intact. A funeral, for example, attracted nearly everybody from the nearby vicinity, and if the person was important, kinfolk and friends came from long dis-

---

[29] Such a ceremony was witnessed by E.J. Glave in 1883. E.J. Glave, *Six Years of Adventure in Congo-Land* (London, 1893), p. 47.

[30] Interview: Lopanda, 7-10-81, Tape 1/2.

tances. Important funeral visitors, such as sons-in-law, daughters-in law, blood brothers, and special friends, all brought a special funeral gift called *mokundu*. A less formal occasion was the drinking party thrown by a wealthy man. Blood brothers and other friends and allies were guests at these parties.[31]

When conflict broke out, it was resolved by force. Winning depended on magical power, on the courage of the soldiers, and on the ability of the alliances to mobilize troops. If one side clearly defeated the other, the conflict was resolved for the time being, although the losing side would hope to revive the conflict when the balance of power shifted. Mumbanza mwa Bawele's description of the river society as a "society of the strong" applies to the southern swamps as well.[32]

If the sides fought to a stalemate, they began to look for a way to end the conflict. Often there were people who had stayed out of the feud because they had relatives on both sides. Such people were called "children of war" because they had the task of convincing the parties to end the fighting. After the fighting stopped, the leaders of each side contacted the guardian of the land in order to begin the mediating process. Because the guardianship was more a ritual position than a political one, the guardian did not mediate disputes himself. That was the job of the *motende,* the judge, who was chosen for his wisdom and eloquence in speaking. The judge carried the *monsasa,* the broom that spoke to him in the voice of the ancestors. It was said that even if the judge did not himself know the laws and precedents of the ancestors, the broom would give him that knowledge. Sometimes the courts were able to resolve disputes before they led to warfare. Often, however, the disputes were judged only after the war had reached a stalemate. Since neither the guardian nor the judge possessed powers of coercion, they could not solve a case unless both sides were willing to submit to the judgment of the court. If the losing party refused to comply with the judgment, the feud could begin anew.

---

[31] Interview: Bampomba, 7-22-81, Tape 11/2.

[32] Mumbanza mwa Bawele, "Histoire des Peuples Riverains de l'entre Zaire-Ubangi" (Diss., Zaire National University, 1980), p. 87.

CONCLUSION

The rules of conflict resolution favored the strong, both on the battlefield and in the courts. As Lila observed:

> Enemies would attack and steal your fields and your fish dams. If you took them to court, they would invent stories about their ancestors being the first settlers in order to steal your land.[33]

In a society characterized by increasing conflict, water lords concentrated on strategies to maintain their strength. By helping kinsmen in need, being generous to loyal clients, marrying women from strategically chosen lineages, making blood brothers, helping allies in battle, throwing palm wine parties, and attending the right funerals, a man could keep up his alliances and repulse challenges to his estate. However, such activities were expensive, and they used up a large share of his expendable resources. This was not a maximal strategy characteristic of the early frontier. It was more like what game theorists call a minimax solution: the least of the favorable strategies.

What kept land and power from being concentrated in fewer and fewer hands was that the strong counterbalanced each other. Each water lord preserved his estate and his autonomy by being ready to fight against rivals and usurpers. Water lords who felt threatened by a powerful rival were likely to band together against him. Thus, the precarious equilibrium among the numerous independent estates was preserved. The society remained decentralized and the institutions of conflict resolution remained weak because the combined actions of the water lords kept things that way.

---

[33] Interview: Lila, 7-10-81, Tape 2/2.

8. The region

CONFLICT AT ONE level enhances solidarity at another. A feud between two families, for example, creates solidarity within each family; a conflict between two villages unifies each of them. This principle was in evidence in the nineteenth century, when the swamps experienced simultaneous conflict on a variety of levels. In addition to the small-scale feuds discussed in the previous chapter, there were wars that pitted neighborhood against neighborhood and environmental zone against environmental zone. These conflicts reflected in part the problems of maintaining order and balance in a society with no centralized institutions. They also reflected the dominant ideology of strength and independence that had motivated earlier generations of settlers to turn swampland into estates. But at a more fundamental level they represented an effort to cope with the effects of overcrowding and lack of new fishing grounds.

NEIGHBORHOOD WARS

Unlike the local feuds, which had identifiable causes and solutions, the larger-scale wars developed an institutionalized, almost ritualized character. The wars that pitted neighborhood against neighborhood became annual events. They were not fought to seize dams, ponds, or fields. They were tests of strength in which the participants fought, killed, and then returned home.

The wars helped create and reinforce neighborhood solidarity. One way in which they accomplished this was to put a disparate group of warriors under the protection of a single charm. Before the warriors gathered for battle, the guardians and charm makers prepared a special charm. In one neighborhood, for example, a charm maker named Manzau devised a charm which he called *Mosunga mo Mpanga Mpanga*, the symbol of the crow. Before a war, the elders gathered at the place where the charm was kept. They drank palm wine, recited certain powerful formulae, and then prepared a specific charm for the upcoming battle. It was believed that the crow symbolized by the charm would then perform a miracle and make the warriors invisible. A more typical practice was to place the new charm near the path the warriors were following to battle. As they passed by the charm, it gave them strength.[1]

By focusing attention on the enemy without instead of on the tensions within, the wars and their accompanying rituals created a common cause that transcended local feuds and disputes. People who were in conflict with each other throughout the year gathered under a single leader and fought side by side during the dry season. Throughout the rest of the year, neighborhood solidarity was reinforced by tales of past battles and boasts of battles to come. The wars were a kind of theater in which neighborhood identity was reinforced with bloody seriousness.

One series of annual wars pitted the people of Mitima, in the core area of the flooded forest, against Minsange, on the eastern fringe. Because most Minsange people could trace their ancestry to Mitima, these wars were literally family quarrels. According to Lila:

> The purpose of the wars was to show who was strong and who was weak. One time, too many [Mitima] people were killed, and so the chief of Mitima ordered that women should bear only male children. For six years women bore only males. These children were born with wounds and scars.[2]

There are many stories of miraculous happenings during these wars. One of them holds that the people of Mitima brought out red soldier ants that bit the legs of the Minsange warriors and sent them fleeing. Another tells how the Mitima people caused water to come and flood the battleground during the dry season.

---

[1] Interview: Lila, 7-12-81, Tape 2/2.
[2] Interview: Lila, 7-14-81, Tape 4/2.

There was a separate tradition of annual wars in the farm-lands of Nkuboko. They were fought between two rival groups of settlers. Oral tradition holds that the lands of Nkuboko were settled by people who came from Mitima via two different routes. One group, led by the Longoko, founded Minsange, and from there people moved inland to settle the southern half of the Nkuboko region. Another group of migrants, led by Eya, settled the northern portion of Nkuboko. The wars were fought between the southern and northern settlements. The story of their origin is as follows:

> The wars began because we sought self-glorification. We wanted to show that we were strong. So the two ancestors made an agreement. Eya [leader of the northern group] and the leader of the southern group agreed that in a certain month, on a certain day, they would gather to fight. So we prepared war charms, and they prepared war charms. Then we fought.[3]

Warfare became an annual event in Nkuboko. In August, after the fishermen had returned from their fishing camps, they began to prepare for war. The warriors went to the war leader and asked when the war would take place. He told them that it would take place on a certain day. When the day approached, he trumpeted the buffalo horn to call people. They gathered at his village and made a plan.[4] The battle plans were relatively simple, indicating mostly the route to travel and the leaders of the attack. The wars in Nkuboko were always fought on the plain of Mongala. The attacks were frontal assaults with spear and shield designed as much to test the bravery of the warriors as to gain a victory.

A second category of wars involved neighborhoods in different ecological zones. Ever since the original settlement, the populations had been developing distinct eco-cultural identities. If language is the fundamental feature of culture, then the differences of dialect among the people of the river, the flooded forest, the flooded grassland, and the dryland forest are a clear sign of eco-cultural differentiation. Although dialectal differ-

---

[3] Interview: Nyangu, 12-15-75, Tape A71.
[4] Interview: Lopanda, 7-10-81, Tape 2/1.

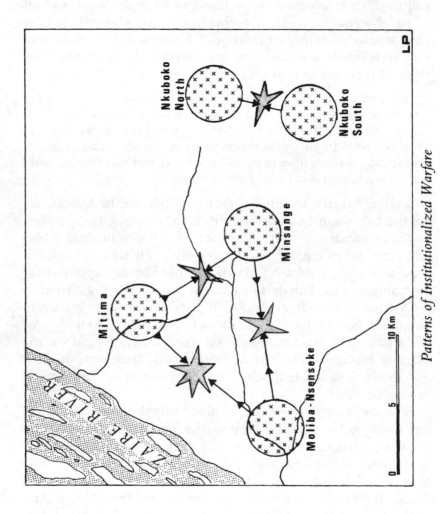

Patterns of Institutionalized Warfare

ences among Nunu subgroups are less a matter of vocabulary than of accent and colloquial expression, most modern Nunu can nevertheless identify a person's zone of origin by listening to him or her speak.[5] A second sign that cultural distinctions correlated with environmental zones became apparent during fieldwork, when informants usually identified their ancestral home in terms of an environmental zone instead of a precise location. To identify their environmental zone was to reveal a great deal about their cultural background.

Each eco-cultural group engaged in a distinct form of economic and social competition. Because they operated in different micro-environments, they used different tactics for exploiting natural resources and they employed different strategies in social competition. In the forest, where up to a hundred people would work on emptying a pond, labor was group-oriented. The owner would maintain ties with large numbers of people in order to ensure that he would have the available labor when harvesttime came. Similarly, landless people would maintain ties with several dam owners in order to work as many dams as possible. The pond system created an enormously complex network of reciprocal work relationships that bound the members of a neighborhood together.

The grasslands were fished mainly through the use of dams that could be worked by a few people. Moreover, a dam was worked regularly throughout the season of the falling water, and regular and steady ties between patron and client were created. Therefore, in the grasslands there were fewer but stronger strands in the web that bound the members of a community together. In a similar way, the farmlands of Nkuboko had small scale dams and ponds in the forests and bogs. A bog pond was usually small enough to be worked by the owner's immediate or extended family, and therefore the large networks typical of the flooded forest never developed.

---

5 Mayaka Ma-Libuka recognizes three modern dialects: the river, Nkuboko, and Nsangasi. Mayaka Ma-Libuka, "Phonologie et Morphologie du Bobangi" (Mémoire de Licence: Institut Superior Pédagogique, Kikwit, 1977), p. 1.

The gender division of labor also differed among ecological zones. In swamp and riverine areas, it was the men who were the providers of meat for the family, while women grew the cassava that provided the starch. The comparative economic value placed on the two could be seen in the marketplaces, where a single fish could be bartered for a much greater quantity of cassava. Because the women in the swamps could not grow enough cassava to feed the family for an entire year, the men helped to make up the shortfall by trading fish in the market for cassava, an action that underlined the economic power of men. No matter what the women produced, the effect was ultimately to provide cassava for the household.

When the Nunu settled the dryland forests of Nkuboko, however, the men fished as before, but their catches were usually inadequate to feed the family beyond the fishing season. The shortfall was made up by the women, who traded their cassava for fish at the market. Women had thus become the providers of meat. This development did not in itself cause a social revolution; women's markets were carried on by barter, and thus women remained providers of food, whereas men sought to build up wealth. Nevertheless, the psychological effect of this change on perceptions of gender roles must have been profound. It may be one of the reasons why the men of Nkuboko today place such emphasis on their warrior tradition.

The earliest remembered wars involving different ecological zones were fought between the people living in the area of Mitima, in the heart of the flooded forest, and the people settled in the floating meadows along the Moliba and the Nsenseke. The beginning of these wars is associated in oral tradition with Nsakansenge, an elder in the Moliba area who lived in the late eighteenth or early nineteenth century.[6] Ekando explained the origins of the wars in terms of a dispute over resources:

> The people of Moliba would complain, "Our fish are being picked up by Mitima people who come to fish with spears during the dry

---

[6] The guardian of the Moliba area when the whites arrived was Manzanga, who was the fourth guardian after Esakansenge. If each guardian served for twenty years, then Esakansenge served at the beginning of the nineteenth century. Interview: Ekando, field notes.

season. The fish are ours." The Mitima people would reply, "You people come into our forest to get raffia fronds to make fish fences and fish traps." So the wars began and people died in droves.[7]

The wars became an annual occurrence. In the month of August when the fishing was over and the water had receded, the people of the flooded forest and the people of the flooded grasslands would gather to prepare for war. The war was always fought at the same site. As Ekando described the battles, "They came with spears to fight. They killed each other, they killed each other." These wars continued into the late nineteenth century.[8] The institutionalized nature of these wars was emphasized by Longwa:

> I don't know why Mitima fought with Moliba. It was the law of the ancestors. During the dry season they would go out and fight. Every dry season they fought. They fought in the month of August. People would die.[9]

The people along the Moliba also carried on dry season wars with the people of Minsange, the crowded and quarrelsome village on the eastern edge of the swamps. Here is how Ekando described the beginning of the wars:

> The people of Minsange were people of the forest. They didn't like the people of the Moliba [a grassland area]. When the Moliba people killed a hippopotamus, the people of Minsange came to take some of it. The Moliba people said, "You are stealing our hippopotamus." So they fought a war. Fight! Fight! Fight! Sixty people from Minsange went out to fight. There were only women left in the village. All sixty men of Minsange died. There was an elder at Minsange named Boyebu who said, "If the people of Moliba come to attack, there is no one here to defend us." So the women quickly gave birth to sixty males, no females. I heard this story from an elder who lived at Minsange. His name was Bobeyu. He was my grandfather.[10]

---

[7] Interview: Ekando, 7-23-81, Tape 12/1.

[8] Interview: Ekando, 7-23-81, Tape 12/1. Ekando's grandfather, Manzanga, had many wounds from these wars. Ekando was born in 1908.

[9] Interview: Longwa, 7-20-81, Tape 9/1.

[10] Interview: Ekando, 7-23-81, Tape 12/1.

After this, the wars became an annual event. When the dry season came and the ground was dry enough to walk on, the people of Minsange gathered for a war with the people of the Moliba. Traveling by land, they walked a full day before camping near the site of the battle. When they arrived, they sang a song:

> The strangers have arrived,
> But they didn't come
> By the stream of Moliba.[11]

They camped for one night and fought the next morning. The battle was often over in a single day. Then they went home.

WAR AS RITUALIZED COMPETITION

One way to approach an understanding of the annual wars is to see them as a form of ritualized competition that condensed and amplified many of the elements of the water lord competition. Although the oral traditions stress the competition between opposing sides, a detailed reconstruction of the ritualized unfolding of the battles suggests that competition between individuals on the same side was perhaps more significant. An annual war unfolded in three stages: preparation, battle, and celebration. At each stage individuals competed to show magical power, knowledge, physical prowess, and courage, the very qualities possessed by successful water lords and guardians.

The first stage was ritual preparation for war. Lopanda described the beginning of the preparation as follows:

> In the eighth month people would go to Monkunungu, the war leader in this area and ask, "When and where is the war?" And he answered, "We will go to battle on such and such a day." When the day approached he blew the antelope horn, "Dee, dee, dee, dee." Everybody came. They said, "Papa, what is the plan? Where shall we go?" He would reply, "The plan is thus."[12]

The days before the battle were filled with dancing and sing-

---

[11] Interview: Lila, 7-11-81, Tape 2/2.
[12] Interview: Lopanda, 7-10-81, Tape 1.

ing to build up the courage of the warriors.[13] They also provided a forum in which individuals competed to display knowledge and magical power. The evening before the battle the warriors began their final preparations by dancing the *mbioki etumba,* a dance to rejoice in the prospect of an upcoming battle. Then they progressed into the *moseto,* a powerful dance in which warriors recounted their previous exploits and commemorated the deeds of their ancestors. Modern Nunu recount that during the *moseto* the warriors began to invoke their fathers, crying "Sango, Sango." Some would begin to recite names of ancestors, names they had not known until the spirit of the dance had possessed them. They would cry, "Kikikiki, kikikiki." They would then start to perform miracles. One warrior would run all the way up to the top of a palm tree; another would swallow hot coals. All the while others were calling, "Sango, Sango; kikikiki, kikikiki." The drums beat louder and faster. The dancing became more frenzied. Courage built up. As the night wore on, the dancers became exhausted by their own exuberance. They fell to the ground and slept. As morning neared, nothing but the polyrhythmic beat of the drums broke the silence of the night.

The next morning the warriors prepared for war. The *mpeti ekobeta bitumba,* the planner of wars, had done his work. Now it was time for the leadership to be taken over by the *ndut'e bamani,* the leader of the warriors, and the *molele o nyembe,* the singer of songs, who kept up the courage of the men. Each warrior dressed himself in battle garb. He wore a feathered headdress, a wide leather belt, and a loincloth of animal pelt. He carried a long, narrow shield, a spear, and a knife. The singer of songs carried with him the *monsasa,* the broom which encapsulated the names and deeds of the ancestors. Holding the broom, it was said, would give him knowledge to sing of the ancestors and their deeds.

---

[13] The account of war songs and rituals comes mostly from Lila, 7-11-81, Tape 2/2; 7-12-81, Tape 3/2; and 7-14-81, Tape 4/2. Lila's praise name was "Ndut'e Bamani," the leader of the warriors, after his grandfather who held that title.

As they proceeded at a half trot toward the battleground, they sang well-known battle songs. One of them emphasized the individual competition among the members of the war party:

Where is the war?
From which direction is it coming?
Who among you will cry with fear?
Who among you will be praised?

Before leaving for battle, the war leader had sent a message to the opponents and told them the time and place of the battle. These were not raids or surprise attacks, but tests of strength fought according to rules. On the path to war, the warriors sang and made noise. Surprise attacks were considered cowardly. When they reached the battlefield, the two sides lined up. Behind each side was the drummer beating courage on the *eyinzako,* the war drum, and the singer of songs holding the broom and singing of the courage of the ancestors. The drummer and the singer were never killed in the battle. They gave courage to everybody and were not fair game for attack.

The battle usually lasted until sunset. By then the losers had retreated, and the winners picked up the spears, shields, and knives of the enemy warriors whom they had killed. They smeared the blood of the dead enemies over their bodies. Although they did not normally take the heads of dead enemies as trophies, they would take the head of the enemy leader if he had been killed in the battle. This act would provoke a return battle, for the losing side would feel obligated to recover the head. Sometimes the day finished with no clear victor. Then the leaders of the two sides would decide if the battle should continue the next day, or if it should be terminated.

After the war both sides returned home, and again they danced. Warriors who had distinguished themselves in battle were heroes, and their feats were acted out in the dances. The results of the individual competition were thus revealed in a public ceremony. Everybody learned who had been strong and who had been weak, who had been brave and who had been cowardly.

Some hints as to the purpose of this competition can be gleaned from an examination of who the participants were. In the first place, they were probably relatively young men who did not own dams and ponds. Because a man could not inherit fishing grounds until the current owner, and perhaps his brothers as well, had died, people seldom became water lords until they were too old to fight. The second feature of the warrior group was that it included sons of both rich and poor families. Manzanga, for example, survived a series of war wounds as a young man and went on to become a wealthy water lord with several dams and several wives.[14] On the other hand, Monku-nungu, a well-known nineteenth century war leader, is remembered as a poor man.[15]

Young men from wealthy families used the competition to prove their worthiness to inherit the family estate. Although in theory estates were passed down along matrilineal lines, the chaotic pattern revealed by the estate histories presented earlier suggests fierce competition for inheritance. On a given estate there would be a number of young men wishing to prove themselves the most worthy of taking over. Because the qualities of magical power, esoteric knowledge, physical strength, and courage were precisely the qualities needed to maintain an estate and defend it from enemies, the annual wars became proving grounds for would-be heirs. A hint of this goal is found in a war song.

> Retreat! Advance!
> To whom will I leave the heritage
> left to me by my ancestors?
> To strangers? To enemies?
> I must fight to protect my birthright.

For young men from landless families, the wars provided a means by which they could gain prestige that would partially compensate for their lack of wealth and status. Nunu oral traditions emphasize the heroism and glory of warfare, and the strategic implications of this ideology were not lost on the poor. They not only participated in these wars, but also provided leaders and heroes. Men such as Monkunungu, who

---

[14] Interview: Ekando, 7-23-81, Tape 12/1.
[15] Interview: Nsamonie, 7-14-81, Tape 5/1.

could never hope to gain prestige in Nunu society through the accumulation of estates, clients, and wives, could become war heroes whose names would be invoked by future generations.

The final aspect of institutionalized warfare to be discussed here is the killing itself. Those were not mere mock battles, but serious warfare in which people died. It is difficult to reconstruct just how many people were killed in these wars. Oral traditions recounting the wars between Mitima and Minsange mention losses of up to 160 men on a single side, and the tradition cited earlier about the wars between Mitima and Moliba mentions 60 men killed on one side. The magical stories about all the men in a village being killed reinforce the general image of the wars as mechanisms for killing off men. Yasi supported this notion by saying that the only thing he knew about Monkunungu, a famous war leader in the Nkuboko area, was that he was responsible for a lot of deaths.[16] However, a very different figure was given by Longwa, who recounted that a typical battle between Moliba and Mitima would continue until about two people had been killed on each side.[17] For purposes of this analysis, it seems prudent to take a low figure and estimate that fewer than a dozen people were killed in a given battle.

One effect of the deaths was to underline the seriousness of the competition. True courage and strength were required in battle, and those who lacked such qualities were at greater risk. The possibility of death was emphasized in the war rituals. The night before the battle, the heroic deaths of past warriors were recounted. On the way to the battlefield, the warriors sang:

We fight as leopards.
We die in the bodies of men.

A second effect of the killing was to reduce the number of competitors for the available estates. Lila emphasized this theme:

---

[16] Interviews: Losengo, 12-10-75, Tape A66; Lila, 7-14-81, Tape 4/2; Ekando, 7-23-81, Tape 12/1; Yasi, 7-13-81, Tape 3/2.
[17] Interview: Longwa, 7-20-81, Tape 9/1.

> In the past people didn't die as much as they do now. The people
> noticed that they had become too numerous. It was necessary for
> some to go and die in wars.[18]

There was not, in ecological terms, an absolute surplus of people who strained the carrying capacity of the land, but there was
nevertheless a growing number of landless men because water
lords controlled estates much larger than were needed to feed
themselves and their families. As a result, competition over inheritance of estates among the nephews and sons of water lords
grew increasingly strident. Young men from landless families
also coveted the wealth of estates. They sometimes stole fish
from dams and ponds or tried to seize fishing grounds. Young
men who lacked money for bridewealth sometimes kidnapped
women whom they would claim as brides. The socially volatile
"surplus" population, therefore, consisted of young males.
Every time a young man was killed in a war, social tension was
reduced.

Even a modest number of deaths per year would have had an
impact on male competition for land because the total population of the swamp in the nineteenth century was relatively low.
A 1909 census that included the entire Moliba area plus the village of Minsange, an area of over 200 square kilometers, revealed 83 adult males. This figure is not representative of the
nineteenth century as a whole because the census came in the
wake of smallpox and sleeping sickness epidemics. Yet even if
the nineteenth-century population was three times as large,
there would have been only 249 adult males in the area.[19] Under
such circumstances, even a relatively small number of deaths
per year would have reduced competition for dams and fishing
rights.

The major compensation for death was glory and fame.
Nunu ideology had elevated death in war to the most noble
way to die. A war song expressed the proposition succinctly:

---

[18] Interview: Lila, 7-11-81, Tape 2/2.
[19] See the 1909 statistical tables for the chiefdoms of Mokongo, Bongamba,
and Moliba-Mitsange, DCMS.

"If I die, let me die as a man in battle." Lila gave a more elaborate explanation:

> If somebody died of disease, it was thought of as a bad thing [because disease was attributed to witchcraft]. People didn't like that at all. They said, "He died of disease? It is better that he had died of a war wound." If somebody died of disease, it was a cause for sorrow. He died for nothing. If he died in war, they rejoiced.[20]

This point of view was reinforced by the rituals of war. The night before leaving for battle the warriors danced the *moseto,* the *nkaki,* and the *mbioki,* in which the heroic deeds of their deceased predecessors were recalled. After the wars, people gathered to dance the *mbioki* (which literally means "rejoicing") to celebrate the deaths of soldiers who died in battle. They danced *limbongo* to praise those who had died in the war. And they danced the *moseto,* flashing their ornately fashioned ceremonial knives and imitating the actions of the deceased in battle. The singer sang of the deeds of the distant ancestors, of the recent ancestors, and finally he added the deeds of the warriors who had recently been killed. A missionary who observed the *moseto* in 1890 described it vividly: "The man in the feather headdress is about to commence dancing and to show how the deceased used to fight in times of war and tell how brave he was. . . . Women also entered the ring and danced and sang of his beauty and strength, and extolled his bravery."[21] All of this must have been heady stuff to the young warriors who observed the ceremonies. Along the trail to the battleground, the lure of glory and immortality must have partially compensated for the fear of death.

UNITY IN DIVERSITY

Despite the antagonism created and reinforced by institutionalized warfare, the dry-season wars did not create a permanent state of war among the neighborhoods and the ecological zones.

---

[20] Interview: Lila, 7-11-81, Tape 2/2.
[21] George Grenfell, "A Funeral Dance at Bolobo, Upper Congo River," *Missionary Herald,* December 1, 1890, p. 450.

People traveled, fished, and traded throughout the rest of the year. The reason that the wars remained limited in both duration and scope was that the different neighborhoods and the zones were intimately bound together by a variety of formal and informal ties. They gave the region a larger unity that could withstand the shocks of annual warfare.

One set of ties was created by marriages between neighborhoods and across environmental zones. People in frontier communities often went back to the core areas to find wives for their sons. Children of trading partners would sometimes marry. During the dry-season wars, people with kinfolk on both sides stayed out of the fighting. The Nunu name for such people, "children of war," points to the role they played in keeping hostilities under control. One oral tradition holds that the annual wars between Moliba and Mitima eventually stopped because a person whose mother came from Moliba and whose father came from Mitima placed himself between the two sides and stopped the fighting.[22]

Another unifying institution was the matrilineage. Because women generally left their homesteads upon marriage to live with their husbands, the members of a matrilineage were widely scattered. Lineage ties therefore formed fine webs throughout the swamps and onto the dry land. The lineage was more than an enlarged version of the household. Indeed, a father who was the head of his household was not a member of the matrilineage of his children, who belonged to their mother's lineage. If he had several wives, his children were divided among several matrilineages. In all cases, they looked to their maternal uncles as male authority figures in lineage affairs.

In practice the matrilineage structured power relationships between two generations of living adults, usually uncles and their nephews and nieces. In theory, however, genealogical reckoning structured a longer list of relationships going back to the founder of the lineage up to six generations before. A lineage segmented frequently as nieces married and nephews moved away to settle on the frontier. Young men who left their

---

[22] Interview: Bampomba, 7-22-81, Tape 11/2.

paternal homestead retained rights in both the homestead and the matrilineage in that they could always be fed and cared for if they returned home. But few of them kept up their claims to rights in ancestral fishing grounds. People of Nkuboko recognized, for example, that they had rights in ponds in the Mitima area, but few of them ever went to help empty them.[23] The result was that rights retained in theory lapsed in practice.

After several generations of living away from the ancestral neighborhood, links to the distant ancestor were still remembered, but ties to the other living descendants of those ancestors were not kept up. Conversely, breakaway segments were usually dropped from the genealogies in the core areas. During fieldwork, informants usually remembered the founder of their matrilineage and other headmen in a single genealogical line down to the current head. They were usually unable to remember the kinsmen in other branches of the lineage. Sometimes they knew that certain people were vaguely related to them, but they were not certain as to how. Thus two people in different parts of the swamp might know very different genealogies that began with the same ancestor.

The largest unit of kin organization was the *likinda*, or clan. The word "*likinda*" has the same root as the word "*nkinda*," which is the charm that was buried when a place was first settled. Therefore the name of one's clan was the same as the name of the place where the *nkinda* charm was buried. A clan was thus composed of all people descended from ancestors who had settled a single area and had shared a protective charm. As these ancestors were not necessarily kinsmen, the clan was not, strictly speaking, a unit of kinship. It was grounded in a place and a shrine, not in blood relationships. As time passed and people migrated or moved because of marriages, members of a single clan became scattered all over the swamps and beyond. Although clans had no formal organization, people who moved to a new area took pains to discover who their fellow clansfolk were and formed friendships or working teams based on clan ties.[24]

---

[23] Interviews: Longwa, 7-21-81, Tape 11/1; Ekando, 7-23-81, Tape 12/2.
[24] Interviews: Bampomba, 7-24-81, Tape 13/2; Longwa, 7-21-81, Tape 11/1.

Old ties to distant kin and friends were renewed from time to time during ceremonial occasions that attracted people from a variety of neighborhoods. Weddings were the most common example of this phenomenon. Longwa, for example, remembers traveling as a young boy with his parents from their home in Mitima to Nkuboko when a distant relative got married.[25] Funerals also brought friends and kinsmen from far and near. In the absence of such occasions, family members often visited one another simply to keep up family ties.

Other opportunities for renewing kin and friendship ties across regional lines resulted from trade. Because of the complementary nature of the economic activities in flooded forests, flooded grasslands, and the farmlands of Nkuboko, the territory as a whole formed an economic region with a lively internal trade. The major impetus for trade was the complementarity in the production of foodstuffs. The flooded forests of Mitima and Nsangasi and the flooded grasslands of Moliba and Nsenseke produced an abundance of fish but a shortfall of cassava. In the drylands of Nkuboko, the opposite situation prevailed. The major flow of trade went east and west between Nkuboko and the swamps. At the eastern end of this network, markets were situated at the places where aquatic trails through the flooded forest led to landing spots near Nkuboko settlements. There was a market near Matende, one near Mongala, one near Pokolo, and so forth. During the dry season when these markets could not be reached by water, the main eastern market was held at Minsange. The main market at the western end of the swamps was at Nkubosaka. Other markets were more centrally located, such as the market at Moliba, located at the point where flooded prairie gave way to the burnt-out flooded forest.

As was customary throughout the southern forest region, the Nunu employed a four-day market week, with different markets meeting on different days so that the markets complemented one another instead of competing. Each market had a *momene liboko,* or owner of the market, whose job was to keep peace and punish those who broke the rules by carrying arms into the marketplace or fighting. As a payment for these ser-

---

[25] Interview: Longwa, 7-21-81, Tape 11/1.

vices, each seller gave him a small percentage of the goods he or she brought to the marketplace. The most important markets, such as the one at Minsange and the one at Nkubosaka, were held on the day of *Mpika,* which was the day of calm and tranquility (the equivalent of the Jewish Sabbath or the Christian Sunday). Fighting, quarreling, and loud talking were not allowed on *Mpika,* and thus these markets became places of peace on days of peace. They were places where normally hostile groups could meet to carry out the exchanges that were vital to the survival of all of them.[26]

The trade in staple items was complemented by trade in a wide variety of foodstuffs and craft items. From Nkuboko came peanuts, corn, red peppers, and sugar cane. Palm oil was the specialty of the Mitima area. The palm fruit was cut by men, but both men and women worked to extract the oil. As men got older, they gradually retired from extracting palm oil and concentrated on making palm wine, whereas the older women continued to make palm oil. Salt was made wherever there was *bikoko* grass, most notably along the Nsangasi, near the Zaire River, and in the flooded grasslands. Nkubosaka was an important center of salt making, as were the villages along the Moliba. While the men fished with the fish fences, the women gathered the *bikoko* grass from behind the fences. This salt would go to Nkuboko and to all of the areas of flooded forest.

Pottery was made from the black clay sediments that underlay the swampland. The early centers of pottery making were two villages located in transitional areas between the Zaire and the swamps: Nkubosaka, located along the stream that went to Mitima, and Yumbi, located near the entrance to the Moliba. The origin of the craft came from upriver, as attested by the name of a major pottery style, *mpoto li Bobangi,* the pots of Bobangi. As women who specialized in pottery moved inland with their husbands, the craft spread up the Moliba and along the routes to Mitima, but Nkubosaka and Yumbi remained the centers of pottery production into the twentieth century. The

---

[26] Interviews: Lopanda, 7-10-81, Tape 1/2; Longwa, 7-20-81, Tape 8/1.

pots were traded to Nkuboko and down the Zaire River, where the sandy bluffs did not provide suitable clay for pot making.[27]

The forest regions supplied other products as well. The raffia palms of the flooded forests of Mitima supplied the material for raffia cloth, which men weaved on looms. Mitima was also a center of canoe making. Although canoes were made on a small scale throughout the flooded forest, the canoes of Mitima were renowned, and production was more concentrated than at other places. In the dryland forests of Nkuboko, men found materials for bark cloth, sleeping mats, and baskets. From the trees they carved canoes and kneading boards for cassava. There was thus a certain degree of complementarity between the dryland forests and the flooded forests.

Institutionalized warfare did not seriously undermine this interdependence. Instead it bound the environmental zones together in a deadly ritual. The oral traditions quoted earlier recounting the origins of certain institutionalized wars do not place blame on one side or the other. Instead, they emphasize that the wars were fought by mutual consent. The common quest and the common rituals created a solidarity of their own that fed into a larger Nunu identity. The songs and dances of war were known throughout the swamplands, the drylands of Nkuboko, and the riverbanks of the Zaire.[28] Out of the six dance forms that informants throughout the Nunu area commonly remembered, four were dances of war. Ceremonial life and public ritual were dominated by the rituals of war. The people of the swamps had turned the conflicts that divided them into a warrior cult that provided a common idiom of ritual and artistic expression.

There was one form of warfare that contributed to solidarity among the Nunu as a whole, and that was war against outside groups. These wars were generally small-scale affairs fought on the borderlands of Nunu settlement areas. Like feuds among the Nunu themselves, they were usually the result of disputes or

---

[27] Interviews: Lobwaka, 8-5-81, Tape 17/1; Etebe, 8-3-81, Tape 15/2; Longwa, 7-20-81, Tape 8/1; Ekando, 7-23-81, Tape 12/2; Lopanza, 7-22-81, Tape 9/2.
[28] Interview: Longwa, 7-20-81, Tape 9/1.

the kidnapping of women, and thus were small and short–lived affairs.[29] There are no remembered wars that pitted the Nunu as a group against other people as a group. There was, however, a series of wars fought in the nineteenth century that pitted Nunu in all parts of the swamps against Lusakani raiders. These wars have become part of a larger Nunu mythology that transcended any given locality.

Lusakani oral traditions hold that their ancestors had migrated southward to their present home, which is situated along the channel between Irebu and Lake Tumba, in the aftermath of bloody defeat in a war with the Tomba. They gained permission to settle along the channel by giving up many women to the owners of the land. Because their population had been greatly reduced by these events, they decided to raid the Mpama, who lived just to the south of them, for women and slaves. So successful was the raid that they launched a series of dry-season raids to the south and east. Some of these raids took them into the territory of the Nunu.[30]

The story of the Lusakani raid along the Moliba provides an excellent example of how the Nunu united in the face of this challenge. To repel the raiders, two elders named Enzie and Maboka united the Nunu of Nsenseke, Bonsoso, Mpokengia, and Nganga. The Nunu triumphed and chased the raiders east toward the Nkuboko villages of Bopyanga, Pokolo, and Mongala. The people of Nkuboko then drove them out of Nunu territory.[31] This single war had thus made allies of Nunu villages which had traditionally fought one another. Another war against the Lusakani invaders involved the people of Moliba, Mitima, Minsange, Bwanza, Mbonga, and Likole, thus uniting

---

[29] Interview: Bampomba, 7-22-81, Tape 9/1.

[30] "Chefferie des Lusakani," 1925, MRAC-E, Prov. Equateur, Dist. Equateur, Terr. Bikoro, 7. Mpela, the chief who led the raids, died shortly after the last raid. His successor, Ibanza, died shortly before the arrival of the Europeans in the 1880s. It therefore seems likely that the raids took place sometime between 1850 and 1870.

[31] Interview: Ekando, 7-25-81, Tape 14/1. Contrary to the Nunu traditions, which show the Nunu winning every encounter, Lusakani traditions hold that *they* won every battle. See "Chefferie des Lusakani."

people of three eco–cultural zones that were traditional enemies.[32]

Nunu oral traditions hold that they won every encounter.
They describe the victories in magical terms to demonstrate the
superior magical power of the Nunu. In one story, the Nunu
caused water to flood the plain in the dry season to drive out
the invaders.[33] The victory in another battle was explained in
the following manner:

> There was a charm maker named Mowibi who called upon all the
> Nunu to prepare a charm. He said, "When the [Lusakani] come,
> keep your eyes to the ground. Don't look at them." They took a
> slave and filled him with medicines. He drank a potion that
> contained the medicines. They left the main body of warriors at
> one spot, and the slave went ahead into the plain. The invaders
> met him and asked him if he was a Nunu. He didn't answer. They
> stabbed him with spears, which caused the medicine to spurt out
> and render them weak. Then the Nunu attacked and won. When
> the [Lusakani] tried to draw their bows, the strings broke.[34]

The battles, and perhaps more importantly, the stories of the
battles helped to create solidarity and a common identity among
the settlers of the flooded forests, flooded grasslands, and the
drylands of Nkuboko. Implicit in the above story is an image
of the Nunu as a single ethnic group.

CONCLUSION

By the middle of the nineteenth century, swamp society was
developing mechanisms to maintain a precarious equilibrium
between the rights of the water lords and the unrest of the landless. The continual warfare that was in part an expression of
this unrest was institutionalized so that it served more to struc-

---

[32] Interview: Longwa, 7-20-81, Tape 9/1.
[33] Interview: Lila, 7-14-81, Tape 4/2.
[34] Interview: Lila, 7-14-81, Tape 4/1. The Lusakani were originally a
subgroup of the Nkundu, hence the confusion of names. For other stories
about the wars, see the 1957 report by DeWeerd, reprinted in J.J.L. Lingwambe, "Histoire Banunu-Bobangi" (mimeographed pamphlet, Kinshasa,
1966), pp. 10–11.

ture competition and to relieve tensions than to foster change. Because warfare was carried out on several levels, large-scale war mitigated the effects of small-scale conflict. Warfare was an appropriate equilibrating mechanism because it fit in well with the strategies of both the water lords and the landless. Each group supported the annual wars for very different reasons. Despite incessant conflict, the fundamental division between water lord and client remained intact.

The warfare did not significantly alter the scale of political authority. On one hand, it did not promote further fragmentation of the swamplands. Although such fighting would probably have destroyed a centralized polity, the decentralized Nunu could tolerate the strife without becoming divided into a series of self-contained warring factions. On the other hand, it did not lead to political centralization. The ritualized form of warfare served more to maintain equilibrium among competing groups than to consolidate the authority of some water lords over others, and the water lords on all sides thus maintained their autonomy of action. The warfare did, however, create ties of solidarity and common identity that transcended the estate or the lineage. The pride with which modern Nunu elders talk of the victories of their ancestors testifies to this enlarged identity.

Just when swampland society was achieving a tenuous balance between conflict and solidarity, the rules of economic and social competition would undergo a change. The impetus behind those changes would come from neither Nunu society nor the swampland environment, but from the Americas and Europe, thousands of miles away.

9. The traders

B Y THE MIDDLE of the nineteenth century, the Nunu had occupied all of the micro-environments that they found hospitable. Each micro-environment had imposed its own rules and had thus forced settlers to alter their goals, strategies, and tactics in the competition to become big-men. Life in the swamps was dominated by two variants of water lord competition: the flooded forest variant, based on ponds, and the flooded grassland variant, based on dams. In the farmlands of Nkuboko, men had tried to create a form of the water lord competition based on control of small streams, but the yield was meager, and household economies depended largely on the agricultural production of women. The final variant was played out along the river. Based on luck and the modest yield of nets and traps, the river variant bore scant resemblance to the water lord competition in the swamps.

The process by which new forms of competition had emerged was, in theory, relatively simple: changes in the rules forced people to develop new tactics and strategies, thereby creating a new form of competition. What made the process complicated in practice was that a variety of factors could influence the rules. Environments, as has been pointed out, impose their own rules. But so do markets, which set the values of commodities; political authorities, who regulate behavior through formal laws; technologies, which determine the limits of production; and religious beliefs, which define the limits of acceptable behavior. A change in any one of these factors could alter the rules and ultimately produce a new variant of the big-man competition.

One factor that had great potential for altering the rules was the world economy, which first began to impinge upon the peoples of the middle Zaire in the sixteenth century. With the growth of sugar plantations in the New World came an increasing demand for African slaves, and Malebo Pool, located just 325 kilometers downriver from Bolobo, became a major interior slave market after 1529, sending some 4000–5000 slaves a year toward the coast for sale to the Portuguese. About one-seventh of those slaves were Tio, who came from the area just north of the Pool, but a few of them were known as "Nubians," who came from north of the Tio. Some "Nubians" may well have been from the general area of the Bolobo-Yumbi Strip.[1]

After 1560 the Pool declined as an inland slave market because warfare in the hinterland of the Kongo Kingdom made the trade routes unsafe and because the Portuguese relocated the hub of their trade at Luanda, some 400 kilometers south of the Zaire. It was during this period of quiescence that the river peoples of the middle Zaire first entered the written record. Portuguese documents from 1612 and 1620 mention a place called "Ibar" or "Ybare," where slaves were traded.[2] They were clearly referring to *ebale,* the term by which the Nunu and their upstream neighbors designated the Zaire River. Slaves from *ebale* probably arrived at the Pool through the intermediary of the Tio, who claimed overlordship of both the Pool and the Channel. Because the slave trade at the Pool was a mere trickle throughout most of the seventeenth and eighteenth centuries,[3] its effect on the people of the Bolobo-Yumbi Strip was minimal.

The middle Zaire became a major exporter of slaves for the first time in the second half of the eighteenth century. The initial impetus came from the Loango coast, north of the Zaire's

---

[1] Joseph C. Miller, "The Slave Trade in Kongo and Angola," in *The African Diaspora,* edited by Martin Kilson and Robert Rotberg (Cambridge, Mass., 1976), p. 82; Philip Curtin, *The Atlantic Slave Trade: A Census* (Madison, Wis., 1969), pp. 97–100; Filippo Pigafetta and Duarte Lopes, *Déscription du Royaume de Congo et des Contrées Environnantes,* trans. and ann. by Willy Bal (Paris, 1965), pp. 32–34.

[2] Antonia Brasio, ed., *Monumenta Missionaria Africana,* 11 vols. (Lisbon, 1953–71) 6:104, 438.

[3] For a summary of the evidence of minimal trade at the Pool, see Robert Harms, *River of Wealth, River of Sorrow: The Central Zaire Basin in the Era of the Slave and Ivory Trade, 1500–1891* (New Haven, 1981), pp. 25–27.

mouth, where the Dutch were buying increasing numbers of slaves. By the 1780s over 2000 slaves a year were sent to the coast from the middle Zaire area by Bobangi merchants, who dominated the river trade from the lower Ubangi down to the southern swamps. The Bobangi traders carried canoeloads of slaves down the Zaire and then up the Alima, where they sold them to other traders who organized caravans that followed the footpaths through Mayombe to the Loango coast.[4]

Malebo Pool began to reassert itself as a major slave market in the late eighteenth century as the ports of Ambriz and Boma, which drew slaves from the Pool area, attracted ships by undercutting the prices of the more established ports. By the early 1800s, their business was bustling. The Pool became even more important after international treaties outlawing the Atlantic slave trade in the early nineteenth century curtailed the trade at the coastal ports and gave rise to a lively smuggling traffic concentrated around the Zaire estuary. As the Atlantic slave trade was coming to an end near the mid-nineteenth century, the world market price of ivory doubled, then doubled again, unleashing a flurry of new commercial activity in the Zaire River basin as traders rushed to capture segments of the ivory market.[5]

Although the Nunu had not been oblivious to these developments, they had not been heavily involved in them either. The Nunu in the swamps remember buying slaves for their own purposes, but they retain almost no memories of selling slaves for the purposes of others. Similarly, oral traditions told by descendants of the Bobangi traders do not mention the Nunu as a source of slaves. Nevertheless, war, famine, crime, and debt had long created slaves among the Nunu, and it is possible that some of those slaves ended up in the wretched holds of trans-Atlantic slave ships.

World markets began to make a significant impact on the people of the Bolobo-Yumbi Strip in the early nineteenth cen-

---

[4] Phyllis Martin, *The External Trade of the Loango Coast, 1576–1870* (London, 1972), pp. 86–87, 124–29.

[5] Harms, *River of Wealth*, pp. 24–47, 99–108.

tury. With the growth of trade at Malebo Pool, the Bobangi traders began to spread out from their homeland along the lower Ubangi and settle at key points along the middle Zaire. Nunu oral traditions recall that the first Bobangi settler in Bolobo was Makwango Nsambo, who came down on a trip and saw that the bluffs of Bolobo made a nice place to settle.[6] He founded the village of Boyambola. Other Bobangi traders soon followed. Bolobo made an ideal site because the river narrowed there, and the faster waters of the narrows contained few islands. It was easy for the Bobangi to monitor the river traffic and to challenge any unauthorized traders who tried to break their monopoly.[7]

Trading, as exemplified by the Bobangi, represented a radical shift in productive tactics. Traders gained wealth, not from exploiting their environment, but by profiting from environmental imbalances between distant parts of the world. In the nineteenth century there was an abundance of ivory in the equatorial African forests, and there was a demand for ivory in Europe. The Bobangi located themselves between the two situations and made profits as middlemen. Their immediate environment mattered little to them. Far more important was their geographical position in relation to the larger patterns of world trade.

Trading also reversed traditional relationships between goods, work, and money. The fishing economy was an economy of use values in which people sold commodities they produced in order to get money to buy other commodities that they did not produce. Money was merely a convenience to facilitate the exchange of one object for another. It did not increase unless production increased. One produced, got money, spent the money, and then had to produce all over again to get more money. Each time the cycle began with production. Trading worked in precisely the opposite way. Capital in the form of money was raised and invested in a stock of trade goods. Then, the trade goods were sold for a profit, resulting in more money than had been originally invested. The cycle

---

[6] Interview: Etebe and Ngamakala, 5-22-75, Tape A4.
[7] Harms, *River of Wealth,* pp. 126-42.

could repeat itself endlessly, and money could increase each time. There was little correlation between wealth and production. Wealth came from playing on the differences among isolated markets, by taking advantage of imbalances between supply and demand—not by producing.

These revolutionary changes in tactics for dealing with the environment were accompanied by equally dramatic changes in strategies for competition among people. Bobangi villages grew largely through influxes of slaves who worked to assist in the primary task of trading. Male slaves paddled canoes on trading trips, while female slaves grew cassava to feed the traders and the paddlers. The society replenished its population by constantly importing new slaves. As a result, the Bobangi did not have kin groups based on blood ties, but rather collections of unrelated and purchased people who addressed one another with kinship titles.[8] Bobangi society, in short, was as divorced from nature as was Bobangi economy.

Although the Nunu disdained the Bobangi for their unorthodox approaches to economy and society, they also envied them. A Bobangi trader could make a 500% markup by carrying a tusk from the equator to Malebo Pool.[9] The Bobangi returned from their voyages with cloth in the most fashionable designs. Wives of chiefs and traders wore enormous brass collars. The Bobangi also had stores of brass rods, the currency then gaining fashion and driving out the *nsi* shells. Wealthy Bobangi trading barons controlled large numbers of slaves and attracted clients. They used their wealth to purchase chiefly titles.

Many Nunu saw trading as an attractive alternative to fishing. Because the waters of the river were open to everyone, river fishing had never lent itself to social strategies whereby one person could gain control over others. The river trade, in contrast, provided the potential for wealth. Wealth gave one control over people, which, in turn, gave one political power. The trading competition thus became a riverine counterpart to the old water lord competition in the swamps.

---

[8] See Harms, *River of Wealth*, pp. 143–59.
[9] Harms, *River of Wealth*, pp. 99–108.

However, the Nunu lacked two things necessary for successful commerce. The first was capital. A trader needed a large canoe, paddlers, and enough money to buy merchandise. The solution to this problem was to form trading companies that were analogous to fishing teams. When a man wanted to undertake a trading trip, he contacted other interested persons who could supply capital and also paddle the canoe. When the trip was over, each person got a share of the profits, but the organizer of the trip got the largest share. A man could thus begin by organizing trading teams and later become an independent entrepreneur with his own trading firm.

The Nunu traders also lacked the contacts that were essential for long-distance commerce. Once they were outside of Nunu territory, which by the nineteenth century stretched less than a hundred kilometers from Bolobo to the upper Nsangasi, they were strangers. They were away from their own *nkinda* charms, and they lacked kinsmen who could serve as their hosts and protectors.

The Bobangi, by contrast, had formed a network stretching over 700 kilometers from Malebo Pool to the lower Ubangi with nodes at Missongo, Tchumbiri, Bolobo, and Lukolela. In addition, they had secured other contacts by ties of blood brotherhood or by marrying wives of prominent traders. The Bobangi jealously guarded the advantages obtained by exclusive contacts. Not only was their network reinforced by ties of marriage and blood brotherhood, but it was also protected by military might. Traders not associated with the Bobangi network who tried to pass the narrows of Bolobo or the extreme narrows at Tchumbiri were heavily taxed or were sometimes simply attacked, their goods confiscated and their crews sold into slavery.[10]

Nevertheless, some Nunu eventually established themselves as traders. A select few, such as Bongoma and Ngonza, managed to join the Bobangi trade network by wearing Bobangi facial markings and speaking with a Bobangi accent.[11] Others

---

[10] Harms, *River of Wealth*, pp. 71–98.
[11] Interview: Etebe and Ngamakala, 5-23-75, Tape A5.

built up their own networks of contacts and became strong enough to challenge the Bobangi monopoly. As the son of a nineteenth century Nunu trader explained:

> When they went with goods to sell at Kinshasa, they passed [Missongo] at night. If they passed in the daytime, Mokemo mo Bolanga [the chief of Missongo] sent his men down to seize them. They took their fish and ivory and put it in his house. If [Nunu traders] went downstream, they went at night and drifted in the current without paddling. When they had Mokemo's people at their backs, they arrived at the mouth of the Kwa River and crossed over to the village of Enkutu Etumba, and the danger was over.[12]

By 1888 a missionary reported that the Nunu traders were remarkably successful in challenging the Bobangi:

> The better morality of the Moie (Banunu) people is telling markedly in their favor; and while the importance of our Bobangi neighbors on the south is waning, that of our Moie friends is increasing. They are more industrious and energetic, making longer journeys and building better houses.[13]

The careers of Mangasa and Elema illustrate how two men of very different backgrounds could attain success as trading barons in the commercial economy of the late nineteenth century. Mangasa, who was born in the Nsangasi area of the swamps, migrated as a young man to Mabwa, one of the Nunu villages that comprised Bolobo. There he became a successful trader. His son recounted that Mangasa would go to the Pool with ivory and dried fish and return with blankets and a wide cloth that the Nunu called *bimbunu bi mbene*. With the profits, he amassed nineteen wives and over a hundred slaves.[14]

Elema was an assimilated newcomer. He had been born along the Alima River among the Likuba. There he met Eyoka, a Nunu trader from Bolobo who had come to the Alima River on a trading trip. He became Eyoka's client and went to live

---

[12] Interview: Mangasa, 5-29-75, Tape A7.
[13] George Grenfell in *The Missionary Herald,* February 1, 1889, p. 50. The parenthetical reference to Banunu is Grenfell's.
[14] Interview: Mangasa, 5-29-75, Tape A7; 5-18-75, field notes.

with him in Bolobo. Working as an agent for Eyoka, Elema
went up the Zaire to buy camwood, ivory, and slaves. He went
to the Pool and traded them for trade goods and slaves from
the lower Zaire region. (As was typical of the internal slave
trade during that period, he took lower Zaire slaves to the upper Zaire, and upper Zaire slaves to the lower Zaire. The purpose was to get them far enough away from home that they
would not try to run away.) At the same time, he was building
up a collection of twelve wives and over a hundred slaves.[15]

As Nunu traders amassed wealth and people, they gained status in their communities that made them strong candidates to
be village guardians. Ngamakala and Etebe explained why:

> To be respected you had to have money. If a man wanted to be
> installed as guardian, he had to have money. If he had a strong
> heart, courage, and a network of friends, he would make money,
> and he would become a guardian.[16]

By the late nineteenth century most guardians of the Nunu villages of Bolobo were traders as well. Ngoie, the guardian of
Bongongo, was a former slave who built up a trading firm that
by 1889 operated along the entire stretch between the lower
Ubangi and Malebo Pool. Ngabosaka, guardian of the village
of Mondanga, was successful enough to be able to go to the
Pool with up to ten tusks of ivory on a single trip.[17] Mangasa
became the guardian of Mabwa, and Elema became the guardian of Bonzongo.

THE PRICE OF POWER

Nunu success in commerce had required a revolutionary re-
orientation of goals, tactics, and strategies. The old productive

---

[15] Interview: Enguta, 4-15-76, Tape A93; 8-3-81, Tape 15/1; field notes, August, 1981; Interview: Esankanga, 4-18-76, Tape A94. Other sources indicate that Elema was a slave of Eyoka. See L. Reynaert, "Histoire Succincte
des Populations Constituant l'Actuelle Sous-Chefferie de Bolobo," 1934, in
Dossier Politique: Bolobo, MZA. Interview: Ngamakala, 3-18-76, Tape
A80.

[16] Interview: Ngamakala and Etebe, 6-25-75, Tape A25.

[17] Reynaert, "Histoire Succincte," MZA. George Grenfell's diary, 6-2-1889,
7-20-1889, and 8-1-1890, BMS Archives, London, A-18.

tactics, characterized by the production of use values, were replaced by the pursuit of exchange values: traders made a profit by buying cheap and selling dear, and they reinvested their profits in more goods, slaves, and canoes. If they were successful, their wealth increased, and this increase was both the goal of the enterprise and the measure of its success.

Strategies in the competition among people also shifted. Capital investment in slaves became dominant, while investment in more traditional social networks declined. Rich traders took slave concubines instead of marrying free women, thus avoiding potential claims from in-laws. For such people, security came more from their stores of wealth than from networks of kinfolk and affines. In the boom climate of the nineteenth century, traders were willing to cut themselves off from traditional support networks in order to maximize their capital investments.

Despite the radical changes in goals, strategies, and payoffs introduced by the commercialization of the region, traders retained a belief in the anti-capitalistic ideology of the zero-sum model, which held that one person's gain was always offset by another's loss. Thus, the fierce commercial competition was accompanied by a frenzy of witchcraft accusations that created a market for itinerant witch hunters. These individuals traveled from village to village to "smell out" witches in response to accusations of witchcraft. Traders sought ever more powerful charms to protect their profits. Wars were fought over charges that one trader was magically preempting the wealth of another.

The internal trade-off between material wealth and wealth in the form of kinfolk, a key feature of the dominant witchcraft models along the middle Zaire, was also seen to be operating. Essential to this trade-off was the correlation of wealth with death: a person who gained wealth caused death among his kin in the process. To the Nunu, the most obvious manifestation of this phenomenon was the low birthrate in trading families. Modern informants recount that the traders killed off their kinfolk by witchcraft in order to gain wealth. Then, having no more kinfolk to give to the spirits, they began to offer up their unborn children.[18] The Nunu hold that many of the children

---

[18] Interviews: Mambula, 5-9-76, Tape A108; Nzolo, 7-22-76, Tape A129.

who were conceived were whisked away by the spirits before
they could be born.

Birthrate was one feature that distinguished trading society
from fishing society. One missionary claimed that there were a
hundred children in Nunu fishing villages for every child to be
seen in Bobangi trading villages. Modern-day Nunu fishermen
brag that because they valued people while the Bobangi valued
money, their populations are increasing while the Bobangi have
almost totally died out.[19] Nevertheless, the low birthrate characteristic of the Bobangi traders is also found in the genealogies
of prominent Nunu trading barons. For some, such as Eyoka
and Ngoie, my research could locate no descendants at all, despite the fact that Eyoka was reputed to have had 30 wives.

Other barons of the river trade left only slight traces. Mangasa, according to his son, had 19 wives, 12 of whose names
are forgotten, probably because they left no children. Of the
seven remembered wives, three of them had no children, two
of them each had one child, one had two children, and one had
three children. That makes seven children from 19 wives. The
genealogy of Elema is remarkably similar. He had 12 wives.
Three of them have been forgotten, having presumably left no
descendants. Five others had no children. One slave wife left
one child. The other three wives, who were free women from
Nkubosaka in the flooded forest, produced a total of eight children. The genealogies clearly show that the slave marriages of
the traders produced very few children.

A modern academic analysis would explain this curious phenomenon in terms of two factors.[20] First, traders often suffered
from venereal diseases, which they passed to their wives and
concubines. Second, slave wives probably aborted many of
their pregnancies in defiance of their masters, who wanted chil-

---

[19] For example, see Interview: Linyanga, 7-2-75, Tape A28.
[20] See Robert Harms, "Sustaining the System: The Trading Towns along the
Middle Zaire," in *Women and Slavery in Africa,* edited by Martin Klein and
Claire Robertson (Madison, Wis., 1983), pp. 95–110.

dren. To nineteenth-century Nunu, however, the lack of children among the trading families seemed to confirm the worst predictions of the zero-sum model.

The Nunu thus continued to believe that wealth could be obtained only at a heavy price. A trading baron was required to constantly search for better charms, to defend himself against witchcraft accusations, to defend himself against armed attacks, and to see death visited upon his town. Yet in comparison with the levels of profit to be obtained in the trade, these costs were not prohibitive: charms could be purchased, and witch-finders could be bribed. Most importantly, people could be purchased. With internal slave prices dropping as precipitously as external ivory prices were rising in the nineteenth century,[21] the "artificial" increase in population due to an influx of cheap slaves into the trading towns outweighed the "natural" decrease in the population due to greed-induced death. By turning people into commodities, the traders bridged the gap between material wealth and wealth in the form of dependents.

THE IMPACT OF TRADE

The rise of the Nunu trading barons had remarkably little impact on the lives of the river fishermen. Unlike the swamplands, where the water lords and the landless lived in a tense symbiotic relationship, the trading barons and the river fishermen operated in almost isolated economic and social spheres. The traders purchased slaves and ivory hundreds of kilometers up the river, and they sold them at markets hundreds of kilometers down the river. Bolobo was merely a convenient stopping point along the way. They amassed followings by purchasing slaves from all areas of the central Zaire basin, and thus they had little need to subjugate members of the local population.

---

[21] By 1854 the price of a slave youth at Luanda had fallen from $70.–$80. to a mere $10.–$12. Joseph C. Miller, "Cokwe Trade and Conquest," in *Precolonial African Trade,* edited by Richard Gray and David Birmingham (London, 1970), pp. 177–78.

The fishermen, on the other hand, continued to make independent livelihoods from their fishing and their wives' cassava fields, and thus they had little need to become clients of the trading barons. Although some fishermen almost certainly sought loans and other forms of support from powerful traders, thus becoming their clients, there is no evidence that the fishermen as a group ever became dependent on traders as a group.

Because the traders based their trading strategies on regional and international markets instead of local ones, they only minimally affected local choices of what to produce and how much. There is no evidence that the Nunu ever produced significant quantities of slaves and ivory, the high-value products in the river trade. While the affluence of the trading barons probably enlarged the market for locally produced fish, pottery, and palm oil, the quantitative change did not lead to a shift in productive tactics.

Perhaps the most significant impact of trading on Nunu riverine society as a whole resulted from the elevation of trading barons to guardianship positions in the Nunu villages of Bolobo. Commercial rivalry among neighboring guardians heightened the normal tensions that were bound to occur when seven independent villages occupied the same bluff. One result was almost continuous warfare among the Nunu villages in the late nineteenth century.

Unlike the ritualized wars in the swamps, these were not limited to the dry season, and they often became wars of attrition instead of the decisive battles. They resulted from disputes over trade or from the social rivalries of trading barons, and they continued until one side capitulated or the matter was settled by arbitration. The opposing militias were largely made up of slaves who fought with guns instead of spears. The outcomes of the battles depended less on the personal courage of the individual combatants than on the ability of the trading barons to mobilize support.

---

[22] George Grenfell, "News from the Rev. George Grenfell," *Missionary Herald,* Jan. 1, 1890, pp. 22–24. See also George Grenfell's diary, May 30–June 19, 1889, in BMS Archives, London, A-18.

A description of one of these wars comes from George Grenfell, who observed its unfolding in May and June of 1889.[22] The fight concerned Ngoie, the guardian of Bongongo, and Eyoka, guardian of Bonzongo, both of whom were active in the river trade. The fight began over Ngoie's failure to pay for a couple of wives he had acquired from Bonzongo, but this may well have been a pretext masking deeper strains in the competitive relationship between the trading barons.

This war, like other wars in the Bolobo area in the late nineteenth century, was fought according to well-known rules. If it rained, they could not fight because the powder in the pans of the flintlock guns would not go off. On market day there was no fighting. At midday the sun was too hot for fighting, and there was no fighting after dark. These and other rules kept down the number of casualties. This war, for example, went on for several weeks but resulted in only sixteen deaths.

The war began with ritualized insults. The Bonzongo warriors, who made the opening move in the war, gathered daily in the grassland behind Ngoie's town and sent out one or two spokesmen to curse Ngoie, who in turn sent out several musketeers to blaze away at the spokesmen. Then the Bonzongo spokesmen dropped behind hills and trees to shoot back, keeping up a steady stream of curses and insults. At this point the two parties were not within musket range, and the shooting was more for psychological effect than for military advantage.

As the days passed, the war entered a second stage. Ngoie's soldiers began to advance to a point just out of rifle range, and they began to send skirmishers to stalk individual soldiers spotted by lookouts stationed safely in trees. The skirmishers on the other side would respond in kind until the bolder army forced the other to retreat. As weeks went by, the Bonzongo warriors seemed to get bolder and bolder, while those of Ngoie became discouraged. Soon the Bonzongo forces were coming close to the narrow belt of forest that separated Ngoie's town from the grasslands and gardens behind it. Fearing an assault on their town, Ngoie's people tried without success to recapture the forest belt.

Ngoie himself did little to help his cause. Instead of going to battle with his warriors, he stayed in the village making medi-

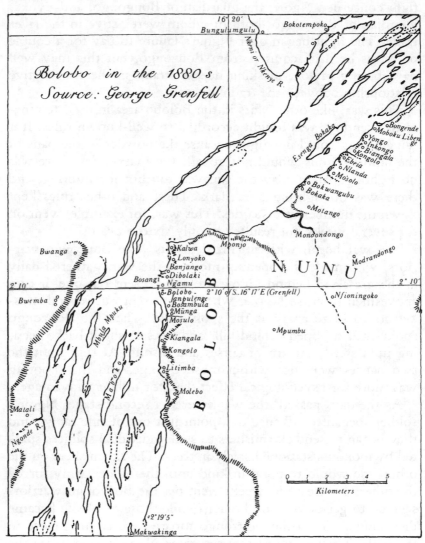

Bolobo in the 1880s

cine to make the bullets strong. He took bullets and made incantations over them. Then the women knelt and received the bullets as he invoked safety for "his children." The medicine was in a bowl set in the middle of four sticks. He cooked the medicine, which he sprinkled over the town to keep it safe and on the women who carried the bullets to the soldiers.

The incantations over the bullets were sealed with a ceremony in which he was assisted by the children of the village, who chanted responses to his incantations. They sat in a circle around Ngoie, who danced around a charm which he had placed between four spears. Then he began chanting:

NGOIE: May the hearts of all our people be strong and all our
             bullets hit our enemies.
CHILDREN: Yes, let it be so.
NGOIE: May the Bonzongo men fear and run away, and none
             of their bullets touch us.
CHILDREN: Yes, let it be so.
NGOIE: May our men kill the Bonzongos and burn their
             town.
CHILDREN: Yes, let it be so.
NGOIE: May our men never fear, and may our town never be
             burned.
CHILDREN: Yes, let it be so.

When Ngoie's side seemed to be losing, some of his warriors chided him for staying in town while they had to fight. To explain their poor record on the battlefield and defend his practice of avoiding the battles, Ngoie accused several of his own men of bewitching the soldiers who had been killed. The accused had to pass through the poison ordeal to prove they were not at fault. By bribing Dingulu, the person who administered the poison, they assured themselves of acquittal on the charges and forced Ngoie to pay an indemnity for false accusation. Ngoie then accused one of his wives of bewitching him and said that her curse would kill him if he ever held a gun in his hands. He sent her away from the village.

After the war had gone on for over a month, Ngabosaka, the guardian of a nearby village, decided that somebody had to intervene to stop it, so he went through the villages beating his double clapperless bell and announcing that the combat must cease and that the two parties must meet him to settle the matter.

Local wars increased in scale when each side sought allies. In 1890 a war began because a person from the village of Mabwa was slow in repaying a debt of 200 brass rods that he owed to Ngabosaka, the guardian of a neighboring village. The debtor was caught by Ngabosaka's men and tied up, but he escaped. Mabwa then attacked Ngabosaka's village as revenge for the indignity of having one of their citizens tied up. Both sides began to look to neighboring villages for help. Three villages—Lonyoko, Ekwayulu, and Bonzongo—agreed to help Ngabosaka. Two other villages—Mulenga and Mumbele—each had citizens that were related to both parties, and so their chiefs agreed to send some combatants to each side when the war began.[23]

Although wars such as these clearly affected the entire populations of the Nunu river towns, it is difficult to determine the extent to which ordinary fishermen were involved in the actual fighting. George Grenfell, a close observer of those wars, once reported that the authority of the trading barons seldom extended beyond their own slaves.[24] It seems likely that many fishermen stayed at their fishing camps as much as possible to avoid the almost continual warfare that plagued the river towns. Despite the fact that the fishermen and the traders lived on the same riverbank bluffs and traveled on the same river, they maintained separate existences.

THE DECLINE OF THE TRADING BARONS

Ironically, the heyday of trading was already coming to an end by the time Nunu traders successfully penetrated the Bobangi networks. The harbinger of these changes appeared on February 26, 1877. A whaleboat, about the length of a medium-sized

---

[23] George Grenfell's diary, Aug. 1, 1890, BMS Archives, London, A-18.

[24] George Grenfell, Response to "Questionnaire Concernant l'Organisation Politique, Civile, et Pénale des Tribus de Territoire de l'Etat Indépendant," AA, A.I. (1370) IX/A/2.

trading canoe and twice as wide, came down the river. It was filled with people who paddled *sitting down and facing backwards*. Those who got a close look might have noticed that two members of the crew had skin that was not black but deep tan from the tropical sun and its reflected glare. One of those white men was Henry Morton Stanley.

Stanley's exploration of the Zaire was to electrify Europe, but his passage along the Bolobo–Yumbi Strip was uneventful. Local tradition recalls nothing other than the astonishment at seeing oarsmen rowing in a seated, back-facing position instead of paddling in a standing, forward-looking position as did the Nunu. Stanley, for his part, recorded little of the passage except to note the cultivated slopes of Bolobo and the "scores of native canoes passing backwards and forwards, either fishing or proceeding to the grassy islets to their fish-sheds and saltmakings."[25]

Stanley returned to equatorial Africa in 1879, this time as a representative of the International African Association (IAA) that King Leopold II of Belgium had founded. Stanley's mission was to lay the foundations for a colonial state. His expedition carried a steamboat, piece by piece, over the Crystal Mountains to Malebo Pool, a sure sign of his intention to make the Zaire River his main communications artery. By November 1882, there was a IAA post in Bolobo headed by Belgian Lieutenant Frederic Orban, who was assisted by 25 Zanzibari soldiers.

The trading chiefs of Bolobo distrusted the agents of the International African Association from the very beginning. Although they did not know that Stanley had brought in trading goods valued at 197,000 Belgian francs in order to buy ivory at the state stations along the middle Zaire, they correctly surmised that the IAA was aiming to penetrate their sphere of influence and to cut in on their profits.[26] Their fears were quickly confirmed when Lt. Orban, the IAA agent, was joined by a Mr. Boulanger of the Dutch Trading Company, who bought

---

[25] Henry Morton Stanley, *Through the Dark Continent,* 2 vols. (New York, 1879) 2:313.

[26] Louis Gann and Peter Duignan, *The Rulers of Belgian Africa* (Princeton, 1979), pp. 119–20.

six hundred pounds of ivory in less than three months.[27] During 1883 and 1884, the IAA post was burned to the ground twice, despite the arrival of Stanley's steamship and an impressive display of the powers of the Krupp gun.

When the IAA became the Congo Independent State after gaining international recognition in 1885 at the Berlin West Africa Conference, it abandoned the post at Bolobo, but it increased river patrols in order to establish control over the ivory trade. In 1890 the missionary George Grenfell reported that "a very considerable amount of ivory falls into the hands of the State."[28] Despite continued hostilities on the part of the African ivory traders, the state gradually increased its control. When Roger Casement went up the Zaire in 1903 he did not see a single African trading canoe throughout the entire 160 mile stretch from Leopoldville to Tchumbiri.[29]

CONCLUSION

Trading, with its heavy capital investment, its slave-powered trading canoes, and its extensive networks of contacts, represented a means by which river fishermen could gain status that equaled or surpassed that of the water lords in the swamps. Control of capital and contacts became the riverine alternatives to the swampland ownership of dams and ponds. Massive importation of slaves became the alternative to the swampland strategies of attracting clients. Success in trade became a stepping-stone to political power, and traders successfully captured the guardianship positions in the Nunu villages of Bolobo.

Despite the similarities between the new riverine trading competition and the old water lord competition, trading nevertheless represented a radical innovation. It was based on exchange instead of production, and it exploited the differences

---

[27] Orban to Stanley, 22 Feb, 1883, MRAC-H, Orban Copie-Lettres, p. 363.

[28] Grenfell to Baynes, June 23, 1890, BMS Archives, London, A-19.

[29] Roger Casement, "Correspondence and Report from His Majesty's Consul at Boma Respecting the Administration of the Independent State of the Congo," *Parliamentary Papers*, Command Paper no. 1933, Africa, no. 1, 1904 (London, 1904), p. 26.

between environments instead of conforming to the imperatives of a particular one. Perhaps its most significant feature was that it allowed individuals to amass wealth at a previously unheard-of pace and scale. It is not surprising that the success of Nunu trading barons was accompanied by a rise in witchcraft accusations and local warfare.

Yet the long-term impact of the trading barons on Nunu life was limited. Because both the productive tactics and the social strategies of the traders depended on resources from outside the immediate area, they could prosper without significantly affecting the lives of the independent fishermen. Their most profound impact on the larger Nunu society resulted from their takeover of the guardianship of the riverine Nunu villages. When the colonial state drove the trading barons out of business, the relatively egalitarian poverty that had long characterized life along the river began to reappear.

10. The troubles

THE COLONIAL CAMPAIGN against the ivory traders was merely the opening move in King Leopold II's attempt to appropriate the resources of the middle Zaire for his own purposes. Leopold was engaged in a competition for wealth and power on an international scale, and the resources of the Congo were the key to his strategy.[1] Soon after Leopold's Congo Independent State gained international recognition in 1885, it proclaimed its ownership of all land not directly occupied by Africans. Four years later it declared an outright monopoly on all products of the forest between Bolobo and the mouth of the Aruwimi, nearly 1200 kilometers up the Zaire. With ownership of the resources came the legal authority to forcibly expropriate them from the inhabitants as "taxes in kind."

The abuses resulting from the forced collection of "taxes in kind" led the Belgian government to take over the Congo from King Leopold II in 1908. One of the first reform measures of the new colonial administration was the abolition of the tax in kind, which was replaced in 1910 by a tax paid in Congolese francs. The money tax was adopted not only to increase revenues, but also because it would force the Africans to enter the cash nexus by working for Europeans or producing cash crops. Governor Fuchs stated the proposition in euphemistic terms:

> The goal of the native tax is not only fiscal: it is also and above all designed to end their apathy, to push them to work and to improve, by working, their material and moral situation.[2]

---

[1] On Leopold's strategies, see Neal Ascherson, *The King Incorporated: Leopold II in the Age of Trusts* (London, 1963).

[2] "L'Impôt Indigène au Congo Belge," *Le Mouvement Géographique,* 1914, col. 290.

In order to ensure that the income-producing activities of the Africans were compatible with the economic priorities of the colonial administration, they introduced obligatory production in 1917. The Africans were ordered to produce specified quantities of commodities that the administration deemed to be important. They could sell the products to licensed European companies for cash, which they used to pay taxes and purchase goods. The free agricultural market gradually disappeared, and by 1935 the administration exercised direct control over African village production and marketing.[3] Added to the normal impositions and restrictions were ad hoc measures such as the "war effort" production during World War II, which closely resembled the old tax in kind.[4] Moreover, the government retained the power to impress gangs of workers for such tasks as making and repairing roads or serving as porters for traveling government officials.

The colonial state intruded on the lives of its subjects in other ways as well. Colonial administrators altered local structures of political authority by appointing "chiefs" who were, in effect, the lowest level of the state administrative apparatus. They suppressed anti-witchcraft rituals as well as ritualized warfare. They dictated settlement patterns and forcibly moved people from isolated estates to consolidated villages. Because the establishment of colonialism coincided with disastrous epidemics along the middle Zaire, many people became convinced that the state was employing a sort of biological warfare against them. It was a time of unprecedented disruption at a variety of levels.

The colonial presence greatly altered the context of decision and action among the Nunu. In precolonial times the rules that had governed choices of tactics and strategies had been derived from the natural environment, religious beliefs, the regional economy, and social institutions. All of those factors had been

---

[3] Bogumil Jewsiewicki, "Rural Society and the Belgian Colonial Economy," in *History of Central Africa,* edited by David Birmingham and Phyllis Martin (New York, 1983), II:101.

[4] See *Le Congo Belge durant la Seconde Guerre Mondiale: Recueil d'Etudes* (Brussels, 1983).

relatively predictable in the short run, and change had come about as a gradual process instead of a decisive rupture. But under the colonial state, life could change drastically and rapidly as a result of a single governmental decree. The Nunu had no way of knowing about the administrative strategies and economic conflicts that lay behind the state actions, and they saw the state policies as capricious and totally unpredictable intrusions into their lives.

Just as people in different environmental zones had employed different kinds of strategies to become big-men, they now employed different kinds of defensive strategies to counteract the effects of the colonialism. The water lords in the swamps sought to defend their estates with armed resistance and with traditional charms and rituals. When these efforts failed, they switched tactics and abandoned their ancient estates, leaving the swamplands almost uninhabited. The river people, in contrast, adopted strategies that took advantage of their nomadic mobility. They were much more successful at resisting the state. As a result, the riverbanks became a haven for displaced water lords from the swamps.

THE SWAMPLANDS

Modern Nunu portray the colonial experience in the swamplands in terms of a series of calamities that demonstrated the declining power of the *nkinda* charms and their guardians. The stories and reminiscences of former swampland inhabitants elaborate the theme of the decline of the old ritual powers and the increasing ritual pollution of the swamplands. As the Nunu saw it, the land was turning against them, and ultimately they were left with no defense except to abandon it.

The first calamity was the colonial conquest itself. In the wake of the international recognition that the Congo Independent State had received in 1885, it began to establish political control over its populations. After establishing a military camp at Yumbi in the early 1890s, the state sent armed expeditions into the swamps to recruit soldiers for the state militia, to obtain workers for the Matadi-Leopoldville railroad, and to collect food and building materials for the military camp. Nunu oral traditions interpret the battles against the soldiers as tests of the power of their *nkinda* charms. The story of the arrival of the soldiers in Bokangamoi illustrates this point of view:

> When the white men arrived, they came to Bokangamoi to recruit soldiers. They had already successfully taken recruits at Nkolo, Nsangasi, and Mpama. At Bokangamoi they were opposed by the local magicians. The magicians went to the forest where our ancestors fought and won wars. They gathered palm oil, cloth, and all sorts of objects which they put into a package and buried. When the white men arrived, they found that their strength was gone, and they retreated.[5]

Often, however, the charms failed. One story tells of a Sengele man who bragged to the state soldiers that the Nunu could not be killed, so powerful were their charms. To puncture Nunu pride, the soldiers attacked the village of Malebo and killed several people. Overall, the soldiers usually won, and the Nunu still remember the names of people who were taken away never to return: Bobika, Eba, Bimpaka, and many others.[6]

The occupation of the swamps put an end to the annual wars. Although modern Nunu generally hold this to be a positive development, it was probably perceived very differently at the time. The *pax Belgica* terminated an important aspect of swampland ritual life. Young people could no longer dream of glory in battle, men could no longer demonstrate their strength, and the power of the charms was no longer tested on a regular basis. A sense of this loss was conveyed to me by Nunu elders who still kept battle regalia in their houses and who could sing the old war songs, even though they themselves had not participated in the old wars. The end of the wars thus brought about an impoverishment of ritual life, which heightened fears about the declining power of the *nkinda* charms.

The colonial conquest coincided with smallpox and sleeping sickness epidemics that were sweeping the area in the late nineteenth century. A smallpox epidemic, first reported at the Pool in 1882, reached Bolobo in 1899. Sleeping sickness swept up the

---

[5] Interview: Lila, 7-12-81, Tape 3/1.
[6] Interview: Lila, 7-14-81, Tape 4/2.

Zaire in the 1890s.[7] Because the swamp people were in regular contact with the river people through trade and familial visits, there were ample opportunities for diseases to be transmitted from the river to the swamps. It seems likely that mortality rates in the swamps were nearly as high as those along the river. A rough estimate of 50% is not out of line. By 1909 the three administrative chiefdoms making up most of the flooded grasslands had a total population of only 187 people.[8]

The Nunu blamed the epidemics on the white people, whom they thought to be spirits returned from the land of the dead. This attitude was evident in 1910, when two young men from Nkuboko decided to go to Bolobo to seek a schoolteacher for their village. When the elders learned of the plan, they refused the boys permission to go, claiming that the missionaries were responsible for the recent epidemic of sleeping sickness. To bring a teacher was to bring sleeping sickness to Nkuboko. The villagers beat the boys with switches to discourage them from going. The young men nevertheless procured a canoe, hid it in the forest, and sneaked away at night. When they stopped at Minsange to rest, people defecated in their canoe to symbolize the polluted nature of their enterprise. The same thing happened the next night along the Moliba. The people of the swamps clearly associated the missionaries with disease and ritual pollution, and they were fighting ritual pollution with literal pollution.[9]

Like the battles against the colonial soldiers, the battle against epidemics was seen as a test of the power of the guardians. In precolonial times one of the main functions of the guardian of the *nkinda* had been to prevent epidemics. One method of doing so was described as follows:

---

[7] Robert Harms, *River of Wealth, River of Sorrow: The Central Zaire Basin in the Era of the Slave and Ivory Trade, 1500–1891* (New Haven, 1981), pp. 231–32.

[8] See the 1909 statistical tables for the chiefdoms Mokongo, Bongamba, and Moliba-Mitsange in DCMS.

[9] Interview: Lila, 7-14-81. One of the young men was Lila's father, Boketa.

> If the diviner foresaw that an epidemic was coming, he told the
> guardian. The guardian then ordered everybody in the
> neighborhood to lie down and keep their eyes to the ground. If
> somebody walked around and saw the disease, he would catch it.
> If the disease came anyway, he called the elders to a council
> meeting. They prepared charms to make the disease go away. The
> guardian placed charms at the end of the villages to make the
> disease go away.[10]

Whether or not such tactics had actually worked, the existence of such stories created the impression that the guardians
of the precolonial era had effectively repelled disease. The
devastation caused by the epidemics was thus seen as further
evidence that the *nkinda* charms and their guardians were losing their power.

The Nunu largely escaped the biggest calamity of the early
colonial period. In the 1890s the state began to get interested in
wild rubber. Although rubber, which was extracted from the
landolphia vine that grew in the forest, had been known to Africans in precolonial times, it had never become a valued commodity, nor had it been the object of trade. Officials of the
Congo Independent State discovered the rubber resources of the
forest at a time when the world market prices were rising rapidly due to increasing demand in Europe for rubber to make
bicycle tires, belts for machines, and other items. Because the
state lacked the manpower to organize the collection of rubber
on a systematic basis, it granted huge tracts of territory to private concession companies in return for shares of company
stock. The companies had the right to force Africans to gather
rubber on their behalf, and they hired private armies to uphold
their authority.

The largest and most notorious concession was the Crown
Domain, a vast territory that was the private fief of King Leo-
pold II himself. Formed by a secret decree in 1896, the Crown
Domain stretched from Lake Mai Ndombe to the Sengele vil-

---

[10] Interview: Lila, 7-14-81. Tape 4/2. A similar account was given by Bampomba, 7-24-81, Tape 13/2.

lages just east of Nkuboko. The inhabitants of the Domain
were at first delighted to be paid in cloth and beads for the
rubber they were ordered to harvest, but the payments were
gradually reduced until they were told to bring rubber for nothing. A.E. Scrivner, a missionary from Bolobo who visited the
Crown Domain in 1903, revealed what happened at the village
of Ngongo when King Leopold's soldiers ordered people to
collect rubber for no pay.

> To this they tried to demur, but to their great surprise several
> were shot by soldiers and the rest were told with many curses and
> blows to go at once or more would be killed. Terrified they began
> to prepare their food for the fortnight's absence from the village
> which the collection of rubber entailed. The soldiers discovered
> them sitting about. "What, not gone yet?" Bang, bang, bang, and
> down fall one and another dead in the midst of wives and
> companions. There is a terrible wail and an attempt made to
> prepare the dead for burial, but this is not allowed. All must go at
> once to the forest. Without food? Yes, without food. And off the
> poor wretches had to go without even their tinder boxes to make
> fire. Many died in the forests of exposure and hunger and still
> more from the rifles of the ferocious soldiers in charge of the post.
> In spite of their efforts, the amount fell off and more and more
> were killed.[11]

The life of rubber gatherers was harsh. Here is how refugees
from the Crown Domain described it to the British Consul:

> It used to take ten days to get the twenty baskets of rubber–we
> were always in the forest and then when we were late we were
> killed. We had to go further and further into the forest to find the
> rubber vines, to go without food, and our women had to give up
> cultivating the fields and gardens. Then we starved. Wild beasts–
> the leopards–killed some of us when we were working away in
> the forest, and others got lost or died from exposure and
> starvation, and we begged the white man to leave us alone, saying
> we could get no more rubber, but the white men and their soldiers
> said: "Go! You are only beasts yourselves, you are nyama [meat]."
> We tried, always going further into the forest, and when we failed

---

[11] Quoted in Roger Anstey, "The Congo Rubber Atrocities: A Case Study,"
African Historical Studies, 4 (1971):67–8.

and our rubber was short, the soldiers came to our towns and killed us. Many were shot, some had their ears cut off; others were tied up with ropes around their necks and bodies and taken away.[12]

The horrors of rubber gathering provoked massive dislocation as people fled the soldiers and the rubber impositions. When Scrivner traveled through the Crown Domain he saw:

. . . still more numerous sites where only recently thousands of people had been living. Cassava still growing in the plantations and bananas rotting on the trees. Here and there a few blackened sticks shewed where the huts had been and sometimes huts were seen fairly well preserved and with cooking utensils lying about. But never a man or woman or child. All as still as the grave.[13]

The Nunu of Nkuboko and the swamps lived just outside the western fringes of the Crown Domain, yet they did not entirely escape rubber gathering. The state officer at Yumbi ordered the Nunu in the swamps to bring in rubber and copal as part of their taxes in kind. When state soldiers came to collect rubber in one village, a village elder beat the dog of a soldier and the soldiers killed several people in retaliation.[14] In general, however, the state seemed more interested in procuring food for the military camp, and rubber was never a high priority.

The entire rubber operation in the Congo had brought fortunes to King Leopold II and a few businessmen, but it was an ecological disaster in that enormous areas were depleted of rubber vines, and it was a demographic disaster for the populations, many of whom became refugees and many of whom died of disease and exposure.[15] So repugnant had been the activity to

---

[12] Roger Casement, quoted in Anstey, "Rubber Atrocities," p. 64.

[13] Anstey, "Rubber Atrocities," p. 69. The figure of "thousands of people" refers to the area as a whole. The population of a single agricultural village rarely surpassed 400. Jan Vansina, "Esquisse Historique de l'Agriculture en Milieu Forestier (Afrique Equatoriale)," *Muntu*, 2 (1985):11.

[14] Interview: Lila, 7-14-81, Tape 4/2.

[15] For detailed descriptions of the rubber-gathering system and its effects in the nearby Abir concession, see Robert Harms, "The World Abir Made: The Maringa-Lopori Basin, 1885–1903," *African Economic History*, no. 12 (1983):125–39; Robert Harms, "The End of Red Rubber: A Reassessment," *Journal of African History*, 16 (1975): 73–88.

the local populations that forced rubber gathering was abandoned after the Belgians took over the Congo in 1908.

Although the Nunu of the swamplands largely escaped the horrors of forced rubber production, they felt the burden of state impositions in other ways. From the beginning of colonial rule, the authorities were concerned with finding foodstuffs and other supplies for the military camp at Yumbi. Ekando remembers that his grandfather, Manzanga, was required to bring regular supplies of fish and cassava to Yumbi. On one trip he did not meet his quota of fish and was imprisoned. He later decided that the burden of supplying food to the military camp was too great, and he refused. As a result, soldiers came and beat him, so he resumed the efforts to supply food to the camp. In addition to fish and cassava, people were asked to bring chickens, palm oil, and *ndele* leaves for the roofs of houses. Lobwaka recounted that every day canoes would arrive in Yumbi bringing supplies for the military camp.[16]

In 1908 Belgium wrested control of the Congo away from King Leopold and began to replace the chaotic plunder of the Independent State with more orderly administration. They divided the swamplands into five small chiefdoms, each headed by a state-appointed chief.[17] The main tasks of the chiefs were to collect taxes and to supply provisions to the military camp. A few years later the Belgians reorganized the administration of the swamps by creating three slightly larger chiefdoms in place of the five small ones. This administrative structure remained stable until the mid-1920s, when the state again reorganized its system of indirect rule. In restructuring the administration of the swamplands, the state undertook two actions that further undermined Nunu confidence in the *nkinda* charms and their guardians.

The first state action was to rearrange Nunu settlement patterns. In 1926 the government decided that in order to facilitate local administration, the people in the swamplands and Nkuboko should be moved from their scattered homesteads into

---

[16] Interviews: Ekando, 7-25-81, Tape 14/1; Lobwaka, 8-5-81, Tape 17/1.
[17] See the map of the Nunu chiefdoms, 1909, DCMS.

concentrated villages. Along the Moliba, where the land was inundated much of the year, the soldiers could not find a site for putting the people into a single large village. They instead opted for about ten small villages on sites that remained dry most of the year. In the flooded forest, the settlements collectively known as Mitima were consolidated into a single large village. On the dry land to the east of the swamps, consolidation was easier to accomplish, and villages such as Bokangamoi and Pokolo were established as people were forced to move their scattered homesteads to designated central places.[18]

The consolidation of the old homesteads further decreased the ritual power of the guardians of the land. As has been previously discussed, the landscape was subdivided into a series of individual forests and grasslands, each with a recognized ritual guardian. These divisions dated back to the earliest settlements and the planting of the first *nkinda* charms. In time a certain forest or grassland would house a variety of settlers from different lineages, all of whom recognized the ritual authority of the guardian of the land. Although guardianship brought few material rewards other than token gifts when animals were killed or when fish were harvested, it carried social and ritual prestige, which were very important to the Nunu. The consolidation of villages removed people from the lands protected by their ancestral *nkinda* charms. It also took away ritual prestige from most of the guardians while greatly enhancing the prestige of the owners of the sites of the new villages.

The ending of scattered settlement made it more difficult for the Nunu to control tsetse flies and animals. Scattered settlement had kept bush cleared over portions of the area and had thus diminished the available habitat for tsetse flies. The abandonment of the homesteads allowed the bush to regenerate and created new habitat for the flies. This factor helps to explain the persistence of sleeping sickness in the swamps even after it had died down along the river. A second function of the scattered settlements had been to control the animal populations.[19] Be-

---

[18] Interviews: Nsamonie, 7-8-81, Tape 1/1; Bampomba, 7-18-81, Tape 7/1; Ekando, 7-25-81, Tape 14/2.

[19] Interview: Mongemba, 7-8-81, field notes.

cause animals tended to avoid places frequented by humans, a pattern of extensive settlement spread thinly over the landscape encouraged the animals to seek habitat elsewhere. The abandoning of the scattered homesteads left the area divided into two zones: small concentrated zones inhabited by people, and vast, uninhabited zones where animals could again roam freely. Elephants, antelopes, buffaloes, and wild pigs could establish themselves in the empty areas and raid fields with impunity at night. To fight them, people dug pits and set traps, but this effort was a constant and often losing battle.[20]

Resettlement altered the rhythms of daily life. Many women who moved into the new villages kept their old fields and made long daily trips to work the land. Men kept their old dams and ponds, but they now traveled much longer distances to go to them. If the distance was too great to go and return in one day, people built small camps near their fields or fishing grounds, where they would stay for a week or two at a time. Life therefore became much more oriented to commuting significant distances between home and workplace; village living also meant less control over the workplace as people were absent for long periods of time during the off seasons.

The consolidation of the villages was quickly followed by a second major state action: the three chiefdoms were abolished and replaced with a single chiefdom encompassing the entire swamp. The state officer in charge of the reorganization, E. Cordemans, undertook some research into the history of the Nunu.[21] He learned the oral traditions about Ngeli, the first holder of the coveted *ngeli* title, who came from upriver and settled at Mitima. He also heard oral traditions about migrations from Mitima to various parts of the swamps. He concluded, with some exaggeration, that "whoever cannot trace his ancestry back to Mitima is not a Nunu." Even though Mitima, located in the inaccessible heart of the flooded forest, had not

---

[20] Interview: Eyongo, 8-4-81, Tape 15/1.
[21] E. Cordemans, "Rapport d'Enquête, Chefferie des Banunu," 1929, DCMS.

been the capital of any of the earlier colonial chiefdoms, Cordemans decided it should be the seat of the new chief. The person
he chose as chief was Lombundja, a matrilineal descendant of a
nineteenth century holder of the *ngeli* title. Thus did the ritual
capital become a political capital and the ritual office become a
political office.

The appointment of a political chief to succeed the old *ngeli*
guardians profoundly disturbed many Nunu. In 1975, when I
did my research, Losengo could still offer a trenchant critique
of the state's actions:[22]

> The state came and ruined our land. They said, "So and so should
> be the chief." However, he was not the appropriate person to rule
> everybody.

One problem with the state's action, according to Losengo, was
that the state had not understood the difference between ritual
guardianship and political chiefship.

> When the state came, they said, "We will give 'chiefship' to the
> *ngeli* because he is the owner of the people." But the *ngeli* was not
> really the owner of the people. He was just their guardian.

Another problem was that the state, believing that the position
was inherited according to matrilineal descent, had chosen
someone from the family of a former *ngeli*. They did not understand that succession to the title was actually the result of
competition among water lords.

> When a *ngeli* died, they would choose another. They wouldn't
> choose a person from the family of the deceased *ngeli*, but from a
> different family instead.

The state, by turning the ritual guardianship into a political
office, had damaged the ritual effectiveness of the *ngeli* of Mitima. Because the *ngeli* at Mitima was the caretaker of the most
powerful *nkinda* charm in the swamplands, the state action had
further damaged the capacity of the swamp dwellers to regulate
the ritual relationship between the people and the land.

---

[22] Interview: Losengo, 12-10-75, Tape A66.

Emptying the Swamps

The consolidation of the villages and the reorganization of the chiefdoms marked the beginning of a process that would result in the depopulation of the swamplands and their reclamation by insects and wild animals. In the 1930s people began to desert the consolidated villages and move out of the swamps altogether. Oral traditions about the emigration from the swamps emphasize that people left in order to escape disease and crocodile attacks. Both of these phenomena symbolized the growing ritual pollution of the land. The main defensive strategies of the water lords had been ritual ones, and the results had not been encouraging.

Disease continued to plague the swamplands as the colonial period progressed. The best documented area is the Nsangasi River valley. In 1928 a visit by a missionary doctor uncovered over two hundred previously unreported cases of sleeping sickness, and missionaries referred to the Nsangasi region as a "heavily infected sleeping sickness area."[23] In 1936 a disease resembling infantile paralysis that swept up the Nsangasi valley caused a large number of deaths among young men and intensified the general feeling that the *nkinda* were losing their power. By 1940 a missionary reported that formerly populous villages were reduced to a handful of diehards as people moved toward the river.[24]

Further evidence of the growing power of evil could be found in the increasing frequency of attacks by crocodiles. The villages in the Moliba area were subjected to repeated attacks in 1939, prompting most of the population to move away. That same year the village of Nganga, near Mitima, was also bothered by marauding crocodiles. Even Yumbi, which was originally along the Moliba, moved to the high bluffs of the Zaire to escape crocodile attacks.[25]

Stories of crocodile attacks had a special symbolic significance for the Nunu. They believed that crocodiles could be controlled

---

[23] *Co-Workers,* Jan., 1928, p. 14; *Co-Workers,* July, 1928, p. 10.
[24] *Co-Workers,* April, 1940, p. 12.
[25] Interview: Ekando, 7-25-81, Tape 14/2; *Co-Workers,* July, 1939, p. 7; Interview: Lobwaka, 8-5-81, Tape 9/1.

by people possessing powers of witchcraft. The crocodiles rendered magical services to their owners and took human lives as payment. A crocodile attack was therefore presumed to have been ordered by an evil person, probably to pay the crocodile for its services. Such attacks in precolonial times could result in family feuds or even intervillage wars.[26] The rampant witchcraft symbolized by the crocodile attacks reflected the inability of the guardians to regulate relations between the people and the land. According to Nunu oral traditions, precolonial guardians had displayed power over witchcraft by decreeing that no person should be attacked by a crocodile. In the 1930s such decrees were no longer believed to be effective.

Perhaps the fate of the *nkinda* and their guardians is best symbolized by the decline of the village of Mitima, ancient seat of the *ngeli* guardians and capital of the modern Banunu Chiefdom. Despite the political and ritual importance of Mitima, its population declined. In 1935 it could boast only 55 men, 70 women, 42 boys, and 52 girls, a total population of 219. In 1940 a Catholic missionary who visited Mitima noted that young people no longer wanted to live there. Five years later the population had declined to 123, only 59 of whom were adults.[27] Longwa recounted that the young men left because "the old men had died," a reference to the traditional practice of waiting until the father had died before moving away from the homestead.[28] By 1958 the entire Banunu Chiefdom contained only 475 adult males. The colonial administration decided that it was no longer administratively viable and abolished it.[29]

People who left the swamps usually settled in the towns along the riverbank. The growing attraction of the river towns

---

[26] Charles Liebrechts, *Souvenirs d'Afrique: Congo, Léopoldville, Bolobo, Equateur (1883-1889)* (Brussels, 1909), pp. 81–83.

[27] J. Paermentier, "Territoire Lukolela, Population du Territoire au 31 Decembre, 1935," BZA; U. Tackx, "Tournée dans les Banunu," 1940, DCMS; J. Calwaert, "Tableau Synoptique de la Population du Territoire de Lukolela au 26 Decembre, 1954," BZA.

[28] Interview: Longwa, 7-20-81, Tape 9/1.

[29] R.V. Godefroid, "Rapport d'Enquête en Vue de la Création du Secteur de Lukolela," 1958, DCMS.

will be examined in the next chapter. The analysis here will focus on the consequences of the migrations for the swamplands themselves.

Although some people simply abandoned their dams and ponds to settle in Bolobo or its surrounding towns, others adopted a compromise strategy by which they could enjoy the advantages of the river towns without giving up their swampland fishing grounds. The ideal resettlement site for such people was Yumbi, a town located on high bluffs at the point where the Zaire met the Moliba. Living in Yumbi gave people access both to the Zaire and to their traditional fishing grounds. During the 1930s and 1940s a series of small villages grew up on the bluffs of Yumbi with names identical to those that had been abandoned. Here is how one man described the move from Nsenseke in the swamps and the founding of the *quartier* of Nsenseke at Yumbi:

> In 1939 Bampomba got tired. All of his friends had died. All that remained was the children. He said, "Let us go to Yumbi. Other elders are already there. So we came to Yumbi. Bampomba became the *capita* of the *quartier* named Nsenseke. A lot of people then came to settle here, but Bampomba was here first. Some of the settlers came from Moliba; others came from Mitima; others came from Nkuboko. They came to build here after us—the people of Nsenseke. The *quartier* is called Nsenseke, but the inhabitants come from various places.[30]

In the early 1940s the government consolidated all of these villages into a single town of some 2000 inhabitants.[31]

Instead of making day trips to the fishing grounds as they had in the past, they now went out during certain seasons of the year to camp for weeks and even months. The abandoned fishing dams and ponds were seldom stolen because there was nobody left to take them. The settled life in the swamps was replaced by transhumance. Palm trees marked the locations of villages that had disappeared as the raffia houses disintegrated and bush encroached on the clearings.

---

[30] Interview: Bampomba, 7-18-81, Tape 7/1.
[31] *Co-Workers,* April, 1940, p. 1.

The people of Yumbi created a new work calendar and new work rhythms that allowed them to fish both in the swamps and in the river. As Bampomba explained the new system:

> In the second month, the period we call *mwanga*, everybody wants to go fish in the river. When *mwanga* finishes in the fourth month we all return to the swamps to fish with dams and traps. In the sixth month dam fishing is finished and we return to Yumbi. In the seventh month some people go out to fish in the river; other return to the swamps to spear fish. In the ninth month we go to fish in the swamps.[32]

For ambitious people like Bampomba who wished to maximize fish production, life was nomadic and difficult, as much of the year was spent at fishing camps either in the river or in the swamps. The old homestead sites in the swamps became known as camping spots, and the term *nganda,* meaning "camp," was commonly added to the old names.

The transhumant rhythms of the new fishing calendar contributed to the physical deterioration of the old fishing grounds. In the days when the swamps had been settled, the off seasons had been spent repairing the dams, dredging the ponds, and cleaning the paths in the brush where fish fences were to be placed. Because the town dwellers now used the off seasons to fish in the river, these maintenance activities were short-changed. As the years went by, dams began to erode and crumble, and ponds began to fill with silt. "The pond is dying," is the way Nunu express the silting process.

The major problem in the twentieth century swamplands was the opposite of what it had been in the nineteenth. Then, there had been an abundance of labor, but a shortage of fishing grounds. In the twentieth century, with the population crowded on the high bluffs overlooking the river, there was a shortage of labor. While ready hands could usually be found to participate in the harvest of a dam or pond for a share of the catch, maintenance activities, which took time away from river fishing, were frequently neglected. Not only were the ponds and dams dying, but the productivity of the swamps was dying as well.

---

[32] Interview: Bampomba, 7-18-81, Tape 7/1.

THE RIVER TOWNS

Although the people of the river towns experienced conquest, epidemics, and impositions similar to those of the swamplands, their responses to the new circumstances were very different. They successfully developed defensive strategies that mitigated the worst effects of colonial rule. The key to their success lay in their nomadic way of life, which allowed them to escape colonial impositions in ways that were not possible in the settled estates of the swamps. The people in the river towns thus describe their experiences of colonialism in very different terms than do the people of the swamps. Whereas the swamp dwellers visualize their colonial history in terms of degradation and decline, the river peoples focus on the strategies by which they resisted colonial intrusions into their lives.

The post at Bolobo which the International African Association (IAA) had established in 1882 had been built primarily so that the IAA could claim effective occupation of the middle Zaire. After the Berlin Conference of 1885 gave international recognition to the Congo Independent State that the IAA had founded, the Bolobo post was abandoned in order to cut costs. Four years later, however, the state began a campaign to recolonize the middle Zaire. The colonial administration sent out a force of 500 soldiers who traveled overland to conquer the east bank of the Zaire from the Pool to Bolobo. In April 1891, they burned and looted Bolobo before boarding riverboats to continue up the river. Although some of the chiefs quickly surrendered in order to save their towns, over a thousand raffia-fround houses were burned to the ground.[33]

As the flames of the houses lit up the night, the Nunu of Bolobo developed a defensive tactic that was to serve them well throughout the colonial period. Knowing that the Zaire River served as the border between the Congo Independent State and the French territories, they moved across the river and rebuilt their villages in an area that was under French jurisdiction, but was not under effective French administration. After living for two years on the French side, the Nunu guardians entered into

---

[33] W. Holman Bentley, *Pioneering on the Congo,* 2 vols. (London, 1900) 2:235; Grenfell to Baynes, April 23, 1891, BMS Archives, A-19.

negotiations with Congo Independent State representatives. Only when they were satisfied with the terms did they agree to resettle in Bolobo. Little by little they trickled back, though the wealthiest guardians such as Mangasa and Elema did not return until after 1908.

The exodus to the French side of the river may have been one of the reasons why the Bolobo area was not included in King Leopold's infamous Crown Domain. In 1896, the same year that the Crown Domain was established, a Baptist missionary at Bolobo wrote:

> In this neighborhood it is impossible for the State to even lightly tax the people, much less can they seriously coerce them, for at the very first appearance of restraint they seek refuge on the French side of the river. A few years ago there was scarcely a village of importance on the French side for upwards of four-hundred miles beyond Stanley Pool. Now there are several, and mainly formed by people who have fled the State administration. As the French do not attempt to administer . . . [the people] simply cross the river and rejoice in absolute freedom.[34]

The privileged status of the Bolobo-Yumbi Strip came to an end in November 1906, when the state granted a concession over all natural products on the left bank of the Zaire for the entire 360 kilometer stretch between Leopoldville and Yumbi to the American Congo Company.[35] By this time, however, the two largest concession companies in the Congo Independent State, Abir and the Société Anversoise, were losing money, and in 1906 they ceased operations, causing the American company to reconsider the advisability of beginning a rubber operation. More importantly, in 1908 the Belgian government took over the Congo and annulled all the rubber concessions. The American Congo Company never began rubber operations, although it did open a few small stores.[36]

[34] George Hawker, *The Life of George Grenfell* (London, 1909), p. 306.

[35] Heinrich Waltz, *Das Konzessionswesen im Belgischen Kongo,* 2 vols. (Jena, 1917) 2:407–27; *Le Mouvement Géographique,* 1906, see map between columns 594 and 595.

[36] Alexandre Delcommune, "La Situation Commerciale du Congo Belge," *Supplément au Mouvement Géographique,* no. 5, Jan. 30, 1921, col. 7.

The people of Bolobo nevertheless felt the burden of state impositions, as their town had become a supply station for passing steamers. In 1903 a missionary described the situation as follows:

> The State government here at Bolobo is almost entirely for the victualizing of the steamers passing up and down, these steamers being used mainly for the transportation of rubber from various points on the river to the Pool. The duties of the official in charge (a lieutenant) consist largely in inducing the people to bring in various food supplies. . . . This demand has been steadily increasing . . . . When on one occasion hints were thrown out that the people were, on account of the demands made upon them, on the point of running to the French side, the officer replied that if they were not useful to the State, they might as well be on the French side.[37]

The missionaries also observed that food procurements by state authorities were exacerbating food shortages in the area.[38]

Another critical need of the state was for wood to fuel the growing number of steamships traveling up and down the river. Fuel wood was first demanded as tax in kind, but later the state set up regular wood posts at Bolobo, Mistandunga, and Yumbi. The state officers asked the village chiefs to forcibly recruit young men to work as woodcutters. Those assigned to the wood post would cut twenty cubic meters of wood per week.[39] They were paid for the work, but they had no choice as to whether to work or not. During the 1930s, the government wood posts were supplemented by private wood stations set up by Portuguese merchants. Viegas set up wood stations at Bolobo, Mistandunga, and Yumbi; Mattos and Martins established wood stations at Bolobo.[40] In 1934 the wood posts in the Bolobo region sold over 52,000 cubic meters of wood.

Securing a wood supply for the steamers became a high government priority during World War II. In 1942 all adult males

---

[37] Scrivner to Baynes, 5-29-1903, BMS Minute Book, Bolobo.
[38] BMS Minute Book, Bolobo, Meeting of July 22, 1902.
[39] Interview: Lobwaka, 8-5-81, Tape 17/1.
[40] Rapport AE/Agri., Mushie Territory, 1938, MZA.

living within ten kilometers of a wood station were required to bring in fifteen cubic meters of wood per month, as were all other men not otherwise engaged in compulsory production. The following year the quota for this latter group was raised to 25 cubic meters per month. Many people migrated to the French side of the river or moved to Leopoldville to escape the woodcutting impositions. So many people left that they caused a serious drop in the wood supply. In Yumbi, the state responded to the shortage by rounding up every available adult male and putting them to work cutting wood.[41] So effective was the opposition to forced woodcutting that after the war the quotas were abolished and the wood stations relied largely on paid labor. In 1946 Bolobo alone had around 300 woodcutters, many of them Mboshi from French Equatorial Africa.[42]

Perhaps the most burdensome of the state impositions were those that affected the fishing economy. From early on the state had required Nunu fishermen to bring fish to the state post as tax in kind. However, it did not attempt to control the market for fish until after 1933, when it awarded licenses to certain Portuguese traders, thus giving them a legal monopoly on the fish trade.[43] Because the authorized fish buyers paid lower prices than those that could be obtained from African merchants, the fishermen avoided the authorized buyers as much as possible, preferring to participate in the free market.

The illegality of the free market, which colonial administrators referred to as the "black market," required Nunu fish traders to take extraordinary measures. Nsamonie explained how he operated.

---

[41] R. Van Acht, "Secteur Mistandunga, Subdivision des Batende," 1947, DMZA.

[42] Rapport AE/Agri., Mushie Territory, 1942, 1943, MZA. On flight from wood production see Interview: Enguta, 5-15-75, Tape A93. For a similar situation at Kwamouth, see Rapport Annuel, CEC Kwamouth, 1942, MZA. On number of woodcutters, see Rapport Annuel, CEC Bolobo, 1946, MZA.

[43] There was, however, an incident in 1920 when the state accused the Nunu fishermen of colluding not to sell fish to Europeans or their staffs. BMS Minute Book, Bolobo, November 17, 1920.

In Leopoldville the soldiers controlled things . . . . If you didn't
have a bill of lading they confiscated everything you had. We sold
our fish at camps on the sandbanks upstream from Leopoldville.
The idea was to sell everything before arriving in Leopoldville, to
arrive with just money and an empty canoe. In Leopoldville we
bought soap, kerosene, and cloth to bring back. There were large
riverboats on the river, but they were not hospitable to people.
They were only for whites.[44]

Soldiers were a constant threat to the Nunu fish merchants,
and Lila, who went to Leopoldville with his father in 1943, recalled hiding in the *bikoko* grass along the edge of the river for
hours with only his head above water until the soldiers passed
on.[45]

The government attempted to tighten its control over fishing
in the early 1940s when it established a post of the *Régie des
Pêcheries* at Bolobo. The *Régie* was in part a response to the
refusal of the Nunu to cultivate the 3000 square meters of peanuts per person that the state had imposed in 1936 as part of the
program of compulsory cultivation. In 1941, after long negotiations with the state, they were allowed to produce smoked
fish, which they were to sell to the *Régie*. The quantity of the
initial imposition is unknown, but by 1945, when impositions
were high because of the war, each adult male was required to
deliver 90 kilograms of smoked fish per year, which was equal
to 360 kilograms of fresh fish.[46] The problem was that the *Régie*
paid prices substantially lower than those obtained on the free
market. In 1943 and 1944, for example, the official price for fish
fluctuated between 1.3 and 1.8 francs per kilogram, while unauthorized local traders were paying 2.5 to 3.0 francs per kilogram. Fishermen who took their fish to Leopoldville could expect to receive at least double that amount.[47]

By 1946 only 254 fishermen had submitted themselves to
state control while another 200 refused. The latter were classi-
fied as unemployed persons and assigned obligatory tasks such

---

[44] Interview: Nsamonie, 7-8-81, Tape 1/1.
[45] Interview: Lila, 7-14-81, Tape 4/1.
[46] Rapport AE/Agri., Mushie Territory, 1936, 1943, 1945, MZA; R. Van
       Acht, "Secteur Mistandunga, Subdivision des Batende," 1947, DMZA.
[47] Rapport AE/Agri., Mushie Territory, 1943, 1944, MZA.

as cutting wood for riverboats and harvesting palm nuts. Most of these fishermen avoided these tasks by fleeing to the islands and living in fishing camps most of the year. By 1949 the number of rebellious fisherman had grown to 410 and the colonial officials were forced to admit that they could do nothing about them. The officials then devised a most ingenious way of solving their problem: they simply stopped counting the rebellious fishermen as part of the population of Bolobo. As far as the administration was concerned, they no longer existed.[48]

The resistance of the fishermen was extraordinarily effective. The 1947 economic report for the Mushie territory, which included Bolobo and Yumbi, estimated that only a tenth of the total catch was being sold to authorized buyers, the remaining 90% being sold to small African traders or taken directly to Leopoldville.[49] The 1949 Annual Report for Bolobo revealed the frustration of the colonial administration:

> Many fishermen live permanently on the islands and sell to passing river boats or to the illegal markets in Leopoldville and Brazzaville. They avoid all control and are reluctant to sell their fish to local markets because here they cannot obtain the exorbitant prices they get elsewhere. Their number has increased this past year as they were joined by some salaried workers who were attracted by the high profits of fishing, its independence, and its leisure time.[50]

During the 1950s, government reports noted that the fishermen of the Bolobo-Yumbi Strip were very independent, avoided all contact with the administration whenever possible, and earned good money from fishing.[51]

CONCLUSION

The different modes of life in the swamplands and along the river help to account for the differing responses of the two populations to colonial rule. Life in the swamps centered on the

---

[48] See the annual reports of the CEC Bolobo for 1946–49, MZA.
[49] Rapport AE/Agri., Mushie Territory, 1947, MZA.
[50] Rapport Annuel, CEC Bolobo, 1949, MZA.
[51] Rapport AIMO, Mushie Territory, 1950, 1954, MZA.

estate, a fixed piece of property protected by a charm and a guardian. When the estates came under attack from both epidemics and the colonial administration, their inhabitants perceived that the swamplands were becoming polluted by evil forces that were no longer held in check by the guardians and the *nkinda* charms. When ritual attempts to purify the land failed repeatedly, they saw little choice but to abandon the estates, often leaving the dams to crumble and the ponds to fill with silt.

Life on the river, in contrast, was nomadic, and this mobility was the key to riverine defensive strategies. Nunu economic life was centered on the river, not the riverbank, and the river was exceedingly difficult for the state to control. The Zaire is ten kilometers wide, and it is dotted with dozens of forested islands. Jurisdiction over the river was divided between Belgian and French colonial authorities. The Nunu fishermen could exploit their fishing grounds equally well from either bank, and they could live permanently on the islands if the need arose. Their strategy of retreat enhanced their bargaining power with the state, and it helped them to avoid or mitigate the burdens of rubber gathering, woodcutting, forced agriculture, and fish-buying monopolies.

Evidence that the Nunu had come to see the river as a more attractive place than the swamps is found in the mass migrations of the swampland people to the riverbanks in the 1930s and 1940s. This migration was a response not only to the troubles in the swampland estates, but also to perceived new opportunities along the river. The strategies developed by the riverine Nunu to exploit the new opportunities is the subject of the next chapter.

11. The opportunities

A s THE SWAMPLANDS were declining in population and production, the Nunu along the river were developing new tactics to prosper despite the restrictions imposed by the colonial state. They borrowed new ritual techniques to replace the declining power of the *nkinda* charms. They learned new industrial techniques and adopted new types of fishing nets to increase their production. They also exploited new markets. As the twentieth century progressed, the new tactics coalesced into a new form of big-man competition that dominated economic and social life along the river.

MISSION TECHNOLOGY

Missionaries from the London-based Baptist Missionary Society (BMS) had first visited Bolobo in July 1884, only two years after King Leopold II's International African Association had established a post there. Four years later George Grenfell returned to build a mission station in the open space between the Bobangi and Nunu towns of Bolobo. In the 1890s more missionaries arrived and built European-type houses. Bolobo became the depot for the two steamships owned by the BMS and the home of the BMS printing press on the upper river. The mission opened a school which enrolled 70 students by 1893.[1]

While the Baptists concentrated on Bolobo, Catholic missionaries focused their efforts on Yumbi. The Mill Hill Fathers opened a station in Yumbi in 1905, which they abandoned two years later.[2] After that the area received irregular visits from the

---

[1] George Hawker, *The Life of George Grenfell* (London, 1909), pp. 272, 277, 350.

[2] R.P. Hijboer, "Mill Hill au Congo," *Lovania*, no. 15 (1er trimestre, 1949):12–13; see also scattered articles in *Missiehuis te Roosendaal*, 1905–06.

Scheutist Fathers until 1929, when responsibility for the region passed to the Lazarists. In the early 1940s, the Lazarists reoccupied the abandoned mission at Yumbi, and they later built a mission station at Bolobo.[3]

The Nunu at first viewed the missionaries as otherworldly beings. When Bentley visited Bolobo in 1887, the Nunu were surprised to see his wife; they had scarcely realized that there were white women as well as white men. And they were utterly amazed by his child.[4] They wanted to know if white babies were born in the normal way. Bentley noted that people in the lower Congo had long believed that white people trafficked in human souls,[5] and such rumors had almost certainly reached the Nunu via the trade routes. The otherworldly status of the missionaries made them feared, but it also brought them respect.

The mission embarked on an ambitious program to bring not only new religious beliefs, but also new industrial techniques and new forms of health care to the middle Zaire. Dr. Girling began a medical practice in Bolobo in 1908, and by 1912 a mission hospital was operating. Mission education grew steadily, and by 1927 Bolobo boasted a nursery school, a primary school for boys, a primary school for girls, an industrial school, and a nursing school.[6]

Although at first the classrooms were filled mostly with the children of slaves, ambitious young Nunu began to recognize the potential advantages that mission education offered. By 1910 young people were coming to the mission schools from all parts of the swamplands and Nkuboko, and they often came despite strong opposition from their parents and village elders. Migration to the mission schools was becoming a twentieth century counterpart to the old migration to the frontier.

---

[3] "Rapport sur la Tournée Fait en Février et Mars 1935 le long des Rives du Congo et du Kasai," DCMS; "Rapport d'un Père de Scheut, 31-10-1922," DCMS; "Tournée Pascale dans la Chefferie des Batende, 1938," DCMS.
[4] W. Holman Bentley, Pioneering on the Congo, 2 vols. (London, 1900) 2:169.
[5] Bentley, Pioneering 2:252–53.
[6] Rapport, Territoire Pama-Kasai - Ensiegnement, 1927, DCMS.

The industrial school, in particular, helped to provide new tactics for prospering under the restrictions of the colonial economy. As George Grenfell explained in 1895:

> Under the old *régime* society was divided into two well-defined classes–the masters, who did the trading, mostly very smart business men, and the slave who did the work. Under the training of the missionaries, a third, and, as it has proved, very important class, has been developed–that of the wage-earning craftsman. Though for the most part this third class consisted of men born of slave parents, it was a class that, in response to training, furnished men who were able to build two-storied brick houses, work a Denny printing press, run a small steam saw-mill, or a small sea-going steamboat, and it can easily be imagined that though it did not constitute numerically a very important community, it was a very different one to be reckoned with as compared with that which furnished paddlers for their master's canoes.[7]

The skills taught in the industrial school were especially useful to the Nunu because the state monopoly on the ivory trade had created an interest in craft production. Because possession of carved ivory was legal, provided that the carver had purchased the raw ivory from the state, craftsmen in Bolobo began to make ivory canes, spoons, bracelets, and necklaces. The founder of the Bolobo ivory carving industry was Fataki Mbala, a Songye slave who had been liberated by the missionary George Grenfell in the course of his travels on the upper Zaire, and who worked as a handyman for the mission at Bolobo. A story told in Bolobo of the beginning of the ivory-carving industry holds that George Grenfell's cane broke and he asked Fataki to make him a new one. Fataki made the shaft out of wood, but he made the handle out of ivory from a hippopotamus tooth. Grenfell was so pleased with the cane that Fataki began to make others to sell to missionaries and administrators. Soon he started selling canes to the Europeans who came upriver on the steamboats that stopped in Bolobo to take on wood. With the cane manufacturing business prospering, Fataki taught the trade to two of his fellow mission employees:

---

[7] Hawker, *George Grenfell*, p. 389.

Lisasi Libondu and Bongudi. When Bongudi went with George Grenfell to England, he returned with a drill to make better joints between the ivory and the wood.[8]

The ivory-carving industry expanded significantly in the late 1920s as more and more people took up the craft. The variety of products increased to include bracelets, necklaces, spoons, and statues. When the production outstripped the market provided by the steamboats, merchants began to take ivory carvings to Leopoldville and sell them door to door in European sections of the city. Some ivory carvers moved to Leopoldville to be closer to their customers, while others moved to Brazzaville. The Zairian ivory carving industry was thus created.

The ivory that was carved was supposed to be purchased from state-authorized ivory merchants, but much of it was smuggled from various places. Nkuboko was an especially good source of ivory, and one of the most prosperous ivory hunters was Boketa, a Baptist catechist who possessed a modern rifle with which he hunted elephants in his spare time. The ivory of Nkuboko attracted even Portuguese traders such as Viegas, who smuggled it to Leopoldville. Still, the state tried to keep a watch over the ivory smuggling, and many ivory carvers in Bolobo suffered the same consequences as Mazeli, who was once fined and had a tusk confiscated by the territorial agent Gustin.[9]

The most successful ivory carver in Bolobo during this period was Eyongo, a man whose biography encapsulates many of the trends in Nunu society at the time. Eyongo had been born in Nkuboko in 1906. At the age of eleven, he heard that the Baptist catechist was starting a school in a nearby village, and he was eager to enroll. He proved to be a good student, and the pastor suggested that he go to the mission school in Bolobo to continue his education. Even though his father opposed the move, Eyongo attended school in Bolobo from 1917 to 1925 while working for the mission and learning masonry

---

[8] Interviews: Mbembo, 8-3-81, Tape 15/1; Eyongo, 8-3-81, Tape 15/1.
[9] Interviews: Lila, 7-14-81, Tape 4/1; Mbembo, 8-3-81, Tape 15/1.

and carpentry. After finishing his schooling, he worked as a carpenter in Bolobo for a couple of years; then he started carving ivory.

Around 1930 he organized a small company of ivory carvers who would produce and market their work as a group. Realizing that the demand for the work of his company went beyond the European quarters in Leopoldville and Brazzaville, he made a trip up the Zaire to Stanleyville to sell ivory, and later made a trip to Elizabethville, the capital of Katanga. One of the men from the company even went to Bujumbura, the capital of Burundi, with a cargo of carved ivory. The company was prosperous throughout the 1930s, after which Eyongo left the ivory business to become assistant chief of Bolobo.[10] Eyongo's progression from economic to political power thus paralleled the careers of Nunu water lords and traders in the nineteenth century.

Although ivory carving was the most prosperous of the new industries, it was not the only one. Lisasi, a friend of Fataki's, taught basket weaving, and later Sengele immigrants to Bolobo began making cane armchairs. By 1926 Bolobo had a cane chair factory.[11] The missionaries in Bolobo supported the new industries by acting as commercial agents for ivory carvers and cane-chair makers. By 1938 the missionaries were complaining that too much of their time was taken up by commercial activities, and that too much of their money was tied up in advances to local artisans on behalf of Europeans who wanted Bolobo-produced goods.[12] One index of the impact of craft production is that the 1952 census of Bolobo listed 277 ivory workers and 17 chair makers as opposed to 356 officially registered fishermen.[13]

Non-Christian Nunu explained the material success of the Christians in terms of the old trade-off between material wealth and human lives. The situation among the Nunu was similar to the one described by Wyatt MacGaffey for the lower Zaire:

---

[10] Interview: Eyongo, 8-3-81, Tape 15/1.
[11] Co-Workers, July, 1926, p. 8.
[12] BMS Minute Book, Bolobo, Sept. 20, 1938.
[13] Rapport Annuel, CEC Bolobo, 1952, MZA.

. . . those who joined the church were seen as having joined a purificatory or anti-witchcraft movement. As initiation fees they handed over, presumably, the souls of relatives, which the missionaries in turn exported to Mputu; in return initiates received schooling, or instruction in the new magic, whereby in due course they might themselves become rich.[14]

The Nunu along the river also discovered that the missionaries possessed useful techniques for health care. Although at first the Nunu had blamed the missionaries and the Congo State for the epidemics of the late nineteenth century, as time passed they began to view the missionaries as healers, not bringers, of disease. The mission hospital established in Bolobo in 1912 began to build up a reputation for healing, and the missionary doctors began to have an impact on sleeping sickness. In 1920 only about 4% of the people of Bolobo had sleeping sickness, while in the region south of Bolobo many villages had sleeping sickness rates of between 15% and 27%. By the mid-1930s the situation had improved remarkably all along the riverbank. Dr. Price reported that sleeping sickness was practically extinguished in the district around Tshumbiri, and Dr. Acres reported that the sleeping sickness rate in Bolobo was down to about 1%. In 1937 the mission opened a dispensary in Yumbi and immediately examined some 1700 people for sleeping sickness.[15]

The surveys were part of a major sleeping sickness eradication campaign that the mission had launched in 1934. It involved all the Nunu populations between Bolobo and Yumbi. Because control of the tsetse fly in this area of tropical rain forest was impractical, the mission doctors concentrated on early diagnosis and treatment of the disease. In the villages that were included in the campaign, each family was noted on an index card and subjected to yearly examinations. Infected individuals were asked to come to Bolobo or to the nearest injection center for a series of injections of tryponarsyl or tryparsamide. Of

---

[14] Wyatt MacGaffey, "The West in Congolese Experience," in *Africa and the West,* edited by Philip Curtin (Madison, Wis., 1972), p. 57.

[15] See *Co-Workers,* July, 1926, pp. 5–7; April, 1936, pp. 1–2; July, 1937; Oct., 1937, p. 13.

those treated, 80% to 90% were cured by the injections, and cured patients were examined frequently for signs of relapse. The first ten years of the campaign saw a decrease in the rate of new cases from 1.55% to 0.48%.[16] Such efforts did not go unnoticed by the Nunu, and the mission gradually acquired a reputation for promoting health instead of causing death.

It was just after the sleeping sickness campaign had begun in earnest that the first indigenous revival movement swept through the river villages. It began in early 1935 when Botendi, a carpenter at the Baptist mission, had a dream in which he was fishing with a line. Sensing a catch, he pulled on the line, and out of the water came a black buffalo followed by a red buffalo, and then a whole group of buffaloes. Each buffalo represented a person. The first one was Botendi himself, but the identities of the others were unclear. At the Sunday morning church service when Botendi got up to recount his dream, he began to speak in strange tongues. Two days later, a mulatto man with reddish skin recounted a vision in which the Holy Spirit descended on him. People remarked that the red buffalo of Botendi's vision had come forward; others would follow.[17]

In the month that followed, over a hundred others came forward to recount their visions and confess their sins. Some people gave back wrongfully gained money; polygynists gave up their extra wives; husbands and wives confessed adultery, often naming their embarrassed lovers in public; workers for the Portuguese merchant Viegas gave back goods they had stolen. Many people burned their charms or threw them in the river.[18]

People who had seen visions traveled to nearby villages to spread the movement. Upriver at Lukolela the number of men seeking church membership increased fourfold; the number of women increased elevenfold. New converts filled a canoe with

---

[16] Ian S. Acres, "A Study of Sleeping Sickness in an Endemic Area of the Belgian Congo over a Period of Ten Years," *Transactions of the Royal Society of Tropical Medicine and Hygiene,* 44 (1950):77–92.

[17] H. Engels, "Visionnaires – Bolobo: Notes de Renseignements," July 12, 1937 (document in possession of author).

[18] A. Windels, "Rapport sur les Visions à Lukolela et à Bolobo," 4/5/35 (document in possession of author).

charms and cast them overboard in midstream. In the hinterland of Bolobo, 400 people in one village began to prepare for church membership; in another village the number was 650. All in all, the Baptist missionaries reported "thousands of enquirers looking to the church for instruction and grounding in the faith."[19] Among the new converts were healers, diviners, and elderly women who had been initiates of local spirit-possession cults.[20]

By June 1936 the movement had run its course. No new visions were reported,[21] and some of the new converts had already begun to drift away from the church. Still, the visionaries movement marked a turning point in Nunu attitudes toward missions and Christianity. At first they had seen Christianity as a ritually dangerous force associated with epidemics and the ravages of early colonialism.[22] By the 1930s the mission was seen as a source of powerful techniques for gaining not only wealth, but health and security as well. The visionaries movement showed that Nunu were beginning to claim these new ritual techniques as their own, as gifts coming to them directly from God.

One result of the visionaries movement was the emergence of a new kind of indigenous healer. Unlike the traditional *nganga* diviners, who were thought to dabble in the dark arts, the new healers claimed to get their powers from God. They were called *batete,* which meant "prophets." The standard procedure for a prophet was to examine the patient, discuss the case with the patient's family, and then retire to a special hut to pray. It was believed that God would give the prophet a vision that would reveal both the cause of the illness and the best form of treatment.

---

[19] "Congo Currents: Baptist Missionary Society," *Congo Mission News,* Jan. 1936, pp. 9–10.

[20] *Co–Workers,* July, 1936, p. 1.

[21] A. Windels, "Bolobo: Suite Visionnaires: Mai–Juin, 1936" (document in possession of author).

[22] Many people held this view well into the 1930s; witness the case of the village that accused the missionary teacher of owning a crocodile. *Co–Workers,* July, 1939, p. 7.

Despite the new tactics by which Nunu Christians dealt with the spirit world, the fundamental paradigm of beneficent and malevolent forces by which they interpreted events in the everyday world remained fundamentally unchanged. The forces of evil were still defined by the metaphor of witchcraft. In 1949 John Viccars, a Baptist missionary in Bolobo, wrote an extremely perceptive article about witchcraft beliefs. He noted that:

> There is no doubt that belief in *boloki* [witchcraft] is extremely widespread to-day amongst all sections of the populace. Young and old people alike have clung tenaciously to the belief in the face of the white missionaries' opposition extending over sixty years.[23]

Viccars reported the words of a respected elder of the church who had been a mission employee for forty years. At a church meeting the man had asked:

> Is it wrong to accuse a friend of *boloki?* If we hear such accusations made by Church members should we remain silent? We all know that this matter still perplexes everyone now here. We believed the early missionaries when they told us that witchcraft was impossible, but the evidence of its working is always before our eyes.[24]

One reason for the persistence of witchcraft beliefs, Viccars suggested, was their role in explaining disparities in wealth. Although the missions had altered the tactics for getting wealth, they had not altered Nunu perceptions of the fundamental trade-offs involved in success. Viccars stated the trade-off in the following terms: "If a certain ivory worker sells his work as fast as he can do it, and at high prices, it is immediately taken for granted that he has surrendered some relative to the *baloki* [witches] as wages for their favorable intervention."[25]

Viccars' second reason involved the easy coexistence of witchcraft beliefs with modern health care. He cited the case of two men who came to the hospital at the same time with ulcers

---

[23] John Viccars, "Witchcraft in Bolobo, Belgian Congo," *Africa* 19 (1949):220.

[24] Viccars, "Witchcraft in Bolobo," p. 221.

[25] Viccars, "Witchcraft in Bolobo," p. 226.

on their legs. One man's ulcers healed quickly, but the other man's resisted treatment. The difference between the two cases was explained in terms of witchcraft: the malevolence of some witch was the cause of the second man's troubles. Hospital care and diviner's charms thus existed side by side. They were complementary sets of tactics for obtaining health.[26]

As the Nunu saw it, Christianity had not abolished the old forces of evil, but it had provided new techniques to keep them in check. In essence, the missions, churches, schools, and hospitals were doing the tasks that had once been left to the *nkinda* charms and the guardians of the land. Whereas the *nkinda* had created the conditions for prosperity in the old water lord competition, the missions were creating conditions that allowed people to prosper in the new economic order. Mission stations, in short, were becoming the twentieth-century counterparts of the old *nkinda* charms.

At the same time that the riverbank was coming to be perceived by the Nunu as ritually safe, the swamplands, for reasons explained in the previous chapter, were perceived as becoming ritually dangerous. Although the Christian message had been preached in the swamps with some success by indigenous evangelists, it had not had enough success to counteract the declining power of the *nkinda*. The differential impact of the missions on the river towns and on the swampland villages can be illustrated by comparing Bolobo, the emerging ritual capital of the riverbank, with Mitima, the old ritual capital of the swamplands. In 1929 Bolobo boasted a mission hospital and five schools. That same year a missionary who visited Mitima could claim to be only the second white person to have penetrated to the ritual heart of the flooded forest.[27]

FISHING INNOVATIONS

At the same time that the new techniques introduced by the missions were making the riverbank ritually safe, new fishing

---

[26] Viccars, "Witchcraft in Bolobo," pp. 226–27. On pluralistic medical care, see John Janzen, *The Quest for Therapy: Medical Pluralism in Lower Zaire* (Berkeley, 1978).

[27] *Co-Workers,* December, 1929, pp. 7–8.

techniques and new markets were making river fishing more lucrative than it had ever been before. Prior to the twentieth century, river fishing had been a poor alternative to swamp fishing. The river did not lend itself to the techniques of dam and pond fishing that were practiced with deadly efficiency in the swamps, and the yield of the fish traps depended largely on luck.

Net fishing had always been the most promising of the available river fishing techniques, but the traditional *malota* and *maya* nets, made from the fibers of the *nkosa* plant, had traditionally had three drawbacks. First, they were difficult to make. The fishermen had to procure sufficient quantities of the plant from the interior, extract the fibers from the bark, twist and roll the fibers together to make string, and only then could they make the net. Second, the effort required for making a net was not well rewarded because they rotted quickly. A fisherman sometimes used up two nets in a single fishing season. Finally, the weakness of the *nkosa* fibers prevented nets from being very long.

Net fishing got a major boost in the early twentieth century when Libasu, a mission worker who came from far upriver, introduced the *nsondo* net with weights on the bottom and holes about 10 centimeters square. Used correctly, it was highly effective in catching *mompongo, mololu,* and *elolo* fish. A second innovation was introduced by a certain Ngangabuka, who learned it up the river and taught it to people in Bolobo. The method used a special net with holes about seven centimeters square called *likoso*. It required two canoes and four men. It was used to catch *ebeye, mololu,* and *mboto,* fish that made a noise something like "bo, bo, bo," as they fed near the surface. Upon hearing the noise, the two canoes began to move in opposite directions, tracing a large circle around the fish as the fishermen let down the net. After they had closed the circle, one man took a long pole and slapped the water to scare the fish. As they tried to flee, their gills got caught in the net.[28]

The most revolutionary changes came during the 1920s. On a trip to Leopoldville, a Bolobo man named Mompango learned

---

[28] Interviews: Etebe and Ngamakala, 1-7-75, Tape A27; Etebe, 8-4-81, Tape 16/1; Lobwaka, 8-5-81, Tape 17/1.

to make and use a large, round cast-net from Senegalese traders. After returning to Bolobo, he had great success with the net, and soon he began to make them for sale. He also introduced imported cord for making nets. Cord nets could last up to four years, and their strength permitted them to be much longer than the old nets made from the *nkosa* plant.[29] This development launched a new round of experimentation and innovation in fish nets. Cord could also be used with imported fish hooks to string trotlines holding up to 300 hooks.

The basic technique of fishing with the long nets was to stretch them out across the current and let them drift downstream. Fish swimming against the current would try to go through the holes and get their fins caught in the mesh. Long nets allowed entire sections of the river to be swept, which was much more effective than the older techniques of traps, spears, and small nets. Young people liked the nets because they required less skill than the old techniques, which had demanded detailed knowledge of the habits of different species of fish. The nets were best used in the low-water season, when the fish were in the sand-covered main channels of the river and the nets could be stretched out without fear of catching them on bushes and grasses. Accordingly, July and August became the peak months of the river fishing season.[30]

As the new nets were making river fishing more efficient, the growth of new markets was making it more profitable. In Leopoldville and Brazzaville, two cities facing one another across Malebo Pool, the demand for fish had been growing rapidly since the beginning of the century. As early as 1909 reports from the French side of the river noted that all of the riparian villages up to the mouth of the Ubangi were bringing fish to Brazzaville, and the practices were similar on the Belgian side of the river.[31] Many Nunu became fishermen-traders who

---

[29] Interviews: Boloba, 5-14-75, field notes; Etebe, 8-4-81, Tape 16/1.

[30] Interview: Paul Jeanfaivre, government fish specialist, in Bolobo, 7-19-76, field notes. For a similar process taking place approximately 500 kilometers upstream from Bolobo, see Pierre Van Leynseele, "Les Transformations des Systèmes de Production et d'Echanges de Populations Ripuaires du Haut-Zaire," *African Economic History*, no. 7 (1979):126–29.

[31] ANSOM-Aix, AEF 4 (2) D 4.

fished until they obtained a canoeload of dried fish and took it
to the capital to sell. Others became full-time traders who visited fishing camps to buy fish for resale downstream.

One of the earliest participants in the fish trade was Elema.
After being driven out of the slave and ivory trade by the state,
he put his slaves to work fishing, and he sent the fish to Leopoldville to be sold. Elema employed a commercial agent, a
Likuba man named Nketa, to direct the trips to Leopoldville
and the selling of the fish. Relations between Elema and his
agent were not always smooth, as the profits from the trips
were not always as large as Elema wanted them to be.[32]

Large firms such as that of Elema were soon challenged by
smaller, independent operators. The situation had changed since
the nineteenth century, when the slave and ivory trade had required large organizations. It had taken large amounts of capital
to buy slaves and ivory, a network of contacts to beat out the
competition, and a fleet of large canoes to ward off attacks from
pirates. Fish trading, however, could be started with little capital and could be carried out on a small scale. In the twentieth
century there was little to fear from pirates. One example of the
new breed of fish trader was Mokoko, a fishermen who fished
mostly with weirs. He began to visit fishing camps to buy
smoked fish, and when he had enough to fill his canoe he paddled to Kinshasa with his sons to sell the fish. He would return
with cloth, soap, and salt, which he sold at Bolobo.[33]

The demand for fish increased steadily as the cities at Malebo
Pool grew and as fish production at the Pool declined due to
overfishing. Symptoms of overfishing first became apparent in
the 1930s, and by 1945 the French began unsuccessful efforts to
decrease the intensity of fishing. As production declined, the
fishermen at the Pool began using nets with finer meshes to
catch the small fish that had previously escaped, thus assuring
even smaller catches in the future.[34] The declining catches at the
Pool increased the demand for fish from the Bolobo area, as the

---

[32] Interview: Enguta, 8-3-81, Tape 15/1.

[33] Interview: Bopopi, 8-6-81, Tape 17/1.

[34] Gilles Sautter, De L'Atlantique au Fleuve Congo, 2 vols. (Paris, 1966) 1:265–
76.

Zaire offered poor fishing between the Pool and the Bolobo area because of its fast flow and barren riverbed.

The people of the river towns profited from their position between the downriver markets for fish and the inland cassava markets. In precolonial times, they had traded a portion of their surplus fish for cassava. Now, however, they sent most of their fish to the Pool, where much higher prices were offered, and they used some of the money thus earned to purchase cassava at the inland markets, where prices were low. Located between the cassava-growing regions to the interior and the urban markets down the river, the Nunu could profit from both. Some traders even bought cassava in the interior and sold it in Leopoldville.

The prosperity of the river towns was thus accompanied by the impoverishment of the people in the agricultural hinterlands. By the mid-twentieth century, fish were seldom sent from the river to the interior. This development caused a severe decrease in the amount of protein flowing toward the inland farming regions. Instead, money and trade goods flowed into the interior, while cassava flowed toward the river. If the people of the interior wanted to buy Nunu fish, they had to compete with the prices being offered by the fish merchants. In short, the inland peoples sold cheap and bought dear, while the riverine peoples bought cheap and sold dear. The result was a net gain for the Nunu, but a significant impoverishment for the inland populations.[35]

Whereas river fishing had once promoted an egalitarianism of poverty, the combination of a booming market and new techniques created a new egalitarianism of opportunity. In contrast to the old estates of the swamps, the waters of the river were open to everybody. People without canoes or nets could work for a kinsman or a patron until they had accumulated enough capital to strike out on their own. It was even possible to rent canoes and nets for a percentage of the catch. The new oppor-

---

[35] In 1938 one kilogram of dried fish at official prices sold for the equivalent of 16 kilograms of fresh cassava. At black market fish prices, the ratio would have been even higher. Rapport AE/Agri., Mushie Territory, 1938, MZA.

tunity offered by the river was a significant factor in migrations from the swamps to the river towns during the 1930s and 1940s.

As a result of increasing net fishing in the river, the riverine fishing grounds of the Bolobo-Yumbi Strip began to get overcrowded, just as the swamps had been a century earlier. In response to this development (and to the safety of travel afforded by colonial control of the river), the fishermen began to travel farther and farther afield during the dry season in search of available grounds in which to spread their nets. Fishermen from Bolobo began to appear along the Kasai in the 1940s. Their activities were viewed with suspicion by state officials:

> The fishermen from Bolobo seldom stay in one place for more than a month. They furnish a portion of their catch to the *Régie,* but the largest part is hidden away in places difficult to reach and far from their fishing camps. As soon as they have enough fish to fill a canoe, they leave in the dark of the night, and by morning they are out of danger.[36]

Other fishermen went upstream to the mouth of the Sanga and even to the lower Ubangi. The dry season diaspora was expanding to incredible proportions.

In the 1950s the fishermen began to make nets out of nylon cord, which was lighter and stronger than the old cord and was almost impervious to rotting.[37] Soon nylon nets up to 600 meters long with names like *cent kilo* and *motelesi moke moke* were in common use along the Zaire. It was said that a serious fisherman needed at least five kinds of nets in order to practice his profession.[38] However, the new nets were potentially detrimental to the environment. Whereas the precolonial nets had openings between four and ten centimeters across that allowed small fish to escape, nets with openings of less than three centimeters

---

[36] Rapport Annuel, Régie des Pêcheries de l'Etat, Mushie Territory, 1948, MZA.

[37] Service des Eaux et Forêts, "Aperçu sur la Pêche Lacustre et Fluviale au Congo Belge et au Ruanda-Urundi," *Bulletin Agricole du Congo Belge,* 50 (1959):1682–83.

[38] Interview: Nzembo, 5-13-75, field notes.

were common by the 1950s.[39] The experience of fishermen at
Malebo Pool in the 1930s and 1940s had demonstrated that
overfishing could cause catches to diminish, but as long as fishing remained lucrative, the fishermen along the middle Zaire
took little notice. Because the new nets were more effective
than the old ones, the catches seemed better than ever. Only
old men such as Etebe, who continued to fish with traps and
fish fences, worried about the environmental consequences.[40]

THE NEW BIG-MEN

By the middle of the twentieth century, the productive tactics
employed along the river differed remarkably from those of half
a century before. Individuals had the choice of craft production,
net fishing, or fish trading, all of which brought good returns.
Some people engaged in more than one activity, alternating according to the seasons. Some people engaged in all three. Along
with the new productive tactics went new social strategies.
Money had always been the key to riverine strategies, and in
the twentieth century people could invest their money in new
ways that would enhance their status and attract clients as well.
The new strategies involved consumer goods that could be obtained via the international market.

One item that became a prized commodity in the new big-
man competition was an outboard motor. Fishermen with outboard motors could not only travel farther to fishing camps,
but they could carry large quantities of fish to the Pool and
bring large amounts of merchandise back. One fish trader described his experience:

> In 1950 I bought a twenty-five horsepower Johnson outboard
> motor for 26,000 francs. In those days a basket of fish cost ten
> mpata (fifty francs) and you sold it for twenty mpata (100 francs). I
> put two large canoes together, side by side. Small merchants
> traveled with me, carrying their own goods. They paid me for
> carrying them and their merchandise.[41]

[39] Service des Eaux, "Apêrçu sur la Peche," p. 1679.
[40] Etebe, personal communication.
[41] Interview: Nsamonie, 7-8-81, Tape 1/1.

Those small merchants became, in effect, his clients. His canoes and motor provided the key to their livelihoods just as the old dams and ponds had supported clients in the swamps. An outboard motor was simultaneously a status symbol and a shrewd investment.

Another important item was a nice house. In the wake of the state-ordered destruction of the old bamboo houses and their replacement with wattle-and-daub houses in the late 1920s, some of the wealthier people began to build houses with corrugated iron roofs.[42] This trend was accelerated in 1948 when Eyongo, the state-appointed chief of Bolobo, built a cement block house with an iron roof and glass windows. He persuaded the Assistant Territorial Administrator to include Bolobo in the new government program of low-interest housing loans. The loan funds were extremely popular, and soon cement and iron houses were springing up all over town.[43] People who were short of funds would collect cement blocks and sheets of corrugated iron slowly over a period of years until they had enough material to build a new house.

Ambitious people built the biggest houses they could afford, or else they built a basic house and then added on little by little. Having a large modern house helped to attract clients. Young people who came to Bolobo and Yumbi for an education would seek to stay with a relative or a patron and help with chores to pay for their keep. Fishermen moving up and down the river according to the luck of the catches would often move in with kinsmen or friends for a month or two and share their catches with their hosts. People with large modern houses could easily attract such clients, whereas those with small houses had a more difficult time of it. Some homeowners even went into the house rental business, building modern houses and renting them out to gain income to build still another house. Like an outboard motor, a house was both a source and a symbol of success in the new big-man competition that had come to dominate river life.

---

[42] *Co-Workers,* December, 1929, p. 4.
[43] Interview: Eyongo, 8-4-81, Tape 15/1.

A variety of other European goods also came into demand. Women wanted sewing machines; men wanted bicycles. Eyongo, the ivory trader who had become chief of Bolobo, even purchased an automobile, as did several other wealthy citizens of the town. Lesser items such as cloth in Dutch wax prints could be purchased by people of more modest means.

The more money that men spent on such consumer goods, the less they could spend on direct social investments. Slavery had been abolished early in the twentieth century, and so the major remaining social investment was in wives. The 1952 census of Bolobo listed 1764 adult males, only 30 of whom had more than one wife. As a group, these 30 men had 68 wives, averaging slightly more than two wives each.[44] The decrease in polygyny was partially the result of missionary activity, but new strategies of gaining power and status through consumer goods played a significant role as well.

Despite the differences in wealth, strategies based on consumer goods did not bring about the types of social inequality that had existed in the old swamplands. The prized objects in the water lord competition had been dams, ponds, wives, and slaves, all entities that were perpetually in short supply. Because consumer goods existed in quantities much greater than the Nunu demand for them, the acquisition of a good by one person did not diminish the chances for another person to acquire a similar item. Each person was, in a sense, competing mainly against himself. Although the inhabitants of a town such as Bolobo exhibited every possible gradation from material poverty to great wealth, the rich did not directly control the poor.

CONCLUSION

Just as the calamities of colonialism affected the inhabitants of different environmental zones in different ways, the opportunities provided by new markets and new techniques had different impacts in different places. While the swamplands were being abandoned, a new form of big-man competition was develop-

---

[44] "Rapport sur le Fonctionnement du Centre Extra-Coutumier de Bolobo, 1952," Dossier Politique: Bolobo, MZA.

ing along the river. It employed techniques of Christian rituals, craft production, net fishing, and fish trading. As a result, the riverbank emerged as the new regional center of economic and ritual power. By the mid-twentieth century, the riverbank had been transformed from a fringe area to a new core, while the old core was progressively abandoned.

The process by which this change occurred was distinctly modern. In precolonial times, changes in the distribution of people over the land, caused mainly by demographic growth, had led to the development of new forms of big-man competition. In colonial times, however, the new form of competition along the river, which the Nunu had developed largely in response to the colonial state and the missions, helped to spark a redistribution of people over the land as people abandoned the swamp for the river towns. It was left to the Nunu themselves to work out the cultural meaning of their new relationship with the land. The struggle to do so would be carried out primarily in the political arena.

12. The battle

DESPITE THE VARIOUS forms of big-man competition that the Nunu had developed over the years, becoming a water lord with estates and clients had always been the Nunu ideal. It had defined the essence of what it meant to be a Nunu male. Even Nunu living in the fringe areas had proudly traced their ancestry back to the water lords in the swamps. But by the mid-twentieth century, old notions of core and fringe were being challenged. The traditional core area of Nunu settlement had literally become hollow, and it was the new competition along the river that was defining the parameters of Nunu life. The redistribution of people over the land forced the immigrants in the river towns to adjust their cultural ideals to the new realities.

This shift in the focus of Nunu identity from the swamp to the riverbanks carried with it the potential for an expanded eco-cultural identity. In contrast to the old swamplands, where a specific variant of big-man competition had been rooted in a geographically isolated micro-environment, the river extended far beyond the territory occupied by the Nunu. For a thousand kilometers upstream from Bolobo, the river environment was relatively uniform, and the strategies of fishing camps, nets, and commerce were common.[1] Notions of a larger riverine community were suggested by the continual mixing of river peoples at fishing camps. Fishermen from Bolobo would fish as far to the south as the Kasai and north as far as the lower Ubangi. Thus, the attachment to estate and homestead that had characterized the Nunu in the swamps was being replaced by the transient camaraderie of river peoples in fishing camps.

---

[1] See Pierre Van Leynseele, "Les Transformations des Systèmes de Production et d'Echanges de Populations Ripuaires du Haut-Zaire," *African Economic History*, no. 7 (1979), 125–29.

Individual musings about identity became transformed into a political ideology as a result of Belgian efforts to establish administrative chiefdoms in the late 1920s. The chiefdom, administered by a native chief, was the lowest unit of territorial administration. As an appointee of the colonial administration, the chief was the conduit by which orders from the colonial authorities concerning taxes, forced labor, required cultivation, relocation of villages, or any other issue were passed on to the inhabitants of the chiefdom. Conversely, taxes and free labor were passed to the colonial administration. Although in theory the colonial rulers were merely incorporating traditional chiefs into a larger administrative framework, in practice they were creating structures of authority that were very different from anything that had been known in precolonial times. The bureaucratic activities of the colonial chiefs bore little resemblance to the largely ritual activities of the precolonial Nunu guardians, and the colonial chiefs themselves were often people with no traditional claims to authority.[2]

The Belgians had appointed chiefs on an ad hoc basis as early as 1908, the year that the Congo ceased to be the private fief of King Leopold II and became a Belgian colony. The original chiefdoms were small, localized entities that raised no issues of ethnic jurisdiction. Along the river the Belgians established chiefdoms centered in the Nunu villages of Yumbi, Nkolo, and Bongende. In Bolobo, each component village was recognized as a separate chiefdom.

The problems began in the 1920s when the Belgians hoped to achieve greater administrative efficiency by creating new and larger chiefdoms. By forcing people to declare loyalty to a single political authority, they also forced people to make decisions about their ethnic loyalties. Their efforts to establish boundaries

---

[2] The chiefs of Bolobo illustrate this point. The first chief of all of Bolobo was Bongudi, a Christian from lower Zaire who worked as a mechanic on George Grenfell's steamboat. He was succeeded by his son Georges. The next chief was Liloko, a former slave of a prominent Bolobo trader. He was followed by Libondu, the son of a Christian Budja slave who had been freed by George Grenfell. The last chief of the colonial period was Eyongo, a native of Nkuboko who had studied at the mission school in Bolobo.

for the new chiefdoms and to select a chief for each unit revealed a profound difference between equatorial African and
European theories of political jurisdiction.

The political theory of the Nunu, like that of peoples in many
parts of Africa, had long distinguished between guardians of the
land and guardians of the people. According to this theory,
strangers who settled in an unoccupied part of a guardian's territory could continue to be governed by their own headmen
provided that they recognized the ritual control of the original
guardian over the land. Thus, when the Nunu settled along the
riverbank, they acknowledged the ritual control of the inland
Tio and Tiene chiefs by presenting them with a leg of every
animal killed.[3] But such recognition in no way implied that the
inland chief had authority over the people in the Nunu villages.

Although colonial authorities certainly understood such sub-
tleties,[4] they did not let their understanding interfere with the
application of government policy. Their approach was to determine which chief claimed control over a certain geographical
space and then to give him authority over all of the people in
that territory. The local guardians and elders quickly recognized
this fact, and they began to manipulate oral traditions in order

---

[3] Evidence left by George Grenfell and confirmed by some Nunu elders indicates that the inhabitants of Bolobo had indeed paid symbolic tribute to
the inland Tio chief after they first settled the riverbanks in the early nineteenth century. Shortly before the Europeans arrived at Bolobo in the 1880s,
the Nunu apparently fought a war with the inland chief. They won and the
tribute was never paid again. Diary of George Grenfell, April 15, 1888,
BMS Archives, London, A-18, shows that the Nunu had formerly sent a
leg of every hippopotamus killed to the inland chief at Bwema. This practice
had been discontinued shortly before the arrival of Grenfell. For oral traditions about the war between Bolobo and Bwema, see Jacob Enzonga's version published in La Voix du Congolais, no. 30 (Sept., 1948):378, reprinted
in Bibaki Ngomwana Wakawe, "La Cité de Bolobo," (Mémoire de Licence:
Zaire National University, 1972–73), p. 29. This same version is reprinted
without attribution in La Voix du Congolais, no. 138 (Sept., 1957):709–10.
See also interviews: Ngamakala, 3-18-76, Tape A80; Esankanga, 4-18-76,
Tape A94.

[4] See E. Cordemans, "Les Batende," 1929, DCMS; E. Cordemans, "Etude
Générale de l'Organisation Politique Coutumière de la Tribu des Bateke,"
1933, DMZA.

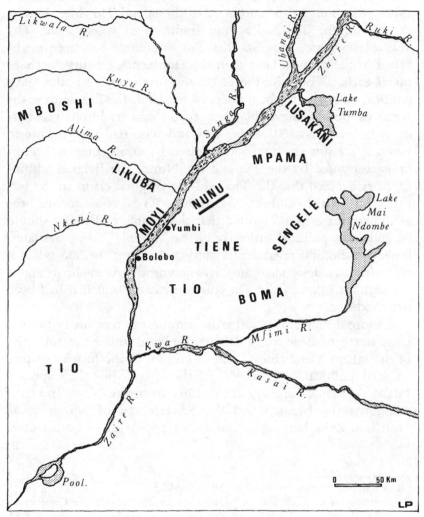

The Nunu and Their Neighbors

to bolster their claims. The government approach created a great deal of dissatisfaction among settler groups such as the Nunu, who lost the right to be governed by their own chiefs.

Bolobo lost its independent status in 1929 when it became a subchiefdom under the authority of the inland Tio chief. Unlike the Nunu, the Tio had a long tradition of chiefly rule. The available evidence suggests that Tio chiefdoms had been established in the area no later than the eighteenth century, perhaps much earlier.[5] Because the colonial administrative policy gave political authority to the owners of the land, the debate over the status of Bolobo inevitably focused on oral traditions recounting who had first settled the land and who had paid tribute to whom.[6] Despite the confusion caused by conflicting oral traditions recounted by the Tio and the Nunu, the Belgian administrators decided that the Tio held the original claim to the territory on which Bolobo was built. As a consequence, the administrator originally ruled that the people of Bolobo should be under the political authority of the Tio chief. Six years later, however, Bolobo regained its autonomy from the Tio when it was officially designated an "urban center." As such, its status was equal to that of the Tio chiefdom from which it had been detached.

A more difficult situation arose among the riverine Nunu villages north of Bolobo, which were placed under the authority of the inland Tiene chief. Little is known of the history or precolonial political organization of the Tiene, but they speak a Lualaba-Atlantic language (as distinct from the Nunu and their neighbors the Mpama and the Sengele, all of whom speak Northern Zaire languages[7]), and they appear to be both cultur-

---

[5] Cordemans, "Tribu des Bateke," 1933, DMZA.

[6] For examples of conflicting oral traditions on this subject, see Cordemans, "Tribu des Bateke," 1933; and the following interviews: Etebe, 8-4-81, Tape 16/1; Ebaka, 6-15-75, Tape A17; Wawa, 8-4-75, Tape A38. For a discussion of these traditions, see Robert Harms, "African Oral Traditions: Indicators of Changing Perceptions," in *The African Past Speaks: Essays on Oral Tradition and History,* edited by Joseph C. Miller (Hamden, Conn., 1980), pp. 194–97.

[7] This classification follows the system outlined in Jan Vansina, "Western Bantu Expansion," *Journal of African History,* 25 (1984):134.

ally and linguistically related to the Boma to the southeast. In precolonial times they apparently lived in small, scattered villages and had no political authority higher than the village headman. As a group, they claimed rights to the land up to the edge of the Zaire River, but they did not live near the water.[8] They feared the mighty river so much that, according to one Tiene tradition, it was taboo for them even to look at it.[9]

When the state conducted an investigation in 1927 to establish the boundaries of a new chiefdom, the Tiene sought the help of a Boma traditionalist to concoct a "tribal history." This history, largely borrowed from the Boma, was replete with tales of powerful chiefs in the past who had ruled over a united Tiene chiefdom.[10] The stories also claimed, probably rightly, that the Tiene had traditionally claimed the land all the way to the riverbank, and that the Nunu were merely squatters. The Nunu countered with "oral traditions" of their own that claimed Nunu settlement of the Bolobo-Yumbi Strip long before there had been any Tiene in the interior. It was the Tiene, they claimed, who were the interlopers. Despite Nunu protests, the boundaries of the new Tiene chiefdom were drawn to encompass the Nunu villages along the riverbank. The state officer chose Sankete, a teacher in a mission school and the grandson of a slave, to be the chief. Sankete duly received his medal in 1929.[11]

State support for the Tiene chief began to wane in 1933 when, as an expression of his own resistance to colonial rule, he "neglected" to collect taxes. Two years later a state investigation of Sankete discovered, among other things, that he had

---

[8] George Grenfell wrote that the Tiene were the "real inhabitants of the country." George Grenfell, "Mission Work at Bolobo, on the Upper Congo," *Missionary Herald*, Feb. 1, 1889, p. 49.

[9] See O.G. Renard, "Rapport d'Enquête Concernant la Création du Secteur de Mistandunga," 1943, MZA, and E. Cordemans, "Les Batende," 1929, DCMS.

[10] The Tiene elders disavowed these stories in 1937. They said that they had invented the "traditions" because they had been afraid of being subsumed by the Tio Chiefdom. H. Engels, "Batende: Autorité Coutumière," 1937, DCMS.

[11] R. Van Acht, "Secteur Mistandunga, Subdivision des Batende," 1947, DMZA.

no traditionally recognized authority over the Tiene (a fact they had known all along), that he had neglected to pursue a murderer who was at large in the area, and that he had again failed to collect the required taxes. When another inspection in 1937 revealed that the paths were overgrown with brush and the villagers were in hiding, Sankete was fired. His successor, Bomwale, also had bad relations with the state administration, mainly because of his tendency to issue orders contrary to those he received from the state agent in Bolobo.[12]

By 1942 the administration, thoroughly dissatisfied with the performance of the Tiene chiefs, began to be receptive to Nunu demands for autonomy. The state proposed that the Tiene chiefdom be dissolved to be replaced by a "sector." In the administrative jargon of Belgian colonialism, a sector, in contrast to a chiefdom, was formed in a multiethnic area where each ethnic group was too small to qualify for its own chiefdom. A sector was subdivided into ethnic "groupings." The new sector, named the Mongama Sector, was to be subdivided into a Tiene grouping and a Nunu grouping. A major argument in favor of the new arrangement was that the Nunu population in the sector had become nearly equal to the Tiene population as a result of the continuous influx of immigrants from the swamps.

The Tiene opposed the new arrangement, primarily because the creation of a Nunu grouping meant that the Nunu were recognized by the state as the owners of the land near the river. By losing political control over the riverbank, the Tiene also lost title to the lands along the river. The situation was aggravated by the fact that some Tiene were beginning to settle along the river to participate in the increasingly lucrative fish production and trade, and they would be ruled by a Nunu chief. Tiene opposition to the new arrangement was so strong that Bomwale, the chief of the defunct Tiene chiefdom, was banished from the region, and soldiers occupied the Tiene area for two months.

In order to placate the Tiene, the state chose a Tiene soldier, Mambiala Timothée, as chief of the Mongama Sector. A Nunu man was appointed to be chief of the Nunu grouping and also

---

[12] R. Van Acht, "Secteur Mistandunga, Subdivision des Batende."

to serve as assistant chief of the sector. Bomwale was to be brought back from exile to serve as the chief of the Tiene grouping. A 1947 government report noted that peace reigned between the Tiene and the Nunu.[13] But the Tiene were only waiting for the appropriate moment to renew the struggle.

The struggle over chiefdom boundaries gave a political dimension to the cultural distinction between river people and land people, thus establishing a political rationale for the development of a larger riverine identity. The first step in this expansion of Nunu identity was the cultural incorporation of the Bobangi. In the nineteenth century the two groups had engaged in very different economic activities and had maintained distinct identities. The Nunu had encapsulated the essence of the relationship in a song:

> Do not descend the river channels
> The Bobangi have blocked the route.[14]

The song referred to the eco-cultural division whereby the Bobangi were lords of the river and the Nunu were lords of the swamp. In practice, it meant that the Bobangi maintained a monopoly on long-distance trade along the river. When the Nunu tried to get into the river trade in the nineteenth century, this division was a constant source of tension. In Bolobo, the Bobangi had a term, *mokwata,* a worthless person, by which they referred to the Nunu. Bobangi and Nunu seldom intermarried, and they rarely set up fishing camps on the same island.

All of this began to change in the colonial period. Having lost their slaves and been forced out of the ivory trade by the colonial administration, the Bobangi adopted strategies of net fishing and small-scale trade. They were, in effect, playing the same game as the Nunu. The two groups began to intermarry, and by the early 1930s a colonial officer could report that there were no ethnic tensions in Bolobo.[15] The merging of identities was

---

[13] Van Acht, "Secteur Mistandunga, Subdivision des Batende."

[14] Interview: Lila, 7-12-81, Tape 3/1. Lila explained that the song meant that Botoke, the founding ancestor of the Bobangi, was lord of the river.

[15] Gustin, "Avant Propos aux Propositions de Création de Centre Extra-Coutumier de Bolobo," n.d., DMZA.

aided by the missionaries, who used Bobangi as the language of evangelism and of education. In 1899 John Whitehead had produced a grammar and dictionary of the Bobangi language,[16] and throughout the colonial period the printing press at Bolobo turned out school textbooks written in Bobangi. Although the language spoken by the Nunu had been very closely related to that of the Bobangi, there had been dialectal differences that were being blurred by education.

In the wake of the struggles over the chiefdoms, Nunu leaders along the river began referring to themselves as Nunu-Bobangi. The addition of the term "Bobangi" not only created a political coalition among the two riverine groups along the Bolobo-Yumbi Strip, but it also had important implications for the stretching of Nunu identity. Whereas the Nunu had traditionally occupied a small geographic area, the Bobangi had been scattered along the river from the lower Ubangi to the mouth of the Kwa River. The addition of the Bobangi name therefore created a larger cultural identification with the peoples of the middle river.

Ironically, the Bobangi name was spreading at a time when the Bobangi population itself had practically disappeared. In the nineteenth century the Bobangi had experienced an almost zero birthrate and had kept up their population by buying slaves.[17] By stopping the internal slave trade the colonial administration had, in effect, decreed the end of the Bobangi as an ethnic group. By 1952 most of the Bobangi had died, leaving no children. The 1952 census listed only 57 adult males, down from 278 in the early 1930s.[18]

The trend toward a larger river identity was accelerated when oral traditions stressing the unity of a variety of river peoples

---

[16] John Whitehead, *Grammar and Dictionary of the Bobangi Language* (London, 1899).

[17] For a discussion of the reasons behind the low birthrate, see Robert Harms. "Sustaining the System: The Trading Towns along the Middle Zaire," in *Women and Slavery in Africa,* edited by Martin Klein and Claire Robertson (Madison, Wis., 1983), pp. 95–110.

[18] "Rapport sur le Fonctionnement du Centre Extra-Coutumier de Bolobo," 1952, Dossier Politique: Bolobo, MZA.

began to be told in the Nunu river towns. It is difficult to determine just when these oral traditions emerged. None of them were collected by colonial administrators when they set up the chiefdoms in the 1920s and 1930s, but by the end of the colonial period they were being written down and disseminated among the Nunu. These stories constituted what Thompson has called political mythology in that they were the historical underpinning of a political ideology.[19]

The first written history of the Nunu was produced by Vincent Bokono, a male nurse at the Baptist hospital at Bolobo. He was the grandchild of Mayenga, who had reportedly settled in Bolobo at the time of Monyongo. In 1956 he wrote a pamphlet in the Bobangi language, the title of which can be translated as "Book of the Voyages of Our Ancestors on the River Congo, and Story of the Chiefs and their Wars."[20] The manuscript was typed in several copies in 1960 and distributed to Nunu leaders. Bokono also prepared a version in Lingala, the regional language spoken by all the river people. The Lingala version had a title that proclaimed the pamphlet to be a history of the "Black People of the Zaire River." Underneath the Lingala title was a French subtitle: "*Histoire Haut-Antiquité des Habitants du Fleuve Zaire en* 1418 *à* 1960." Below that was the claim: "Edition Baptist Missionary B.M.S. par G. Grenfell en 1901 à Bolobo."[21] Bokono claimed that the text had originally been written in 1901 by the missionary George Grenfell, who had given it to Bokono's grandfather. It had later come down to Bokono who recopied it and had it typed. The claim of Grenfell's authorship was a piece of fiction designed to lend authority to the pamphlet.

The history itself was organized around a core cliché, a stereotyped story, which by the time I did fieldwork in the mid-1970s was so widely known among the Nunu that it was im-

---

[19] Leonard Thompson, *The Political Mythology of Apartheid* (New Haven, Conn., 1985), p. 1.

[20] Vincent Bokono, "Monkama mo Mibembo mi Bankoko o Ebale e Congo, Bibo be Makonzi na Bitumba bi Bango" (Typescript: Bolobo, 1960).

[21] A copy of the Bobangi version is in the possession of the author. The Lingala version is on microfilm. See DCMS.

possible to determine how it originated or spread.[22] The cliché described the migrations of a group of ancestors from the Ubangi who descended the Zaire River together, with different members of the group stopping off at various points to found ethnic groups. Bokono's history in this way accounted for the common origins of seven ethnic groups in the middle river area: Lusakani, Mpama, Likuba, Mboshi, Bobangi, Moyi, and Nunu.

In many cases the story given by Bokono differed from the stories told by the groups themselves. Bokono, for example, wrote that all seven groups came from the Ubangi, whereas the Lusakani themselves claim an origin in the Maringa River valley, the Mpama claim a homeland along the lower Sanga, and the Mboshi claim to have migrated overland from the east to arrive at their present location.[23] Moreover, Bokono presented the Nunu and the Bobangi as equal partners along the river, whereas Bobangi oral traditions emphasized Bobangi dominance of both the river and the Nunu.[24]

Despite the contradictions between Bokono's history and the oral traditions of the other river groups themselves, the pamphlet accomplished two goals. First, it articulated a vision of a larger identity group of which the Nunu were a part. The new form of big-man competition based on river fishing and trade was now supported by a new mythology. Second, it advanced

---

[22] For written versions of this story, see Bokono, "Monkama mo Mibembo," typescript in possession of the author; Bompinda, Fédor, testimony, in "Procés-Verbal d'Audition sur le Conflit du Pouvoir Coutumier," 1971, MZA; J.J.L. Lingwambe, "Histoire Banunu-Bobangi" (mimeographed pamphlet: Kinshasa, 1966), pp. 1–3; Lila Ndut'e Bamani, "Ekumela e Banunu-Bobangi," manuscript in possession of the author. All of these versions are in substantial agreement with one another.

[23] On Lusakani, see "Chefferie des Lusakani," 1925, MRAC-E, Prov. Equateur, Dist. Equateur, Terr. Bikoro, 7. On Mpama, see A. Windels, "Chefferie des Pama-Bakutu," manuscript in possession of the author. On Mboshi, see Théophile Obenga, La Cuvette Congolaise (Paris, 1976), pp. 5, 51; Gilles Sautter, De l'Atlantique au Fleuve Congo, 2 vols. (Paris, 1966) 1:246.

[24] Interviews: Ebaka, 6-15-75, Tape A17; Wawa, 8-4-75, Tape A38; Bomele, 9-25-75, Tape A57; Yangawa, 3-21-76, Tape A81; Mambula, 5-3-76, Tape A96.

Nunu claims to being the owners of the riverbanks on which they had settled. The dichotomy between river people and inland people, which lay at the heart of the new mythology, would be an important weapon in future political struggles.

But the new mythology also created a dilemma because the Nunu were themselves divided between river people and land people. As the 1950s came to a close, the geographical division was becoming less and less important—by then most Nunu lived in the river towns—but the ideological division remained. While members of old riverine families enthusiastically supported the new riverine ideology, many of the recent immigrants still retained a strong identification with the old estates. For them, identification with the larger world of the river peoples constituted a denial of their swampland heritage. Other immigrants, however, embraced the new mythology. The Nunu of the river towns were thus split into two ideological camps.

With the approach of political independence in the late 1950s, the ideological conflict became transformed into a life and death struggle over the spoils of political power. This contest forced the Nunu living in the river towns to choose between the old eco-cultural identity that focused on ties with the old estates and the new eco-cultural identity that stressed the river and the unity of its peoples. The narrative that follows will thus focus on three political issues that precipitated the Nunu identity crisis: the reforms of 1957, the accession to independence in 1960, and the creation of *provincettes* in 1962. By forcing the Nunu to make decisions about their eco-cultural identity, these political issues divided the Nunu community and ultimately led to civil war.

REFORMS AND INDEPENDENCE

The reforms of 1957 constituted a rather vague attempt by the colonial administration to make local government more democratic. At the time the reforms were announced, the colonial administration had no idea that the country would be independent by the time they were fully implemented. The reforms limited the term of a chief, abolished the position of assistant chief, and created a *collège permanent,* a body that would assist the chief in his daily administrative duties. Because the exact arrangement in any locality was left to the local state officer, the reforms were applied in different ways in Bolobo and in the Mongama sector. In both cases, however, they created tensions that would continue even after independence had been achieved.

Bolobo

In Bolobo the decree was implemented by the state agent, who appointed Eyongo, the sitting chief, to a five-year term, fired Ngondola, the assistant chief, and announced city-wide elections for the town council. By this act he created a split among the Nunu of Bolobo that was to animate local political strife for the next eight years. The problem was that Ngondola, the assistant chief who had lost his job, was from an old Nunu family that had settled Bolobo in the nineteenth century. His identity as a river person was total and long-standing. His rival, Eyongo, who had just been appointed to a five year term, had been born in Nkuboko and strongly identified with his kinsmen who remained in the innermost reaches of the swamps. After Ngondola lost his job, he began to agitate to replace Eyongo; he argued that the town should be governed by a native of Bolobo rather than an immigrant from Nkuboko. Although this agitation did not seriously threaten the position of Eyongo, who had already been appointed to a five-year term as chief, it did cause both men to look for support within the community, and it caused a split between those Nunu who still looked toward the swamps for their cultural identity and those who looked to the river.[25]

The immediate test of strength between the two factions was the upcoming city council election. Each quarter in the town was to elect a councilman, and two of the councilmen would become members of the *collège permanent*. This body's main function was to assist the chief in his daily administration. The council would also have an important voice in the choosing and firing of chiefs. Ngondola, who had lost his job, decided not to run for the city council himself, but to support his son, Momai,

---

[25] Bibaki Ngomwana Wakawe, "La Cité de Bolobo" (Mémoire de Licence: Zaire National University, 1972–73), p. 26.

who was better educated and who could thus more effectively represent the riverine faction. As the election neared, the two groups put up candidates for the city council. The immigrants from Nkuboko supported candidates favorable to Eyongo; the riverine Nunu favored Momai, who pledged to work for the ouster of Eyongo if elected to the *collège permanent*. Both sides sought to form coalitions with the Tiene, Tio, and Sengele minorities that had settled in Bolobo during the colonial period. (It is not surprising that the Sengele, who had close relations with the Nunu of Nkuboko, supported the Nkuboko faction in Bolobo politics.) When the election was held in 1959, the Nkuboko faction lost heavily, and Momai, supported by the riverine faction, became a member of the *collège permanent*.[26]

What had started out as a fight over local political offices escalated in 1960 when the Round Table discussions in Brussels resulted in the unexpected announcement of Congolese independence to come on June 30, 1960. In May 1960 there would be an election for the provincial assembly of the new independent nation. Various political parties scrambled to gain the allegiance of the Nunu, and again the Nunu split along eco-cultural lines. The immigrants from Nkuboko, led by Eyongo, supported the Lumumba branch of the *Mouvement National Congolais* (MNC), the only truly national party. The riverine Nunu, led by Momai, supported the *Parti de l'Unité Nationale* (PUNA), which set up offices in both Bolobo and Yumbi.

Adherence to PUNA represented a further increase in the scale of cultural and political identity for the riverine Nunu. Like most political parties formed in the Congo at the time, PUNA had an ethnic base. It was the party of the people known as Bangala, a loosely defined term that the Belgians had used to designate the fishing peoples between the mouth of the Ubangi and Stanley Falls. The myth of Nunu origin written in Bokono's history had promoted the unity of the river peoples below the mouth of the Ubangi, but adherence to PUNA would unite all the river peoples of the middle Zaire. In order to give political structure to this ethnic unity, PUNA advocated

---

[26] Bibaki, "Cité de Bolobo," pp. 27–28.

the creation of a new province stretching along the riverbanks
that would unite the river peoples.

Bolikango, the leader of the PUNA party, had forged close
ties with the riverine Nunu. When he went to the Round Table
discussions in Brussels in early 1960, he took along as his secretary a Nunu from Bolobo. The way in which Bolikango
viewed the Nunu can be seen in a statement he would make in
the House of Representatives two years later:

> Mr. Manote speaks in his report of the Bangala who live in the
> Lake Leopold II district. Each time someone makes an allusion to
> that ethnic group, I always see myself as obligated to defend
> them. . . . I insist on the fact that the Banunu–Bobangi are mine.[27]

The coming of independence and the prospect of a radical
restructuring of local governmental institutions prompted the
riverine Nunu to escalate their campaign against Chief Eyongo
and his Nkuboko supporters. Momai told the people of the
town not to pay taxes because the Lumumba government was
only temporary; everything would change when PUNA took
power. He even gathered up the identity cards of his supporters
to make sure that they did not pay local taxes. The drive was
so successful that in late 1960 the city offices closed for lack of
funds.[28]

Eyongo and his Nkuboko supporters lacked adequate popular
support. When an order came from Mushie in October to hold
a new election for chief, the council cast four votes for Momai
versus none for Eyongo. Before he could assume office, however, Momai received word from Mushie that he had been appointed *chef de poste* of Bolobo to replace the European administrator who had left. In colonial times the job of the *chef de
poste* was to oversee the work of the African chiefs, and so this
meant a promotion for Momai. One of his first official acts was
to order the arrest of ex-chief Eyongo, who had retained an

---

[27] J.C. Williame, *Les Provinces du Congo: Nord Kivu–Lac Léopold II*, Cahiers
Economiques et Sociaux, Collection d'Etudes Politiques, no. 3 (Leopoldville, 1964), p. 107.

[28] Eyongo, 9-2-1960, DMZA; "Population de Bolobo," 10-21-1960, DMZA;
Telegram, 6-9-61, DMZA.

important following despite his ouster from office. In fact, Eyongo was telling people that he was merely on vacation, and that he would be back in office soon. The police chief refused to make the arrest, and Eyongo remained a free man.[29]

The Nkuboko faction reassumed power in 1962 when personnel changes at the administrative headquarters in Mushie and Inongo brought people who sympathized with Eyongo and his Nkuboko faction. Momai, the *chef de poste,* was accused of financial irregularities and transferred to Mushie. The man who had replaced him as chief of Bolobo was also accused of financial irregularities and was fired. The new *chef de poste* was a Sengele man who sympathized with the Nkuboko faction.[30] He simply appointed a new chief and three new city councilmen, all supporters of Eyongo and the Nkuboko group.

The forced reinstallation of the Nkuboko faction was not a popular move. The PUNA party held large meetings in Bolobo at which the town officials were regularly denounced. The new chief, Ngambomi, was unsuccessful in his attempts to collect taxes. Territorial officials declared Bolobo to be "ungovernable."[31] Still, the new chief was not entirely impotent. When a smallpox epidemic broke out, he ordered the houses of suspected witches to be burned. One of the houses set ablaze belonged to the father of Momai.

The Mongama sector
North of Bolobo in the Mongama sector, things were no less tense. In implementing the 1957 reforms, the state administrator did not have to deal with incumbents because the sector chief, who was getting old and blind, agreed to step down, and the assistant chief had recently died. The state administrator, for purely administrative reasons, chose Paul Kumbale, an educated Tiene man who had previously served as secretary of the sector, as the new sector chief. For the Nunu and Tiene groupings that made up the sector, he decided that new "customary" chiefs were needed. He called meetings of Tiene and Nunu "notables"

---

[29] Bokeyala, 10-26-1960, DMZA; Kuzengedila, 1-3-1961, DMZA.
[30] Bibaki, "Cité de Bolobo," p. 45.
[31] Ngambomi, 8-3-1962, DMZA; Telegram, Mushie, 10-29-1962, DMZA.

to choose the new "customary" chiefs. The Nunu chose Fédor Bompinda, an itinerant trader from Yumbi, and the Tiene chose Paul Mbongo, a male nurse who worked in the hospital at Bolobo.

Mbongo, the new "customary" chief of the Tiene grouping, had political ambitions. In order to gain the solid support of the Tiene, he called for the reestablishment and the enlargement of the old Tiene chiefdom. At his installation in January 1959, he made a speech pressing Tiene claims to the land occupied by the Nunu.[32] In November of that year, he went to Leopoldville to present his claims to the governor of the province.[33] He left the meeting hopeful that he would succeed in getting the riverside land occupied by the Nunu returned to Tiene jurisdiction.

Bompinda, the new "customary" chief of the Nunu grouping, likewise had political ambitions. As an active supporter of Bangala unity, he disliked being under the authority of a Tiene sector chief, and he sought to create an independent Nunu chiefdom. He was a solid supporter of PUNA, which opened an office in Yumbi in early 1960. Immediately after the Congo became independent, he announced to the people of Yumbi that the central government had given him independent authority over the Nunu. To implement this newly claimed authority, he personally hired six judges and two policemen who worked for him alone. To gain popularity, he legalized the poison ordeal as a way of suppressing witchcraft. To increase his base of support, he encouraged Moyi and Mboshi from the French Congo to move into Yumbi.[34] The ethnic ties celebrated in Bokono's "history" solidified into concrete political alliances.

Bompinda actively rejected any symbolic recognition of Tiene guardianship of the land on which Yumbi was built. Shortly after independence, he ordered all the palm trees in Yumbi to be cut down. This was an act of defiance against the Mbieme Mayala, the Tiene guardian who claimed ritual own-

---

[32] Procés Verbal d'Audition sur le Conflit du Pouvoir Coutumier, 5-7-1971, DMZA.

[33] J. Luste, 1-9-1960, DMZA.

[34] Mwata, 9-29-1960, DMZA; DMZA; Kumbale, 10-21-1960.

ership of all the trees of Yumbi.[35] The symbolic defiance escalated in August when the Tiene guardian died. In preparation for the funeral, the Tiene followed their custom of harvesting a little food from each field on the land claimed by the deceased guardian. Denying the dead guardian's claim to the land near the river, Bompinda forbad the customary symbolic harvest on lands under his jurisdiction. Tension rose to the point at which numerous fistfights broke out.

The territorial officials in the newly independent government were disturbed by Bompinda's attempt to create de facto an independent chiefdom. To reassert their authority, they arrested him for cutting down the palm trees and kept him in prison for 17 days. When he returned from prison, he renewed his call for an independent Nunu chiefdom, and he ordered the Nunu not to pay taxes to representatives of the sector chief. Instead, they were to wait for the formation of a new province that would unite all the Bangala peoples. In July 1961, the territorial officials ordered Bompinda arrested, but he fled to Leopoldville and used his political connections to get the order rescinded.[36]

Although Bompinda's defiance of the sector chief and the territorial authorities was popular with the majority of the Nunu, there was a substantial minority that disapproved. These were mostly recent immigrants from Nkuboko who did not want to see the riverbanks separated from the inland regions. Many of them paid their taxes despite Bompinda's orders to the contrary. As a result, they found themselves insulted and threatened in bars and on the streets.[37] By 1962 many of these people supported the Association Banunu-Bobangi, which opposed the creation of a separate river province and called for the removal of Bompinda. Thus, in the Mongama sector, as in Bolobo, the Nunu were divided into two factions: one that identified with the river peoples, and one that wished to maintain ties with the inland regions, especially the swamps and Nkuboko. Again, popular opinion favored the river faction.

---

[35] Mwata, 9-29-1960, DMZA; Mbongo, 8-2-1960, DMZA.
[36] Bompinda, 11-2-1960, DMZA; Representatives of Banunu-Bobangi, 1-6-1961, DMZA; Mbo, 6-11-1961, DMZA; Telegram, 7-11-1961, DMZA.
[37] Lingwambe, 10-26-1962, DMZA.

THE *PROVINCETTES*

The conflicts simmering in the Bolobo–Yumbi area escalated in 1962, when the entire country was divided into 21 small provinces, or *provincettes,* as they were called. This move was largely designed to secure power bases for the various ethnically based political parties and to better distribute the political spoils of national independence. The Congo would become a loosely organized federation, and the highest office in each *provincette* bore the title of "president."

One of the proposed new provinces consisted of a long narrow strip of land that ran along the Zaire River for over a thousand kilometers from Bolobo upstream to past Lisala. This province would not only unite the river peoples politically, but also give them unquestioned rights over the land along the river. The problems encountered by the Nunu of the Bolobo–Yumbi Strip are but one example of the kinds of problems caused by colonial chiefdom organization all along the river. Everywhere the river people were essentially squatters on land claimed by the inland populations, and this fact, according to colonial administrative theory, disqualified them from having their own chiefs. The proposal of a province called Moyen Congo (Middle Congo) was the united response of the river people to this situation. They would put themselves in a separate province from their inland neighbors, and their claims to sovereignty over the land on which they lived could never again be questioned.

The cause of the Moyen Congo province had been championed by Bolikango and the PUNA party. Moyen Congo would be more than a province; it would be a quasi-state with its own president, and would be loosely federated with the other states of the Congo. The formation of the province would give substance to the political ideology of Bangala ethnicity; the cultural unity of the river people would have a political framework. The Nunu participation in the notion of a larger Bangala cultural identity can be seen in a petition signed in 1962 by a delegation of river people that included Nunu from Bolobo and Yumbi. The declaration ended by saying:

Our populations are firmly dedicated to see their regions
integrated purely and simply into the province of the Bangala
from whence they originated.[38]

Not only physically, but also psychologically, many of the
Nunu had emerged from the swamps and had come to identify
strongly with the larger culture of the river people.

Not all of the Nunu living along the river supported the idea
of Bangala ethnicity and its manifestation in the creation of the
Moyen Congo province. Many immigrants from Nkuboko, a
region located too far inland to be included in the proposed
Moyen Congo province, preferred to remain in the same province with their relatives in the hinterland. They called for peace-
ful relations between riverine people and inland people. To this
end they developed a political organization called the Committee for the Defense of the Banunu-Bobangi, created in Leopoldville by immigrants from Nkuboko.

J. J. L. Lingwambe, the head of this committee, wrote his
own history of the Nunu. This mimeographed booklet, which
did not appear until 1966, reflected the positions of the committee on questions of ethnic identity and political affiliation.
The booklet itself consisted largely of reproductions of various
colonial reports on the history and customs of the Nkuboko
region. In the preface, Lingwambe recounted the story of the
founding ancestors coming down the river. Although brief, his
account was almost identical to the one by Bokono, discussed
earlier. Nevertheless, the bulk of the text dealt with the Nunu
of Nkuboko and stressed cultural continuities between them
and their inland neighbors, the Sengele. The river and the riverine populations were scarcely mentioned after the preface.
The booklet made it clear that the Nkuboko area was the center
of Nunuhood and that there could be no true Nunu identity if
the Nkuboko area were cut off from the rest of the Nunu.

The conflict over Nunu eco-cultural identity became bloody
after 1962 when, by a quirk of the national House of Representatives, the Bolobo-Yumbi Strip became simultaneously part of

---

[38] Dossier 575, Affaires Politiques, Archives Nationales du Zaire, Kinshasa.

two provinces. It became part of the Moyen Congo province, which ran primarily north and south along the river, and it became part of the Lake Leopold II province, which ran east and west inland from the river. The question of whether the Nunu living along the river identified primarily with the other river people or with their inland kinsmen could not have been posed in a starker fashion.

While the creation of the Moyen Congo province was still being debated in the House of Representatives in Leopoldville, the House created the Province of Lake Leopold II on August 14, 1962. This new province was identical to the old Lake Leopold II district, and it included the Bolobo-Yumbi Strip. The Nunu who favored the Moyen Congo province began to fear that, being a minority in the Lake Leopold II province, they would again fall under the domination of the Tiene and Tio. They immediately began to agitate for removal of the Bolobo-Yumbi Strip from the Lake Leopold II province pending the formation of the future Moyen Congo province. A delegation from the area traveled to Leopoldville and presented a petition to the minister of the interior demanding this action. The minister never responded to the petition.

On February 5, 1963, approximately six months after the creation of the Lake Leopold II province, the House of Representatives passed a bill creating the Moyen Congo province. The boundaries of the new province were drawn to include the Bolobo-Yumbi Strip. They included not only the riverbanks, but many of the Tiene and Tio villages in the interior. The Tiene and Tio immediately realized that in the new province they would lose all jurisdiction over land that they had traditionally claimed. In a petition to the central authorities in Leopoldville, they declared:

> We will spare no effort in order to combat our enemies because we are defending our land rights. It is a noble cause . . . . Must we demand the return of the Belgians who, despite the difference in color, nevertheless recognized our land rights which are being thrown away by our unfortunate parliamentary representatives?[39]

---

[39] Williame, *Les Provinces,* p. 108.

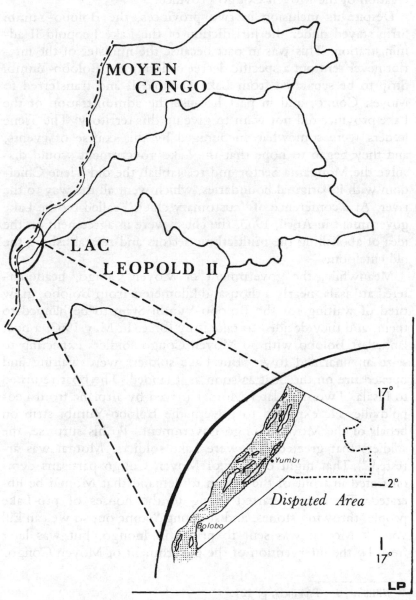

Provincettes Moyen Congo and Lac Léopold II

In Bolobo many Tiene and Tio began plotting to kill members of the riverine faction of the Nunu, many of whom fled to Leopoldville to join Momai, who had settled there to await the creation of the Moyen Congo province.

Despite its inclusion in two provinces, the Bolobo-Yumbi Strip stayed under the jurisdiction of the Lake Leopold II administration. This was in part because the minister of the interior never sent out a specific decree ordering the Bolobo-Yumbi Strip to be separated from Lake Leopold II and transferred to Moyen Congo, and in part because the administration of the Lake province did not want to give up this territory. The Tiene leaders were somewhat encouraged by this course of events, and they began to hope that the Lake government would dissolve the Mongama Sector and reestablish the old Tiene Chiefdom with its original boundaries, which went all the way to the river. At a conference of "customary chiefs" called by the Lake government in April, 1963, the chiefs were in agreement on the idea of abolishing the multiethnic sectors and reestablishing the old chiefdoms.[40]

Meanwhile, the government of Moyen Congo, headquartered at Lisala, nearly a thousand kilometers from Bolobo, grew tired of waiting for the Bolobo-Yumbi Strip to be handed to them, and they decided to take it by force. In May 1963, a boat landed at Bolobo with 30 Moyen Congo soldiers expecting to seize an unarmed town. But Lake soldiers were waiting and opened fire on the boat as soon as it landed. The boat returned to Lisala. Two days later Momai arrived by airplane from Leopoldville. He expected to govern the Bolobo-Yumbi strip on behalf of the Moyen Congo government. To his surprise, the soldiers that greeted him were Lake soldiers. Momai was arrested.[41] That night crowds of Moyen Congo partisans demonstrated in front of the prison to demand that Momai be liberated. Then they started going to the houses of pro-Lake people, throwing stones, and shouting "come out so we can kill you."[42] Momai was sent to prison in Inongo, but was later freed by the intervention of the government of Moyen Congo.

[40] Williame, *Les Provinces,* p. 121.
[41] A.T. Mushie, 5-13-1963, DMZA; Bibaki, "Cité de Bolobo," p. 52.
[42] Interview: Mbembo, 5-4-76, field notes.

The exiling of Momai did not quiet the Moyen Congo partisans. They formed mobs to menace the Lake soldiers stationed in the Bolobo-Yumbi area. In Bolobo the local police were totally neutralized by pro-Moyen Congo mobs. In Yumbi the Lake soldiers faced a hostile crowd that they estimated, with some exaggeration, at ten thousand people. The soldiers fired in self-defense, killing six Nunu.[43] This pro-Moyen Congo sentiment continued at a high pitch even after the Senate reversed itself on June 6, 1963, and voted to return the Bolobo-Yumbi Strip to the Lake province.

Despite the Senate action, Moyen Congo made a second attempt to occupy Bolobo on December 19, more than six months after the Senate vote. They brought the commander of the fifteenth infantry battalion of the Congolese Army, and this time they succeeded. Two days later an airplane arrived in Bolobo carrying Momai and Bompinda. Momai was installed as chief of Bolobo, and almost immediately he began to arrest pro-Lake people. The ousted chief of Bolobo, Ngambomi, fled to Mushie, as did ex-chief Eyongo.[44] Other pro-Lake partisans sought refuge in Tio villages. Mobs roamed the streets of Bolobo and burned the abandoned houses. In an attempt to drive out the Moyen Congo soldiers, a group of Tiene attacked Bolobo, but withdrew after four of their number were killed. Young Tio men paddled along the river between Bolobo and Tchumbiri looking for Nunu to kill.[45]

In Yumbi, Chief Bompinda, backed by Moyen Congo soldiers, began taking land titles away from the Tiene chiefs and giving them to his Nunu supporters. In response, the Tiene attacked Yumbi, but were driven back. They then attacked Nkolo and the Nunu section of Mongama. In both cases they drove out the Nunu, who fled to islands. Nearly a hundred people were killed in the fighting.[46]

The Moyen Congo administration of the Bolobo-Yumbi Strip lasted only two months. On February 20, 1964, President

[43] A.T. Mushie, 5-15-1963, DMZA.
[44] Jean Sébastien Buala, "Rapport Administratif sur l'Installation de l'Administration du Moyen-Congo au Bolobo," Dec., 1963, DMZA.
[45] Bibaki, "Cité de Bolobo," p. 55.
[46] Nkanda, 1-27-1964, DMZA.

Kasa Vubu declared a state of emergency and placed the entire strip under the direct control of the central government. A special commissioner arrived to govern the area.[47] Momai was arrested and sent to Kinshasa, where he was released. Bompinda fled to Lisala, the capital of the Moyen Congo province, where he would spend the next seven years. The state of emergency remained in effect until June 16, 1965, when the Bolobo-Yumbi strip was reintegrated into Lake Leopold II province. The Nkuboko faction in Bolobo was restored to power. Scarcely had this change been made official when General Mobutu came to power in a coup d'état. In an effort to centralize his authority, Mobutu eliminated the *provincettes* and reinstated the pre-independence administrative divisions.

CONCLUSION

When the old divisions were restored, it was almost as if the effects of eight years of conflict had been erased. The riverine Nunu had lost their province, and the chiefship of the Nunu grouping in the Mongama Sector remained vacant till 1971. But if the activity had accomplished little, it had revealed a great deal. The Nkuboko faction, with its ties to the deepest recesses of the swamps, had clearly shown itself to be a minority that could hold power only with the intervention of outside authorities. The vast majority of the Nunu had identified with Bangalahood and with the river peoples. They had shown themselves willing to be cut off from the ancestral *nkinda* charms buried in deserted swamp villages.

During the colonial period the Nunu had developed new forms of economic and social competition that reflected new relationships with the land, the market, and the spirits. They had created an ideology that encapsulated these changes and a political program to give the ideology concrete reality. They had risked their lives to defend their program. The Nunu were no longer the people of swamplands, water lords, and scattered estates. In both action and consciousness, they had become people of the river and the towns.

---

[47] Bibaki, "Cité de Bolobo," 122–25.

13. Conclusion: nature and culture

THE RELATIONSHIP BETWEEN people and their environment has been a topic of discussion throughout human history. It is an implicit theme of many myths collected throughout the world,[1] and it has been a subject of ongoing debate in Western scholarship. In ancient Greece, it was discussed by philosophers; during the Middle Ages, it was debated by theologians; during the Enlightenment, it was scrutinized by men of letters; in the nineteenth century, it was examined by geographers; and in the twentieth century, it has been analyzed by anthropologists and ecologists. Throughout this long period, the debate has focused on three propositions: that people are geographic agents who can alter or even transform the earth; that individuals and societies are influenced and perhaps shaped by their environment; and that nature manifests a coherent design.[2]

Ever since Hippocrates wrote *Of Airs, Waters, and Places,*[3] comparative ethnography has been used to test these propositions. Comparing the cultures of peoples living in different environments is a useful way to separate cultural features that seem related to specific environments from those that seem independent of any given type of natural setting. In the twentieth century, the ethnographic case study, which permits relations between a specific culture and a specific environment to be explored in greater depth, has emerged as an alternative approach.

---

[1] See Edmund Leach, *Claude Lévi-Strauss* (New York, 1970), pp. 15–91; Luc de Heusch, *The Drunken King, or the Origin of the State,* trans. by Roy Willis (Bloomington, Ind., 1982).

[2] Clarence J. Glacken, *Traces on the Rhodian Shore: Nature and Culture in Western Thought from Ancient Times to the End of the Eighteenth Century* (Berkeley, 1967), pp. vii–viii.

[3] See Glacken, *Traces,* pp. 82–88.

The two approaches are complementary. Whereas comparative ethnography can focus our attention on certain cultural or environmental features, only a detailed case study can reveal the actual relationships.

This book has drawn from both traditions. On one hand, it is a comparative study of adaptations to four environments: flooded forest, flooded grassland, dryland forest, and riverbank bluffs. On the other hand it is a case study of adaptation within a single cultural tradition. What differentiates this study from many of its predecessors in both traditions, however, is the emphasis on change over time. The relationship between culture and environment is a dynamic one, and the Nunu case permits comparisons across time as well as across space. It therefore seems useful to explore the implications of the information gathered on the Nunu as it relates to the three propositions listed above.

CULTURE AND NATURE

The first proposition—that people transform the earth—is at the forefront of current discussions about environmental degradation. The industrial societies of the world provide ample evidence that people not only transform, but also destroy the land. In our justifiable concern over what is happening to the environment, it is tempting to look to non-industrial societies in search of models of harmonious relationships between people and nature.

There is a growing body of literature that emphasizes the ecological wisdom of non-industrial peoples who have ordered their activities in ways that maintain harmony with the environment.[4] Although such studies provide us with useful alternative models to the greedy exploitation of resources in the West, there is nevertheless a danger of romanticizing non-industrial peoples, of projecting onto them a moral innocence and a nat-

---

[4] See, for example, Roy Rappaport, "Ecology, Adaptation, and the Ills of Functionalism," *Michigan Discussions in Anthropology*, 2 (1977): 161.

ural intuition that makes them less than complex human beings. The "noble savage" of the eighteenth-century French philosophers can easily become the "conservationist savage" of twentieth-century environmentalists.[5]

The Nunu data show that people who lived in a tropical rain forest and wore few clothes sometimes acted very much like people in Western societies. There are numerous parallels between the seventeenth- and eighteenth-century Nunu settlers in the southern swamps and their contemporaries, the European colonists in New England who bounded the land and turned its products into commodities.[6] In a manner roughly analogous to that of the colonists, the Nunu water lords claimed individual ownership of forests and grasslands, they channeled the waters with dams and ponds, and they turned fish into commodities to be manipulated in the struggle for power and prestige. The Nunu traders of the nineteenth century went even further, acting as middlemen in the export of ivory collected by Pygmy hunters in the heart of the tropical rain forest.

The Nunu were not oblivious to conservation. They used wide-mesh nets that let small fish escape, and they constructed their fish traps with openings to let out the fingerlings. However, the short-term requirements of social competition sometimes took precedence over long-term strategies of environmental management. When the price of fish went up in the twentieth century, the meshes of the nets got finer.

The Nunu were neither natural conservationists nor inveterate maximizers. Because their production decisions were influenced by technology, markets, socioeconomic competition, and other factors, their methods and priorities were subject to change over time. It is not surprising, therefore, that conservation declined in the twentieth century as fishing technology im-

---

[5] On this point see Jonathan Friedman, "Hegelian Ecology: Between Rousseau and the World Spirit," in Social and Ecological Systems, edited by P.C. Burnham and R.F. Ellen (New York, 1979), pp. 264–66.

[6] See William Cronon, Changes in the Land: Indians, Colonists, and the Ecology of New England (New York, 1983).

proved, commodity markets grew, and consumer goods became status symbols. Yet even these developments had contradictory consequences: by maximizing production along the river, the fishermen were allowing the swamplands to revert to their natural state.

NATURE AND CULTURE

The second proposition—that environments influence human societies—is still with us as well. In its most mundane form, it has been expressed by the "possibilist" position, which holds that although placing limits on what humans can do, environments do not determine what people will do within those limits. The possibilist approach has been criticized as a crude type of analysis that discovers the obvious,[7] but the obvious is nevertheless a useful starting point. In the Nunu case, a possibilist analysis would conclude that the swamps did not support an agricultural way of life, that Nkuboko could not sustain a fishing way of life, and that the river did not lend itself to dams and ponds. These points are so obvious that they seem trite, yet they provide the key to understanding the differences in Nunu life among the various micro-environments.

A more sophisticated approach has been articulated by Julian Steward, whose "cultural ecology" distinguished between those cultural elements that were related to environmental adaptations and those that were not. Cultural ecology focuses on the "cultural core," which Steward defined as:

> . . . the constellation of features which are most closely related to
> subsistence activities and economic arrangements. The core
> includes such social, political, and religious patterns as are
> empirically determined to be connected with these arrangements.
> . . . Cultural ecology pays primary attention to those features

---

[7] For critiques of possibilism, see John W. Bennett, *The Ecological Transition: Cultural Anthropology and Human Adaptation* (New York, 1976), pp. 210–12; Clifford Geertz, *Agricultural Involution* (Berkeley, Cal., 1963), pp. 1–3.

which empirical analysis shows to be most closely involved in the utilization of the environment in culturally prescribed ways.[8]

By comparing the cultural cores of a large number of groups, Steward hoped to determine "whether similar adjustments occur in similar environments."[9]

The Nunu data lend themselves to the kind of analysis that interested Steward. Because the Nunu successively settled a series of distinct micro-environments, one can distinguish those cultural features that varied from environment to environment from those that remained relatively constant. One conclusion that emerges from a comparison of the various Nunu groups is that the Nunu maintained great cultural continuity despite their dispersion over radically different micro-environments. Kinship systems, religious beliefs, marriage customs, structures of authority, and even ritualized warfare were common to a variety of environmental zones and cannot be seen as adaptations to any one of them.

The historical process by which the various micro-environments were settled helps to account for the continuities. The people who left a given environment were mostly losers in the competition to become big-men. In entering new environments, settlers did not simply seek to adapt in random ways, but in ways that would allow them to become big-men. They therefore sought to replicate insofar as possible the institutionalized patterns of the areas they had left. Geographical proximity also played a role in maintaining continuity. Because the various micro-environments settled by the Nunu were so small, a person in one zone usually had kinfolk and friends in other zones less than 20 kilometers away. The proximity factor helps to explain why there were great cultural similarities among the various Nunu groups, whereas there were significant cultural

---

[8] Julian Steward, *Theory of Culture Change: The Methodology of Multilinear Evolution* (Urbana, Ill., 1955), p. 37. See also Julian Steward, "The Concept and Method of Cultural Ecology," in *Evolution and Ecology: Essays on Social Transformation*, edited by Jane Steward and Robert Murphy (Urbana, Ill., 1977), pp. 43–57.

[9] Steward, *Theory of Culture Change*, p. 42. For a critique of Steward, see Bennett, *Ecological Transition*, pp. 212–17.

differences between the Nunu and the people of the Ngiri River, which Nunu claim as their ancestral home.

The influence of the different micro-environments was seen less in formal structures of society than in the everyday activities of ordinary people. The swamps were inhabited by settled fish farmers; Nkuboko was populated with settled agriculturalists; and the river was home to nomads. Ironically, it was the town-dwellers who led the nomadic lives, while the most sedentary people were the water lords on the scattered swampland estates. The balance between men's and women's production in the household economy also varied with the environment. In the swamplands, men were the primary producers; in Nkuboko, women contributed most; and along the river, men's and women's contributions were relatively equal.

Because success in becoming a big-man depended on extracting resources from the environment, there was a close correspondence between environmental zones and competitive strategies. The flooded forest fostered a form of competition based on collective harvesting of ponds, whereas the flooded grasslands depended on individual clientship of dams. The farmlands of Nkuboko did not allow the types of clientship that prevailed in the swamps, and the river provided the basis for a more egalitarian competition than did the swamplands. Each micro-environment thus generated its own form of big-man competition.

All of this suggests that the institutions and ideologies of forest societies acted less as determinants of action than as flexible frameworks that could encompass a wide variety of life-styles and competitive strategies. A common kinship system, for example, was followed in all of the micro-environments, but people in the swamps traced their genealogies over several generations, whereas fishermen along the river maintained kinship networks that were much more restricted, and traders circumvented the kinship system altogether by marrying slave women. Similarly, the ideology of guardianship was common to all the Nunu groups, yet guardians in the swamps concentrated on ritual control of the land, whereas the trading guardians along the river depended more on slave armies.

Comparison across micro-environments is a useful way to identify cultural adaptations that seem related to specific environmental conditions, but this form of analysis can only partially account for cultural variation and change. The Nunu data show that many other factors were involved as well. For example, between the mid-nineteenth and the mid-twentieth centuries, life along the Zaire River was dominated by three successive forms of big-man competition, each of which entailed different adaptations to the same environment.

SYSTEMS

The third proposition—that nature manifests a coherent design—has resurfaced in the twentieth century in the form of sophisticated ecosystem models that see human individuals and societies as components of a larger ecosystem. An ecosystem is an interdependent biotic community that exists in a bounded space such as a pond, a forest, or a field. The links that bind the components of the system together can be found in the exchange of energy and nutrients: plants absorb energy from the sun and take nutrients from the soil, animals eat plants, and carnivorous animals eat herbivorous ones. Energy is dissipated as it passes up the food chain and needs to be replenished continually by the sun. Nutrients, on the other hand, are recycled as they return to the soil in the form of wastes and decaying organisms. An ecosystem, in short, can be pictured as a black box, and its behavior can be measured in terms of inputs and outputs of nutrients and energy.[10]

The notion of an ecosystem has been around since Sir Arthur Tansley coined the term in 1935,[11] but it is only in recent decades that human factors have been included in the equations. In the 1960s two ecologists, S. D. Ripley and H. K. Buechner, concluded that human *societies,* not simply human individuals, "are an integral component of the highest level of biological integration." They suggested that ecosystem science could provide a sort of master model that would integrate the natural and

---

[10] Frank B. Golley, "Historical Origins of the Ecosystem Concept in Biology," in *The Ecosystem Concept in Anthropology,* edited by Emilio F. Moran (Boulder, Colo., 1984), pp. 43–44.

[11] Golley, "Historical Origins of the Ecosystem Concept," pp. 33–49.

human sciences.[12] In the 1970s several anthropologists proposed that instead of talking about environment and culture, we simply talk about ecosystems and component populations,[13] and thereby see the human community as one of a variety of populations coexisting within the framework of the larger ecosystem.

Because the ecosystem thus defined provides an inclusive framework for the analysis of nature-culture interaction, debate over the "design of nature" proposition has in recent years subsumed much of the debate over the two propositions discussed earlier.[14] The ecosystem approach to nature-culture interaction differs from the other approaches primarily in terms of its focus. It tries to place specific relationships between people and their environment in the larger context of the ecosystem as a whole.

One useful application of the ecosystem concept has been to trace the complex chains of environmental consequences of human activity. When the Nunu altered the land, for example, they were also initiating complex ecological processes. When they cleared a field and left it fallow, they initiated processes of floral succession and regeneration that could take nearly two centuries to complete. Along with the successive changes in vegetation came changes in the animal life that inhabited the patch. With the construction of dams and ponds, new patterns of silting and sedimentation were initiated that would alter the landscape and influence the aquatic vegetation and the kinds of fish and insects that it attracted.

Despite the insights which ecosystem studies have contributed to our understanding of such processes, environmental responses to human activities are not completely mechanical and predictable. Unlike the relatively simple successions found in temperate-zone forests, the astonishing floral diversity of tropi-

---

[12] S.D. Ripley and H.K. Buechner, "Ecosystem Science as a Point of Synthesis," in *America's Changing Environment,* edited by Roger Revelle and Hans Landsberg (Boston, 1967), pp. 20–27.

[13] See Andrew Vayda and Roy Rappaport, "Ecology, Cultural and Non-Cultural," in *Introduction to Cultural Anthropology* edited by James Clifton (Boston, 1968), pp. 477–97.

[14] See the essays in Moran, *The Ecosystem Concept in Anthropology.*

cal rain forests creates processes of regeneration so complex that they are only vaguely understood. Tropical botanists have discovered that instead of reaching a competitive equilibrium in which each ecological niche is filled by a single species, tropical forests develop a dynamic equilibrium in which a number of species coexist in each niche. The exact composition of the regenerated stand will be influenced by historical occurrences such as seed predation, periodic floods, periods of relative dryness, and other unpredictable factors. Regeneration, in short, is a historical phenomenon as well as an ecosystemic process.[15]

The ecosystems approach has also been applied to the analysis of human culture, most notably through attempts to identify cultural mechanisms that regulate the balance with the larger ecosystem much as a thermostat regulates a heating unit. Roy Rappaport, for example, has suggested that religious belief and ritual in decentralized societies may serve as mechanisms that regulate relations between people and their environment.[16] Similarly, Betty Meggers has interpreted the religious beliefs of the Amazon Basin peoples as "a translation into cultural terms of the checks and balances that exist on the biological level to maintain the equilibrium of the ecosystem."[17]

The Nunu had institutions that some analysts might interpret as system-level environmental regulating mechanisms. One of them was the landholding pattern in the swamps. Because each water lord in the swamps controlled not only dams and ponds, but their drainage areas as well, the number of landowners was reduced to well below the carrying capacity of the swamplands. However, it seems clear that this result was an unintended by-product of an institution that was devised and perpetuated for

---

[15] See Patrick S. Bourgeron, "Spatial Aspects of Vegetation Structure," in *Tropical Rain Forest Ecosystems*, edited by Frank B. Golley (New York, 1983), pp. 38–43.

[16] This view was set out in Roy Rappaport, *Pigs for the Ancestors: Ritual in the Ecology of a New Guinea People* (New Haven, Conn., 1968). This study generated an enormous debate. For a summary of the debate and Rappaport's defense, see the epilogue and the supplementary bibliography to the 1984 edition of *Pigs for the Ancestors* (New Haven, Conn., 1984). For an elaboration of Rappaport's views, see the essays in Roy Rappaport, *Ecology, Meaning, and Religion* (Richmond, Cal., 1979).

[17] Meggers, *Amazonia*, p. 2.

other purposes. When those other purposes shifted, as in the twentieth century swamplands, the landholding pattern shifted as well. Two religious institutions—the *nkinda* charm and the day of rest—could perhaps be seen as environmental regulators. However, there is no evidence that the *nkinda* ever influenced the way people hunted, fished, and farmed, or that observing a day of rest enhanced the productivity of the land. Nunu religious practices were aimed more at the ritual regulation of society than at the preservation of the environment.

The small-scale warfare found in decentralized societies has been identified by some anthropologists as an environmental regulating mechanism. Marvin Harris has proposed that such warfare can be a control mechanism that keeps the population in balance with the carrying capacity of the land.[18] Andrew Vayda has interpreted warfare in Oceania as an adaptive response to perturbations induced by population pressure.[19] Roy Rappaport has explained Maring warfare in New Guinea as part of a ritual cycle that served to keep the pig population under control and to redistribute people over the land.[20]

At first glance, Nunu warfare appears to lend itself to this type of analysis. The wars apparently became institutionalized at a time when there was a growing population in the swamplands, and one Nunu informant explicitly stated that war was a population-control mechanism. A closer look reveals, however, that the growing population posed less of a threat to the ecosystem than it did to the landholding class. Warfare provided a competitive arena that mirrored the socioeconomic competition among water lords. The wars can certainly be interpreted as a regulating mechanism, but it was the regulation of social competition, not ecosystemic regulation, that predominated.

Instead of seeking ecosystemic explanations for cultural phenomena,[21] it is perhaps more useful to see Nunu interaction with nature as embedded in two contexts. The first consisted of

---

[18] Harris, *Cannibals and Kings*, pp. 33–54.
[19] Andrew Vayda, *War in Ecological Perspective* (New York, 1976).
[20] Rappaport, *Pigs for the Ancestors*.
[21] See John W. Bennett, "Ecosystem Analogies in Cultural Ecology," in *Population, Ecology, and Social Evolution*, edited by Steven Polgar (Chicago, 1975), p. 284; Friedman, "Hegelian Ecology," pp. 259–66.

ecosystemic processes. The yearly cycles of climate, water levels, growing seasons, and movements of fish and animals affected one another in complex ways, and the Nunu planned their productive activities accordingly. In a similar manner, they took advantage of long-term processes of forest regeneration in order to renew the fertility of their fields, and they interrupted natural processes of succession to keep the forest from invading the grasslands. At the same time, however, the Nunu saw nature as something to be manipulated in accordance with strategies of social and economic competition. Decisions about where to settle, what and how much to produce, and which methods to employ were influenced by competitive considerations as well as by ecosystemic processes.

CHOICE

This book has focused on the options available to individuals and the factors impinging on their choices. I have sought to integrate system and action by seeing systems as contexts for choice and action, not determinants of them.[22] The central issue is not how nature, as a system, affects culture, or how culture, as a system, affects nature. Rather, it is how natural and cultural considerations come together at the moment of choice, and how the resulting actions alter the context of future choices.

Some historical moments of decision making were more critical to the Nunu than others. When settlers entered a new environment, for example, they had great latitude to make new choices and set precedents. A key decision concerned which resources of the environment to exploit. The Nunu did not gather rubber in the eighteenth century, for example, even though it grew wild in the forest. They also made choices about whether the exploited resources should be collectively owned or individually claimed. Individual ownership of fishing grounds in the swamps provided the basis for the water lord competition, whereas the open waters of the river encouraged a more egalitarian society. Finally, they made choices about which tech-

---

[22] This approach is somewhat analogous to what John W. Bennett has called "adaptive dynamics." See Bennett, *Ecological Transition,* p. 166.

niques to use to exploit the environment and how labor was to be mobilized. Pond fishing required the efforts of a large numbers of workers, whereas river fishing was most efficiently done with small, flexible teams. Both productive efficiency and the possibilities of mobilizing labor were important considerations in the choice of techniques.

The generations that followed the early settlers, although more constrained by patterns of behavior that were already in place, were not without choices. Environment is usually treated as a given factor in ethnographic studies, but in fact each Nunu had a choice of several environments. People who had little chance of succeeding in one environment retained the option of moving to another. Family genealogies show a great deal of back-and-forth movement among the different micro-environments inhabited by the Nunu, and they indicate that the natural environment in which an individual lived was often a matter of conscious choice.

Although the environments themselves remained relatively constant over the period covered in this book, many other factors that influenced individual decisions changed over time, and those factors help to explain why people made different adaptive decisions in different historical periods. In the first place, trade networks and markets influenced decisions as to which resources should be exploited and which environments should be settled. Ivory did not become valuable until the early nineteenth century; rubber did not become valuable until the end of the nineteenth century; and the rising value of fish in the twentieth century influenced the move toward the river.

Second, technological innovations influenced not only how an environment would be exploited, but also which environments would be settled. The introduction of cassava from the New World in the seventeenth or eighteenth century certainly influenced production and settlement decisions in a variety of ways, most of which can no longer be reconstructed. The technology of the fish dam made the flooded grasslands attractive in the eighteenth century; modern nets made the river attractive in the twentieth.

Third, religious and political authorities altered the context of decision making and thus influenced adaptive decisions. The actions of the eighteenth-century guardians made the swamplands seem safe for settlement; the actions of the colonial government, in contrast, created an emigration out of the swamps. Fourth, population densities influenced settlement decisions. The swamplands attracted immigrants in the seventeenth and eighteenth centuries when the population density was low, but they created emigrants in the nineteenth century when the density was much higher.

A final factor influencing adaptive decisions was the divergent interests of the various social groups in Nunu society. It is not adequate merely to deduce that a certain custom or institution was adaptive to a certain environment. One must ask, "adaptive for whom? and for what purpose?"[23] Dam fishing and individual ownership were highly adaptive for the water lords, but they increased the problems for younger sons and people from landless families, and they reduced the human carrying capacity of the swamps. In the twentieth century, fishing with fine-meshed nylon nets has had clear advantages for young men eager to buy consumer goods, but it is not necessarily adaptive to long-term ecological stability.

To sort out the ways in which such factors interacted with individual choice and action, I have used concepts and vocabulary borrowed from game theory to distinguish among cultural goals, various types of rules, social strategies, and productive tactics. Each of these elements changed at a different pace and in a different way, resulting in a continually changing context of decision making. The goal of becoming a big-man persisted, though the definition of a big-man changed considerably from the eighteenth century to the twentieth. The rules imposed by nature varied significantly over space, but remained relatively constant over time. The rules imposed by regional economies and political authorities, however, showed remarkable uniformity over space, while varying widely over time. Individuals adjusted to the different sets of rules by developing appropriate

---

[23] See P.C. Burnham, "The Explanatory Value of the Concept of Adaptation in Studies of Culture Change," *The Explanation of Culture Change,* edited by Colin Renfrew (Pittsburgh, 1973), pp. 93–102; Friedman, "Hegelian Ecology," pp. 261–62.

strategies and tactics. As might be expected, strategies and tactics showed great variation over both time and space.

Just as rules influenced tactics and strategies, tactical and strategic decisions also influenced rules. The migratory strategies in the eighteenth and early nineteenth centuries led people into new environments and generated new variants of the big-man competition. Conversely, the development of net fishing and black-market trading techniques in the twentieth century had a major impact on people's choices of environment and form of competition.

Because the relationship between nature and culture is mediated by human choice, it is both dynamic and unpredictable. Just as economists admit that they cannot account for consumer taste, historians and ethnographers must admit that they can only partially account for cultural choices. The ultimate answers as to why a certain group of people adapted to a particular environment in a particular way probably lie hidden in the imponderables of the human spirit. Stephan Jay Gould has captured the essence of the problem as eloquently as anyone:

> We live in essential and unresolvable tension between our unity with nature and our dangerous uniqueness. Systems that attempt to place and make sense of us by focusing exclusively either on the uniqueness or the unity are doomed to failure. But we must not stop asking and questioning because the answers are complex and ambiguous. We can do no better than to follow Linnaeus's advice, embodied in his description of *Homo sapiens* within his system. He described other species by the numbers of their fingers and toes, their size and their color. For us, in place of anatomy, he simply wrote the Socratic injunction: Know thyself.[24]

---

[24] Stephan Jay Gould, *Hen's Teeth and Horse's Toes* (New York, 1983), p. 250.

Abbreviations

AA	Archives Africaines. Brussels, Belgium.
ANSOM-Aix	Archives Nationales, Section Outre-Mer. Aix-en-Provence, France.
ANZ	Archives Nationales du Zaire. Kinshasa, Zaire.
ARSC	Académie Royale des Sciences Coloniales. Brussels, Belgium.
ARSOM	Académie Royale des Sciences d'Outre-Mer. Brussels, Belgium.
BMS	Baptist Missionary Society. London, England.
BZA	Bikoro Zone Archives, Bikoro, Zaire.
DCMS	"Documents from Catholic Mission Stations. Bandundu, Equateur Provinces, Zaire," compiled by Robert Harms (Microfilm: Center for Research Libraries, Chicago, film no. 4980).
DMZA	"Documents from Mushie Zone Archives, Zaire," compiled by Robert Harms (Microfilm: Center for Research Libraries, Chicago, film no. 4979.)
INEAC	Institut National pour L'Etude Agronomique du Congo. Kinshasa, Zaire.
IRCB	Institut Royal Colonial Belge. Brussels, Belgium.
MRAC	Musée Royal de l'Afrique Centrale. Tervuren, Belgium.
MRAC-E	Musée Royal de l'Afrique Centrale, Section d'Ethnographie. Tervuren, Belgium.
MRAC-H	Musée Royal de l'Afrique Centrale, Section d'Histoire. Tervuren, Belgium.
MZA	Mushie Zone Archives. Mushie, Zaire.

The following abbreviations are found in the citations of colonial administrative reports:

AIMO   Affaires Indignes et Main d'Oeuvre.
AE/Agri.   Affaires Economiques et Agricoles.
CEC   Centre Extra-Coutumier.

Sources cited

PUBLISHED SOURCES

Acres, Ian S. "A Study of Sleeping Sickness in an Endemic Area of the Belgian Congo over a Period of Ten Years." *Transactions of the Royal Society of Tropical Medicine and Hygiene,* 44 (1950):77–92.

Allison, A.C. "Malaria in Carriers of the Sickle-Cell Trait and in Newborn Children." *Experimental Parasitology,* 6 (1957):418–46.

Anstey, Roger. "The Congo Rubber Atrocities: A Case Study." *African Historical Studies,* 4 (1971):59–76.

Ascherson, Neal. *The King Incorporated: Leopold II in the Age of Trusts.* London, 1963.

Bailey, F.G. *Strategems and Spoils: A Social Anthropology of Politics.* Oxford, 1970.

Bates, Robert. *Essays on the Political Economy of Rural Africa.* New York, 1983.

Bennett, John W. *The Ecological Transition: Cultural Anthropology and Human Adaptation.* New York, 1976.

————. "Ecosystem Analogies in Cultural Ecology." In Steven Polgar (ed.), *Population, Ecology, and Social Evolution,* pp. 273–303. Chicago, 1975.

Bentley, W. Holman. *Pioneering on the Congo.* 2 vols. London, 1900.

Bequaert, Maurice. "Contribution à la Connaissance de l'Age de la Pierre dans la Région de Bolobo." *Bulletin de la Société Royale Belge d'Anthropologie et de Préhistoire,* 60 (1949):95–115.

Bouillenne, R., J. Moreau, and P. Deuse. *Esquisse Ecologique des Faciés Forestiers et Marécageuses des Bords du Lac Tumba.* ARSC, Classe des Sciences Naturelles et Médicales, n.s., vol. 3, no. 1. Brussels, 1955.

Bourgeron, Patrick S. "Spatial Aspects of Vegetation Structure." In F.B. Golley (ed.), *Tropical Rain Forest Ecosystems,* pp. 29–47. New York, 1983.

Bràsio, Antonia (ed.). *Monumenta Missionaria Africana.* 11 vols. Lisbon, 1953–71.

Brown, H.D. "The Nkumu of the Tumba." *Africa,* 14 (1943–44): 431–47.

Bulletin Administrative du Congo Belge. Brussels.

Bultot, Franz. *Atlas Climatique du Bassin Congolais.* 3 vols. Kinshasa, 1971.

Burnham, P.C. "The Explanatory Value of the Concept of Adaptation in Studies of Culture Change." In Colin Renfrew (ed.), *The Explanation of Culture Change,* pp. 93–102. Pittsburgh, 1973.

Carneiro, Robert. "Cultivation of Manioc Among the Kuikuru." In Raymond B. Hames and William T. Vickers (eds.), *Adaptive Responses of Native Amazonians,* pp. 65–111. New York, 1983.

Casement, Roger. "Correspondence and Reports from His Majesty's Consul at Boma Respecting the Administration of the Independent State of the Congo." *Parliamentary Papers.* Command Paper no. 1933, Africa, no. 1. London, 1904.

259

Le Congo Belge Durant la Seconde Guerre Mondiale: Receuil d'Etudes. n.a. Brussels, 1983.

"Congo Currents: Baptist Missionary Society," *Congo Mission News,* Jan., 1936, pp. 9–10.

Conklin, Harold. "An Ethnoecological Approach to Shifting Agriculture." In Andrew Vayda (ed.), *Environment and Cultural Behavior,* pp. 221–31. Garden City, N.Y., 1969.

Coquery-Vidrovitch, Catherine. *Brazza et la Prise de Possession du Congo.* Paris, 1969.

Co-Workers. Bolobo, Belgian Congo.

Cronon, William. *Changes in the Land: Indians, Colonists, and the Ecology of New England.* New York, 1984.

Curtin, Philip. *The Atlantic Slave Trade: A Census.* Madison, Wis., 1969.

De Craemer, Willy, Jan Vansina, and René Fox. "Religious Movements in Central Africa." *Comparative Studies in Society and History,* 18 (1976):458–75.

de Heusch, Luc. *The Drunken King, or the Origin of the State.* Translated by Roy Willis. Bloomington, Ind., 1982.

Delcommune, Alexandre. "La Situation Commerciale du Congo Belge." *Supplement au Mouvement Géographique,* no, 5, Jan. 30, 1921.

Devroey, Egide. *Le Bassin Hydrographique Congolais.* IRCB, Sciences Techniques, vol. 3, no. 3. Brussels, 1941.

Dupré, Georges, *Un Ordre et sa Destruction.* Paris, 1982.

Duren, A. *Un Essai d'Etude d'Ensemble du Paludisme au Congo Belge.* IRCB, Sciences Naturelles et Médicales, vol. 5, no. 5. Brussels, 1937.

Elster, John. "Marxism, Functionalism, and Game Theory." *Theory and Society,* 11 (1982):455–82.

Evrard, C. *Recherches Ecologiques sur le Peuplement Forestier des Sols Hydromorphes de la Cuvette Centrale Congolaise.* INEAC, Série Scientifique, no. 110. Kinshasa, 1968.

Friedman, Jonathan. "Hegelian Ecology: Between Rousseau and the World Spirit." In P.C. Burnham and R.F. Ellen (eds.), *Social and Ecological Systems,* pp. 253–70. New York, 1979.

Froment, E. "Trois Affluents Franais du Congo: Rivières Alima, Likouala, Sanga." *Bulletin de la Société de Géographie de Lille,* 7 (1887):458–74.

Gann, Louis, and Peter Duignan. *The Rulers of Belgian Africa.* Princeton, 1979.

Geertz, Clifford. *Agricultural Involution: The Processes of Ecological Change in Indonesia.* Berkeley, Cal., 1963.

Germain, R. *Les Biotopes Alluvionnaires Herbeux et les Savanes Intercalaires du Congo Equatorial.* ARSOM, Sciences Naturelles et Médicales, n.s., vol. 15, no. 4. Brussels, 1965.

Glacken, Clarence J. *Traces on the Rhodian Shore: Nature and Culture in Western Thought from Ancient Times to the End of the Eighteenth Century.* Berkeley, 1967.

Glave, E. J. *Six Years of Adventure in Congo-Land.* London, 1893.

Godelier, Maurice. *The Making of Great Men: Male Domination and Power among the New Guinea Baruya.* New York, 1986.

Goldschmidt, Walter. "Game Theory, Cultural Values, and the Brideprice in Africa." In Ira Buchler and Hugo Nutini (eds.), *Game Theory in the Behavioral Sciences*, pp. 61–74. Pittsburgh, 1969.

Golley, Frank B. "Historical Origins of the Ecosystem Concept in Biology." In Emilio F. Moran (ed.), *The Ecosystem Concept in Anthropology*, pp. 33–49. Boulder, Colo., 1984.

Gosse, J.P. *Le Milieu Aquatique et l'Ecologie des Poissons dans la Région de Yangambi*. MRAC, Sciences Zoologiques, no. 116. Tervuren, 1963.

Gould, Stephan Jay. *Hen's Teeth and Horse's Toes: Further Reflections in Natural History*. New York, 1983.

Gourou, Pierre. *La Densité de la Population Rurale au Congo Belge*. ARSC, Sciences Naturelles et Médicales, n.s., vol. 1, no. 2. Brussels, 1955.

Grenfell, George. "A Funeral Dance at Bolobo, Upper Congo River." *Missionary Herald*, Dec. 1, 1890, p. 450.

———. *A Map of the Congo River between Leopoldville and Stanley Falls, 1884–1889*. London, n.d.

———. "Mission Work at Bolobo on the Upper Congo." *Missionary Herald*, Feb. 1, 1889, pp. 48–51.

———. "News from the Rev. George Grenfell." *Missionary Herald*, Jan. 1, 1890, pp. 21–25.

Hames, Raymond, and William Vickers. "Introduction." In Raymond Hames and William Vickers (eds.), *Adaptive Responses of Native Amazonians*, pp. 1–26. New York, 1983.

Harms, Robert. "Bobangi Oral Traditions: Indicators of Collective Perceptions." In Joseph Miller (ed.), *The African Past Speaks: Essays on Oral Tradition and History*, pp. 178–200. Hamden, Conn., 1980.

———. "The End of Red Rubber: A Reassessment." *Journal of African History*, 16 (1975):73–88.

———. *River of Wealth, River of Sorrow: The Central Zaire Basin in the Era of the Slave and Ivory Trade, 1500–1891*. New Haven, Conn., 1981.

———. "Sustaining the System: Trading Towns along the Middle Zaire." In Martin Klein and Claire Robertson (eds.), *Women and Slavery in Africa*, pp. 95–110. Madison, Wis., 1983.

———. "The World Abir Made: The Maringa-Lopori Basin, 1885–1903." *African Economic History*, no. 12 (1983):125–39.

Harris, Marvin. *Cannibals and Kings*. New York, 1977.

Hawker, George. *The Life of George Grenfell*. London, 1909.

Henrard, C.L. *Notice de la Carte des Tsé-Tsé au Congo Belge et au Ruanda-Urundi*. IRCB, Atlas Générale du Congo, vol. 11. Brussels, 1952.

Hijboer, R.P. "Mill Hill au Congo." *Lovania*, no. 15 (1er trimestre, 1949):12–13.

Hulstaert, Gustave, "L'Evolution de la Production Alimentaire des Nkundo (XIXe–XXe Sicles): Un Bilan Partisant." *African Economic History*, no. 7 (1979):171–81.

"L'Impôt Indigne au Congo Belge." n.a. *Le Mouvement Géographique*, 1914, col. 290.

Janzen, John. *The Quest for Therapy: Medical Pluralism in Lower Zaire*. Berkeley, 1978.

Jewsiewicki, Bogumil. "Rural Society and the Belgian Colonial Economy." In David Birmingham and Phyllis Martin (eds.), *History of Central Africa*, 2 vols., pp. 95–125. New York, 1983.

Jewsiewicki, Bogumil, and Mumbanza mwa Bawele. "The Social Context of Slavery in Equatorial Africa during the 19th and 20th Centuries." In Paul Lovejoy (ed.), *The Ideology of Slavery in Africa*, pp. 73–98. Beverly Hills, Cal., 1981.

Johnson, Allen. "Machiguenga Gardens." In Raymond B. Hames and William T. Vickers (eds.), *Adaptive Responses of Native Amazonians*, pp. 29–63. New York, 1983.

Jones, William O. *Manioc in Africa*. Stanford, 1959.

Kuper, Adam, and Pierre Van Leynseele. "Social Anthropology and the Bantu Expansion." *Africa*, 48 (1978):335–52.

Laburthe-Tolra, Philippe. *Les Seigneurs de la Forêt*. Paris, 1981.

"Le Confluent de l'Ubangi et du Congo et la Rivière N'Ghiri." n.a. *La Belgique Coloniale*, 1 (1895):52.

Leach, Edmund. *Claude Lévi-Strauss*. New York, 1970.

Lebrun, J. "La Forêt Equatoriale Congolaise." *Bulletin Agricole du Congo Belge*, 27 (1936):163–92.

Lerner, Gerda. *The Creation of Patriarchy*. New York, 1986.

Letouzey, R. "Végétations." In *Atlas de la République Unie du Cameroun*, pp. 20–24. Paris, n.d.

Liebrechts, Charles. *Souvenirs d'Afrique: Congo, Léopoldville, Bolobo, Equateur (1883–1889)*. Brussels, 1909.

Lloyd, P.C. "Conflict Theory and Yoruba Kingdoms." In I.M. Lewis (ed.), *History and Social Anthropology*, pp. 25–61. London, 1968.

Luca da Caltanisetta, Fra. *Diaire Congolaise, 1690–1701*. Translated by François Bontinck. Louvain, 1970.

MacGaffey, Wyatt. "Lineage Structure, Marriage, and the Family amongst the Central Bantu." *Journal of African History*, 24 (1983): 173–87.

———. "Oral Tradition in Central Africa." *International Journal of African Historical Studies*, 7 (1974): 417–26.

———. "The West in Congolese Experience." In Philip Curtin (ed.), *Africa and the West*, pp. 49–74. Madison, Wis., 1972.

Marlier, G. "Limnology of the Congo and Amazon Rivers." In Betty Meggers, Edward Ayensu, and Donald Duckworth (eds.), *Tropical Forest Ecosystems in Africa and South America*, pp. 223–38. Washington, D.C., 1973.

Martin, Phyllis. *The External Trade of the Loango Coast, 1576–1870*. London, 1972.

Meggers, Betty. *Amazonia: Man and Culture in a Counterfeit Paradise*. Chicago, 1971.

Meillassoux, Claude. "Essai d'Interpretation du Phénomène Economique dans les Sociétés Traditionnelles d'Auto-Subsistance. *Cahiers d'Etudes Africaines*, 4 (1960):38–67.

Miers, Suzanne, and Igor Kopytoff. "African 'Slavery' as an Institution of Marginality." In Suzanne Miers and Igor Kopytoff (eds.), *Slavery in Africa*, pp. 3–81. Madison, Wis., 1977.

Miller, Joseph C. "Cokwe Trade and Conquest." In Richard Gray and David Birmingham (eds.), *Precolonial African Trade*, pp. 75–113. London, 1970.

_____. "The Slave Trade in Kongo and Angola." In Martin Kilson and Robert Rotberg (eds.), *The African Diaspora*, pp. 75–113. Cambridge, Mass., 1976.

Miracle, Marvin. *Agriculture in the Congo Basin*. Madison, Wis., 1967.

_____. "The Congo Basin as Habitat for Man." In Betty Meggers, Edward Ayensu, and Donald Duckworth (eds.), *Tropical Forest Ecosystems in Africa and South America*, pp. 335–44. Washington, D.C., 1973.

Motulsky, Arno. "Heredity Red Cell Traits and Malaria." *Supplement to the American Journal of Tropical Medicine and Hygiene*, 13 (1964):147–61.

Mumbanza mwa Bawele. "Fondaments Economiques de l'Evolution des Systèmes de Filiation dans les Sociétés de la Haute-Ngiri et de la Moeko, du XIXe Siècle à nos Jours." *Enquêtes et Documents d'Histoire Africaine*, 2 (1977):1–30.

_____. "La Production Alimentaire dans les Marais de la Haute Ngiri de la XIXe Siècle à nos Jours." *African Economic History*, 7 (1979):130–39.

Patterson, Orlando. *Slavery and Social Death*. Cambridge, Mass., 1982.

Pigafetta, Filipo, and Duarte Lopes. *Déscription du Royaume de Congo et des Contrées Environnantes*. Translated and annotated by Willy Bal. Paris, 1965.

Rappaport, Roy A. "Ecology, Adaptation, and the Ills of Functionalism." *Michigan Discussions in Anthropology*, 2 (1977):138–90.

_____. *Ecology, Meaning, and Religion*. Richmond, Cal., 1979.

_____. *Pigs for the Ancestors: Ritual in the Ecology of a New Guinea People*. Enlarged edition. New Haven, Conn., 1984.

Rey, Pierre Philippe. "L'Esclavage Lignager chez les Tsangui, les Punu et les Kunyi du Congo Brazzaville." In Claude Meillassoux (ed.), *L'Esclavage en Afrique Précoloniale*, pp. 509–28. Paris, 1975.

Richards, Paul W. "Africa, the Odd Man Out." In Betty Meggers, Edward Ayensu, and Donald Duckworth (eds.), *Tropical Forest Ecosystems in Africa and South America*, pp. 21–26. Washington, D.C., 1973.

_____. *The Tropical Rain Forest*. London, 1964.

Ripley, S.D., and H.K. Buechner. "Ecosystem Science as a Point of Synthesis." In Roger Revelle and Hans Landsberg (eds.), *America's Changing Environment*, pp. 20–27. Boston, 1967.

Roberts, Tyson R. "Ecology of Fishes in the Amazon and Congo Basins." In Betty Meggers, Edward Ayensu, and Donald Duckworth (eds.), *Tropical Forest Ecosystems in Africa and South America*, pp. 239–54. Washington, D.C., 1973.

Sahlins, Marshall. "Poor Man, Rich Man, Big Man, Chief: Political Types in Melanesia and Polynesia." *Comparative Studies in Society and History*, 5 (1963): 285–303.

Sautter, Gilles. *De l'Atlantique au Fleuve Congo*. 2 vols. Paris, 1966.

Scott, James. *The Moral Economy of the Peasant*. New Haven, Conn., 1976.

_____. *Weapons of the Weak*. New Haven, Conn., 1985.

Serpenti, L.M. *Cultivators in the Swamps*. Assen, Netherlands, 1965.

Service des Eaux et Forêts. "Aperçu sur la Pêche Lacustre et Fluviale au Congo Belge et au Ruanda-Urundi." *Bulletin Agricole du Congo Belge*, 50 (1959): 1665–90.

Shubik, Martin, "Game Theory and the Study of Social Behavior." In Martin Shubik (ed.), *Game Theory and Related Approaches to Social Behavior*, pp. 3–77. New York, 1964.

Stanley, Henry Morton. *Through the Dark Continent*. 2 vols. New York, 1879.

Steward, Julian. "The Concept and Method of Cultural Ecology." In Steward, Jane, and Robert Murphy (eds.), *Evolution and Ecology: Essays on Social Transformation*, pp. 43–57. Urbana, Ill., 1977.

_____. *Theory of Culture Change: The Methodology of Multilinear Evolution*. Urbana, Ill., 1955.

Thomas, Jacqueline M.C. *Les Ngbaka de la Lobaye*. Paris, 1963.

Thompson, Keith, and Alan C. Hamilton. "Peatlands and Swamps of the African Continent." In A.J.P. Gore (ed.), *Mires: Swamp, Bog, Fen, and Moor*, 2 vols., B:331–73. New York, 1983.

Thompson, Leonard. *The Political Mythology of Apartheid*. New Haven, Conn., 1985.

Thornton, John. *The Kingdom of Kongo: Civil War and Transition, 1641–1718*. Madison, Wis., 1983.

Tonnoir, René. *Giribuma*. MRAC, Archives d'Ethnographie, vol. 14. Tervuren, Belgium, 1970.

Van der Kerken, Georges. *L'Ethnie Mongo*, 2 vols. Brussels, 1944.

Van Gele, Alphonse. "L'Exploration de l'Oubangi et de ses Affluents." *Le Mouvement Géographique*, 4 (1887): 40–41.

Van Leynseele, Pierre. "Ecological Stability and Intensive Fish Production: The Case of the Libinza People of the Middle Ngiri (Zaire)." In P.C. Burnham and R.F. Ellen (eds.), *Social and Ecological Systems*, pp. 167–84. New York, 1979.

_____. "Les Transformations des Systèmes de Production et d'Echanges de Populations Ripuaires du Haut-Zaire." *African Economic History*, no. 7 (1979):117–29.

Vansina, Jan. *The Children of Woot: A History of the Kuba Peoples*. Madison, Wis., 1978.

_____. "Comment: Traditions of Genesis." *Journal of African History*, 15 (1974):317–22.

_____. "Esquisse Historique de l'Agriculture en Milieu Forestier (Afrique Equatoriale)." *Muntu*, 2 (1985):5–34.

_____. "L'Homme, les Forêts, et le Passé en Afrique." *Annales: Economies, Sociétés, Civilizations*, 1985:1307–34.

_____. "Lignage, Idéologie, et Histoire en Afrique Equatoriale." *Enquêtes et Documents d'Histoire Africaine*, 4 (1980):133–45.

————. "The Peoples of the Forest," In David Birmingham and Phyllis Martin (eds.), *History of Central Africa,* 2 vols., 1:75–117. New York, 1983.

————. "Towards a History of Lost Corners in the World." *The Economic History Review,* 35 (1982):165–78.

————. "Western Bantu Expansion," *Journal of African History,* 25 (1984):129–45.

Vayda, Andrew. *War in Ecological Perspective.* New York, 1976.

Vayda, Andrew, and Roy Rappaport, "Ecology, Cultural and Non-Cultural." In James Clifton (ed.), *Introduction to Cultural Anthropology,* pp. 477–97. Boston, 1968.

Viccars, John. "Witchcraft in Bolobo, Belgian Congo." *Africa,* 19 (1949):220–29.

Von Neumann, John, and Oskar Morgenstern, *Theory of Games and Economic Behavior.* Princeton, N. J., 1944.

Waltz, Heinrich. *Das Konzessionswesen im Belgischen Kongo.* 2 vols. Jena, Germany, 1917.

Whitehead, John, *Grammar and Dictionary of the Bobangi Language.* London, 1899.

Williame, J.C., *Les Provinces du Congo: Nord Kivu–Lac Léopold II.* Cahiers Economiques et Sociaux, Collection d'Etudes Politiques, no. 3. Leopoldville, 1964.

Wilverth, E. "Au Lac Ibanda et la Rivière Ngiri." *La Belgique Coloniale.* 1 (1896):576.

UNPUBLISHED SOURCES

Bibaki Ngomwana Wakawe, "La Cité de Bolobo." Mémoire de Licence, Zaire National University. Lubumbashi, 1972–73.

Bokono, Vincent. "Monkama mo Mibembo mi Bankoko o Ebale e Congo." Typescript. Bolobo, 1960.

Harms, Robert (Compiler). "Documents from Catholic Mission Stations. Bandundu, Equateur Provinces, Zaire." Microfilm, Center for Research Libraries, film no. 4980. Chicago, 1977.

Harms, Robert (Compiler). "Documents from Mushie Zone Archives, Zaire." Microfilm, Center for Research Libraries, film no. 4979. Chicago, 1977.

Lingwambe, J.J.L. "Histoire Banunu-Bobangi." Mimeographed pamphlet. Kinshasa, 1966.

Mayaka Ma-Libuka, "Phonologie et Morphologie du Bobangi." Mémoire de Licence, Institut Supérieur Pédagogique. Kikwit, Zaire, 1977.

Mumbanza mwa Bawele. "Histoire des Peuples Riverains de l'entre Zaire-Ubangi: Evolution Sociale et Economique (ca. 1700–1930)." Dissertation, Zaire National University. Lubumbashi, Zaire, 1980.

Van Leynseele, Pierre. "Les Libinza de la Ngiri: L'Anthropologie d'un Peuple des Marais du Confluent Congo-Ubangi." Dissertation, University of Leiden. Leiden, Holland, 1979.

Archives

Archives Africaines. Brussels, Belgium.
Archives Nationales, Section Outre-Mer. Aix-en-Provence, France.
Archives Nationales du Zaire. Kinshasa, Zaire.
Baptist Missionary Society. London, England.
Bikoro Zone Archives. Bikoro, Zaire.
Equateur Région Archives. Mbandaka, Zaire.
Mushie Zone Archives. Mushie, Zaire.
Musée Royal de l'Afrique Centrale. Tervuren, Belgium.

Index